WOMEN TRADERS IN
CROSS-CULTURAL PERSPECTIVE

Women Traders in Cross-Cultural Perspective

MEDIATING IDENTITIES,
MARKETING WARES

Linda J. Seligmann, *editor*

STANFORD UNIVERSITY PRESS
STANFORD, CALIFORNIA
2001

Stanford University Press
Stanford, California

© 2001 by the Board of Trustees of the Leland Stanford
Junior University

Printed in the United States of America
On acid-free, archival-quality paper

Library of Congress Cataloging-in-Publication Data
Women traders in cross-cultural perspective : mediating
    identities, marketing wares / Linda J. Seligmann, editor.
        p. cm.
    Includes bibliographical references and index.
    ISBN 0-8047-4052-6 (alk. paper)—
    ISBN 0-8047-4053-4 (paper : alk. paper)
        1. Women merchants—Developing countries.
    2. Markets—Developing countries. 3. Women—
    Developing countries—Economic conditions.
    4. Women—Developing countries—Social conditions.
    I. Seligmann, Linda J., 1954–
        HF4055.W66 2001
        381′.1′082—dc21   00-059509

Designed by Janet Wood
Typeset by G & S Typesetters, Inc. in 11/14 Garamond

Original printing 2001

Last figure below indicates year of this printing:
10 09 08 07 06 05 04 03 02 01

Frontispiece: *Informal vendors sell fruit and potatoes on Santa
Clara-San Pedro Street near the Central Market of Cuzco, Peru,
1993 (detail). Photo credit: Linda J. Seligmann*

Contents

List of Illustrations

Preface

As I write these words, I feel a bit like one of the market women that the Kumasi traders of Ghana, Africa, describe as "nursing mothers." Nudging this manuscript along through several years of twists and turns until it emerged as a coherent piece of work was hardly what I expected when I undertook the project. The wide-ranging comments, questions, and interest generated by an invited session I organized at the Annual Meeting of the American Anthropological Association (AAA), sponsored by the American Ethnological Society and the Society for the Anthropology of Work, prompted me to consider transforming our session papers into an edited volume. This turned out to be harder than beginning with three oranges to sell and ending with five more and enough to spare for the family breadbasket. So be it. Working to understand the intimate intersection of culture and economy in the context of women traders was a relatively uncommon thing to attempt to do. I am indebted, as I always will be, to the many women in Cuzco's markets who, with laughter, pride, and not a few tears, have shared with me the stories of their work and lives. These stories were a principal impetus for organizing the AAA panel and they inform the theoretical construction of this volume. I also issue a special thanks to Teófila Huáman who has consistently assisted me in my market research in Peru.

The contributors to this volume always cooperated with my many demands and tolerated not a few unexpected delays. Working with them has been an enjoyable learning experience. Theodore Bestor and Florence Babb were the discussants at our session. Florence also contributed a chapter to this volume. Both of them offered comments and perspectives that illuminated connections among the papers and specified areas to which we needed to dedicate more attention. Hanna Lessinger, also a contributor to this volume, could not resist exercising her journalistic penchant for clarity, and the Introduction which follows has benefited from her editing pencil. Ayesha Aliana did the legwork of tracking down sources on markets as my graduate research assistant. Laura Kaplan, also my graduate research assistant at George Mason University, went to work organizing my database for another project in the works but stopped in the middle to help me do one last round of editing on this book. Her editorial skills are impressive and are matched by her kindness. Kathleen Fine and I have held long and stimulating conversations about our respective research. I am lucky to have a good friend who is also intellectually inspiring. Susan Russell and two anonymous readers offered many helpful suggestions to improve the manuscript; I am grateful to them for reserving time from their busy schedules for this task. Many thanks to John Stone, my colleague at George Mason, who urged me to act and who has always been smart and fair, judicious to an extent I rarely see in the academy. Alex Giardino did a careful job of copyediting. Kate Washington and Kate Warne have been supportive, efficient, and pleasant in facilitating the publication process. Muriel Bell told me it would not be easy and saw it through. The encouragement and empathy I have received from my parents, Albert L. Seligmann and Barbara B. Seligmann, and my sisters, Susan Moreno, Ann Lyons, and Wendy Seligmann, have helped to keep my spirits high. John Cooper, Marina Cooper, and Gus are my family. As I occupy the roles of being professor, wife, and new mother, I understand better what it means to juggle identities and mediate among them, particularly in the context of social expectations. My family has brought me joy and a sense of well-being; I value their presence in my life more than the words on this page can convey.

L.J.S.

About the Authors

Jennifer Alexander, formerly an Australian Research Council Fellow, held her award at the University of Sydney, Australia, where *Paul Alexander* teaches social anthropology. Their numerous individual and joint publications have been based on extensive fieldwork in Sri Lanka, Indonesia, and Malaysia. They are currently engaged in research on the export furniture industry of Indonesia and the destruction of small-scale communities in Central Borneo.

Florence E. Babb is an associate professor of anthropology at the University of Iowa, where she has also served as director of women's studies and of Latin American studies. She is the author of *Between Field and Cooking Pot: The Political Economy of Marketwomen in Peru* (University of Texas Press, 1989; rev. ed., 1998), based on research carried out between 1977 and 1997. She is presently completing a book entitled *Mapping Gender and Cultural Politics in Neoliberal Nicaragua*. She has recently published articles in *Identities*, *Latin American Perspectives*, and *Cultural Survival*.

Gracia Clark is an assistant professor in anthropology at Indiana University. Her fieldwork with market traders in Kumasi Central Market, Ghana, began in 1978 with her Ph.D. research for the University of Cambridge. She has also done development consulting with UNIFEM and the ILO. Her 1994 book, *Onions Are My Husband* (University of Chicago Press), integrates these two interests. Presently she is editing life histories of Kumasi market women and analyzing their economic ideas.

Éva V. Huseby-Darvas received her Ph.D. in cultural anthropology from the University of Michigan at Ann Arbor and teaches at the University of Michigan at Dearborn and University of Michigan at Ann Arbor. Since the early 1980s she has been conducting research in rural Hungary and among Hungarian Americans. Her publications include "Elderly Women in a Hungarian Village: Childlessness, Generativity, and Social Control" (*Journal of Cross-Cultural Gerontology*, 1987); "Migrating Inward and Out: Validating Life Course Transitions Through Oral Autobiography" in *Life History as Cultural Construction/Performance* (Hungarian Academy of Sciences, 1988); and "Migration and Gender: Perspectives from Rural Hungary" (*East European Quarterly*, 1990).

Deborah A. Kapchan is an associate professor of anthropology at the University of Texas at Austin. She has been the director of the Center for Intercultural Studies in Folklore and Ethnomusicology since 1996. The chapter in this volume grows out of her fieldwork in the Moroccan marketplace, documented in her 1996 book, *Gender on the Market: Moroccan Women and the Revoicing of Tradition* (University of Pennsylvania Press). She is currently working on Moroccan popular culture and oral poetry.

Johanna Lessinger is an anthropologist who has worked in South India since 1971. Her initial investigation of the men and women employed in Madras City's marketing system, carried out during a period when feminist analyses were just entering anthropology, led to a larger interest in women's employment within the Indian urban working class. Her work on Madras markets has been followed by more recent research into the employment of women in the city's export garment factories. She has also carried out research on Indian immigration to the United States. Her ethnography, *From the Ganges to the Hudson, Indian Immigrants in New York City*, was published by Allyn and Bacon in 1995. She is a research associate in the Department of Anthropology at Barnard College, Columbia University, and a visiting professor of anthropology at the University of New Hampshire.

Judith Marti is an associate professor of anthropology at California State University at Northridge. She has pioneered the use of archival and photographic materials for researching gender roles. Together with Mari Womack, she edited *The Other Fifty Percent: Multicultural Perspectives on Gender Relations* (Waveland Press, 1993). She is currently working on a book on nineteenth-century market women in Mexico.

B. Lynne Milgram is a lecturer in anthropology at the University of Toronto, where she held a postdoctoral position. She is also a research associate at the Royal Ontario Museum, Toronto. Among her most recent articles on women and crafts in Southeast Asia are "Craft Production and Household Practices in the Upland Philippines" in *Transgressing Borders: Critical Perspectives on Gender, Household and Culture* (Bergin and Garvey, 1998) and

"Locating 'Tradition' in the Striped Textiles of Banaue, Ifugao" in *Museum Anthropology*. Her current research on women's craft cooperatives and microfinance projects in the northern Philippines addresses issues of gender and development and tourist art production.

Linda J. Seligmann is an associate professor of anthropology at George Mason University. Her current research concerns women in markets as cultural, political, and economic mediators. Among her publications are "Survival Politics and the Movements of Market Women in Peru in the Age of Neoliberalism" in *The Costs of Modernization in Latin America* (Jaguar Books, 1998), *Between Reform and Revolution: Political Struggles in the Peruvian Andes, 1969–1991* (Stanford University Press, 1995), "Between Worlds of Exchange: Ethnicity among Peruvian Market Women," (*Cultural Anthropology*, 1993), and "To Be in Between: The *Cholas* as Market Women in Peru" (*Comparative Studies in Society and History*, 1989).

Lynn Sikkink is an assistant professor of anthropology at San Jose State University, California. She has carried out research on ethnoarchaeology and household studies in Peru and Bolivia, respectively. Her publications include "The Household as the Locus of Difference: Gender, Occupational Multiplicity and Marketing Practices in the Bolivian Andes" (*Anthropology of Work Review*, 1995) and "Water and Exchange: The Ritual of *Yaku Cambio* as Communal and Competitive Encounter" (*American Ethnologist*, 1997). Her current research is on women's work and vending traditional medicines.

WOMEN TRADERS IN
CROSS-CULTURAL PERSPECTIVE

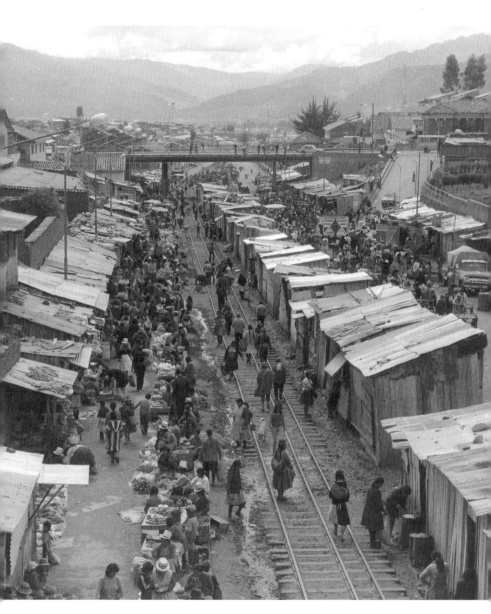

The sprawling informal market of Avenida del Ejército, along the railroad tracks, Cuzco, Peru, 1991. Photo credit: Linda J. Seligmann.

Introduction: Mediating Identities and Marketing Wares

LINDA J. SELIGMANN

Hagglers, peddlers, hawkers, traders, market women, "higglers," and queens are among the many labels scholars have assigned to the women who work in the marketplaces of the world. Such terms seek to describe the complex, varied activities of buying, selling, trading, gossiping, and mothering. Yet few researchers have focused on the kinds of larger mediating roles—those extending beyond economic functions—that market women play in merging disparate social spaces, gendered identities, supposedly separate kin-based, religious, or economic values, as well as different ethnicities and language genres.[1] Little in the way of previous scholarship on markets has examined market women's lives comparatively, across multiple geographic locations. An important exception is Gracia Clark's (1988) edited volume that explores women traders' relationships to the state in several different societies.

Much of what has been written about market women has used the framework of political economy, a theoretical approach that tends to concentrate narrowly on the economic dynamics of market women's activities and on the ways in which women have been able to establish themselves as entrepreneurs in the informal sector.[2] Often missing in such work is an extensive exploration of how a particular set of economic behaviors, found globally, are shaped by local cultural practices and values, especially those pertaining to gender.

In contrast, the contributors to this volume, some of whom also use political economy as a framework, treat as an analytic whole both the economic and cultural practices that shape the lives of women who work in markets in a wide range of societies—Bolivia, Ecuador, Ghana, Hungary, India,

Indonesia, Mexico, Morocco, Peru, and the Philippines. The collection of work presented here grew out of an invited session of the 1995 annual meetings of the American Anthropological Association, cosponsored by the American Ethnological Society and the Society for the Anthropology of Work. Although contributors to this volume approach the subject of market women from different analytical traditions, they share the assumption that market women are not simply traders or vendors of economic wares. Rather, they seek to demonstrate the complexity of the positions these women occupy, to explain how and why their positions change over time, and to specify the structural conditions that inhibit or enhance market women's activities. These chapters are informed by newer trends in anthropology that look at personal agency and at the cultural construction of identity. Many of the contributions consider the cultural dimensions of a changing global economy and of interventions of the state and of international aid and lending agencies, and their effects upon market women's work.

By demonstrating the critical importance that cultural values and practices have in shaping economies, the contributors challenge established anthropological and sociological paradigms of how economies work. Rather than assuming a simple dichotomy between substantivist and formalist approaches to economic dynamics, or adopting economic determinist explanations of market activities, the authors offer in-depth examples of how market women impose cultural calculations that may manipulate and transform the laws of supply and demand. The work on women and markets in this volume speaks most eloquently to the usefulness of *not* disengaging economic from political and cultural processes if one is to understand how economies work.[3] The contributors uncover refreshing evidence of the interplay of culturally constructed categories and ideologies within the organization of labor, production, and exchange, and in processes of economic development and nation building. They also show how activities that are often considered to unfold in separate spheres—for example, in the market or household, in rural or urban spaces, or in local, national, or global domains—actually interact and shape the activities that take place in all of these domains. In short, the authors in this volume, through an examination of the identity, position, and activities of market women, disrupt neat sociological categories. They call into question many widely held assumptions about how economies work and they employ research methodologies that situate the lives of market women within complicated webs of social ties, institutional structures, and economic forces.

All of the contributors seek to integrate multiple levels of analysis and to explore comparatively a cluster of issues centering around the complexity of market women's social identities. By using this approach, we hope the chapters comment on one another, thereby exposing readers to more than one perspective. Despite the specificity of gender relations and historical processes that shape how market women are situated in each society, it is possible to discern general patterns that characterize most, if not all, women's participation in markets everywhere. From there it is possible to venture theoretical explanations for why these patterns emerge.

GENDER IDEOLOGIES, HOUSEHOLD MODELS, AND MARKET DYNAMICS

Women vendors move between and knit together household and marketplace activities in intriguing ways.[4] The very participation of women in markets is determined in part by household structures, sexual divisions of labor, and marriage, residence, and inheritance patterns. Household and market interact dialectically as kinship dynamics, gender ideologies, and household practices and economies are translated or transferred to the market. Meanwhile market practices and economic principles become integral to the reproduction of the household and the nature of the activities that take place within it. Where women's work in markets is negatively sanctioned because of gender ideologies operating within the household as well as in the larger society, particular conditions or strategies may nevertheless permit some women to enter the workplace as vendors.

Frequently women will enter the market as an extension of household tasks they perform as well as to make possible the economic survival of those households and, particularly, to secure the survival of their children. While women are often socialized to contribute the largest share of their labor to the household in order to ensure children's welfare, in many societies that work is not conceptualized as physical caretaking but rather as the economic maintenance of children. In this volume, Alexander and Alexander, in their work in Indonesia, Clark in her research in Ghana, and Huseby-Darvas's work in Hungary all find this to be the case. That is, women enter the market as "mothers" and do not necessarily assume that the actions they must take to ensure the welfare of their children occur solely within the home.

At the same time that gender ideologies may not necessarily prohibit women from pursuing particular kinds of economic activities, they may create intense conflicts along class and gender lines. Lessinger in this volume traces the way cultural values about appropriate female activities in Madras, India, are stretched to their limit when women enter vending. Because it has such low entry barriers, vending is one of the few occupations available to Madras households struggling to counteract widespread unemployment. Nevertheless, women's entry into vending when cultural values and gender ideologies disapprove of it causes great stress within households. Huseby-Darvas in this volume explores how gender ideologies as well as notions of appropriate generational demeanor stigmatized middle-aged Hungarian women who embarked on marketing activities in the late socialist period, even though their income was of tremendous value to family members.

In contrast, Milgram finds that because there are no ideological constraints on women seeking upward economic mobility through commerce in the upland Philippines, women traders have become the main risk takers and the gateways to cash earnings through the handicraft industry. In fact, where trade is both an economic imperative and a cultural tradition in which generations of women have engaged, women are able to accumulate considerable capital for themselves and even to move into wholesaling (see Alexander and Alexander; Milgram, this volume).[5] Marketing activities among women are hardly unusual in societies where women are "naturally" considered to be economically autonomous. This contrasts with the negative attitudes of most men toward women's engagement in paid work in Latin America and India and the consequent restriction of women to the lowest levels of marketing where they have little opportunity for accumulation of capital (see, for example, Pescatello 1976; Guttman 1996).

Women become vendors, rather than pursuing more lucrative occupations, for many reasons. For instance, men often monopolize or jealously guard employment in better-paid work; it is thus easier for women with little capital to pursue vending. Lineage and inheritance dynamics may also encourage women to enter marketing.[6] Furthermore, jobs with more flexibility, like trading, enable women to combine their household and work responsibilities; as vendors, they may already have rights to certain kinds of crops, especially perishable food products within the household economy, that they can market. However, ambivalence may surround these women's economic activities if their incomes begin to surpass those of men and if they gain access to their own capital rather than depending on male kin to supply it. The economic fertility associated with capital accumulation is considered to be appropriate for men, not women, whose work should be primarily directed toward biological reproduction and economic reproduction of the household.

Despite societal or male disapproval, women may be compelled to enter the workplace as vendors because of economic conditions eroding the ability of the household to survive. The implementation of structural adjustment programs (SAP) in so many societies being drawn into the global capitalist system initially puts men, with their more established employment, out of work. The dire needs of the household then begin to take precedence over cultural sanctions or gender ideologies that prohibit women's entry into the marketplace. Women, operating in the most flexible end of the informal sector, have begun to take up the slack (see Babb; Clark; Lessinger, this volume).

Many of the volume's contributors find that drawing a clear boundary between "private" and "public" spheres of economic activity is not helpful.[7] Ideologies of appropriate female or male labor may clash with the actual economic activities that both men and women perform, as the above examples demonstrate. The lack of a clear boundary also means that gender ideologies, as they structure the sexual division of labor within households, do not *determine* cultural rules about labor. Women who enter a new workplace sometimes devise creative ways to challenge restrictive gender ideologies. Likewise, men may take on tasks formerly considered to be women's. Depending on the value attached to the goal of a task, a man's activities may come to be not only socially tolerated but also admired. A case in point is that of a man in Ghana whose "nursing-mother" work in maintaining his children economically was highly regarded (see Clark, this volume).

The patterned links between women's vending activities and household dynamics demonstrate that women may seek work in the marketplace as a means of achieving or maintaining autonomy, alleviating poverty, and protecting children, even as their actions may perpetuate the very systems that disadvantage them. Whatever the specific motivation for women's entry into marketing activities, the cases in this volume demonstrate that gender ideologies and economic forces intervene to shape women's experiences as vendors. In turn, women's marketing activities may occasionally have an impact on the cultural values that structure the sexual division of labor. The studies thus suggest, if sometimes obliquely, the sources of change in gendered employment structures and work cultures.

IDENTITY, ECONOMY, AND SURVIVAL IN THE MARKETPLACE

> Though theoretically the market is indifferent to personal social characteristics, the societies into which it is introduced are not. They are deeply gendered and this fact affects how market institutions bed down.
>
> — J. SHAW

Contributors to this volume address the cultural dimension of women's trading and emphasize how the identities of traders and their participation in markets are affected when they straddle cultural spheres and shuttle between them. Some chapters offer examples of how cultural values and practices affect commodity exchanges in such a way that they are neither wholly commodified nor wholly without calculation. These conditions (mediating between worlds and using at least two different modes of calculating value) sometimes lead to the emergence of new kinds of hybrid identities *and* new economic practices.

Once women enter the market as vendors, they establish themselves using both economic and instrumental strategies of identity. They interweave household economic dynamics with those of a market economy. In particular, women traders in many areas incorporate reciprocity as a primary aspect of their transactions rather than reducing all exchanges to the law of supply and demand. This reliance on reciprocity has multiple advantages, as both Milgram and Sikkink show in this volume. The producers who supply market women may feel a greater loyalty to them, thus providing a more constant and cheap supply of goods if a kinship or fictive-kinship relationship already exists between supplier and vendor. This reciprocity will ensure that vendors continue to return to the same producers. Reciprocity may also play a critical role in the way that market women organize among themselves, a subject to which I shall return in the section below on political activities among market women.

The breadth and depth of social networks constitute a rich source of capital for market women as the chapters by Milgram, Babb, Clark, and Alexander and Alexander show. These networks have particular characteristics. Often originally established for noneconomic purposes, they draw on long traditions and on ethnically specific means of constituting social life. Such networks are not available to just anyone; they can be inherited by subsequent generations and can be converted into economic, symbolic, or political capital (see Steinhauf and Huber 1996).

Gender ideologies, which in some societies hamper market women, can also be a source of strength as female vendors draw on them in constructing presentations of self that facilitate successful sales or offer protection in the face of frequent legal difficulties. Contributors found two common presentations of self among women vendors: (1) the motherly but shrewd and tough entrepreneur; and (2) the helpless victim of circumstance. Distinguishing between these self-presentations as deliberate and manipulative, or as a perpetuation or transfer of gender ideologies from the household to the marketplace, is not a simple task (see Clark; Marti, this volume). Marti, drawing from historical records, offers a particularly useful view of the interplay between these two stereotypical presentations. She traces society's views of market women in nineteenth-century Mexico, specifically the ways in which different media represented market vendors as well as how market vendors presented themselves to city government officials. She concludes that, deliberately or not, tremendous ambiguity surrounded the figure of market women; it is unclear whether the dominant society wanted to portray market women as vulnerable, helpless, and dependent, or whether the vendors themselves manipulated that representation for their own purposes. Marti also presents evidence of the ways female vendors and their activities were construed to support or criticize local government. Vendors could be lauded for being shrewd and enterprising, yet those same qualities could be ruthlessly condemned in battles for control over revenues from street markets and fairs.

One of the most important findings of contributors to this volume is that market women value their social skills, information, and social networks more than they value economic capital in enhancing their ability to make a livelihood. Often, vendors form trading partnerships in order to maximize these resources that are particularly critical to women's abilities to obtain loans, given the reluctance of banks to offer market women credit. While social skills, information, and social networks are crucial to both men and women petty entrepreneurs, gender ideologies force women to value social capital more heavily and to do so in three ways: women tend to have less economic capital available to them; they encounter greater obstacles to entry into alternative occupations; and they are more knowledgeable than men about the gossip and ties of daily life that constitute the material of social information and networks.

In practice, a vendor depends heavily on personal style to supplement general marketing skills. She needs social skills to bargain well, persuading her client that she is well aware of price ranges and is embedded in an extensive array of social relationships. Buying cheap and selling dear requires superb bargaining skills and constant testing of knowledge about price ranges. Alexander and Alexander (this volume) find that trade in the Javanese *pasar* (marketplace) is characterized by unstandardized products, ranges in value, a high number of selling points and traders, and traders who often come from different economic classes. These features inhibit the spread of accurate prices so that competition takes place between individual traders and customers, rather than between traders of the same commodity. To do well in these conditions, traders have to control the flow of information through a highly complex and far-flung market system.

The Alexanders also observe that, in comparison to the unwieldy requirements for obtaining bank loans, the credit and debt agreements among wholesalers, trading partnerships, and petty traders provide cheap and efficient distribution of scarce financial resources through the marketing and production systems as a whole (see also Clark; Milgram, this volume). While large loans may not be so common in these more informal arrangements, agreements structured by interpersonal considerations may allow women without a credit history to obtain needed capital at particular moments, on short notice, and on more flexible terms.

Identity strategies seem to prevail most in the instrumental efforts of market women to establish themselves and expand their entrepreneurial activities by gaining control over niche markets. These identity strategies often reveal the ability of global economic and cultural currents to insert themselves in local environments. Sikkink finds that Bolivian women from rural communities who sell herbal remedies in urban markets inhabit class/regional/ethnic identities that are fluid and contextual. The identity vendors adopt depend greatly on the scale at which they sell, how separated they are from rural households, the frequency of their vending activities, and how they are perceived by consumers of their products.[8] Exchange itself and the kinds of goods involved in the exchange shape identity as tourists and urbanites attribute the efficacy of herbal medicinal remedies to rurality and exotic, potent, mysterious Indianness. Even though some regular vendors identify themselves as shrewd entrepreneurs engaged in a business venture, the products they sell, their knowledge of traditional healing practices, and the views of their consumers, including tourists, root the vendors in an ultra-traditional, indigenous rural identity. If these traders want to continue to do well in the marketplace, they must offer more than herbal remedies; they must also wear the trappings of knowledgeable native medicine women.

In the Philippines, Milgram observes that the style adopted by women intermediaries seeking to purchase weavings and woodcarvings from producers plays a huge role in their ability to make a living. It is not only a question of the amount of credit or raw materials they might have to offer but also *how* they offer them. Abundant generosity, maternal protectiveness, and a willingness to create an intimate and sociable environment for exchange serve both parties, especially when competition becomes fierce and brokers want to assure themselves of a reliable and loyal group of producers. Social skills then—a culturally informed understanding of how to ensure access to credit, how to establish trust for a transaction, how to make a culturally grounded calculation of reciprocity and its timing, as well as a sensitivity to the nature of consumer demands—are critical to market women's economic relationships.

A related factor in the success of women in marketing is their ability to learn the culture of the marketplace, which includes acquisition of the appropriate language and aggressive behavior characterizing so many marketers. These skills may be acquired through either an informal socialization process or formal apprenticeship. Market women with firm roots in a particular marketplace appear to share cultural practices and values, some of which are predicated on their command of a special language or slang. Market women often have a distinctive way of talking among themselves, especially if they are quarreling, discussing prices, or assessing customers. (They may also use a number of slang words and expressions familiar to customers.) Customers themselves acknowledge the unique site that market women occupy by developing their own slang to let market women know their financial difficulties (Musisi 1995, 132; and Alexander and Alexander; Clark; Kapchan; Milgram, this volume).

The interconnections between gender ideologies, the use of culturally and gender-specific speech genres, and the economic survival of women as vendors is particularly intriguing in Kapchan's comparison (this volume and 1996) of Moroccan men and women vendors. Kapchan shows how women vendors, working against gender ideologies, have carved out a niche for themselves in the Moroccan *suq* (bazaar). Although economic necessity may play a role, the verbal artistry that these women have mastered has permitted them to challenge the traditional local assumption that the marketplace is a male domain. Male vendors draw on a discourse grounded in such conventional symbols of legitimacy and power as diplomas, religious literacy, and code switching among French, English, and Moroccan Arabic. Women, in contrast, draw on more popular discourses, challenging their clients to place their trust in the magic of healing, the herbalist herself, and in God. Men have generally always denigrated women's belief in magic. Rather than abandoning this domain of discourse as they enter the marketplace, Moroccan women have made their beliefs public. In so doing, they have succeeded in stealthily gaining ground in the market, thus expanding the space in which women are able to move without constraint. Moroccan women vendors face two paradoxes, however. By putting their belief and knowledge of magic in the public domain, they have succeeded in validating it while simultaneously undermining its power, since magic is supposed to be secret. Secondly, the bazaar itself is becoming peripheral as modernization and late capitalism herald the rise of supermarkets. Hence, while Moroccan women who enter marketing have succeeded in challenging gender ideologies and male control of public space through performative genres, the space itself is being consigned to the economic and social margins.

FIELDS OF POWER

Market women, in their experiences as economic and cultural brokers, perform contradictory and ambivalent roles. The contributors to this volume inquire into the political philosophy and consciousness of market women. To what problems or challenges do market women direct their political activities? What kinds of ties of solidarity do they have with others, and on what basis? Finally, what is the relationship between their trading, their participation in grassroots political movements, traditional electoral campaigns, and formal political parties? Platt remarks that what we imagine as "the market" is a "field of power," certainly not one that operates in terms of unfettered and unbiased market forces (1992, 152). Indeed, markets are sites of power that are linked to local and national politics and may often be the hubs where the majority of "community" wealth circulates.[9]

Market women the world over are the target of attacks by municipal agents and police attempting to collect taxes, raise revenues, and relocate or control marketplaces. Because they are women, traders are frequently harassed, physically and sexually, or forced to engage in prostitution if they want to retain their goods. In cases where societies are ethnically or racially divided, race constitutes another weapon that authorities can use (and justify using) against market women. If the economic activities of market women present competition to established businesses, then women's success is jeopardized because of the close links between the forces of law and order and the bourgeoisie. What, then, does this mean politically for women who trade?

Market women do not have a monolithic response to these conditions. In some cases, because of these kinds of attacks on their persons and livelihood, they begin to develop a political consciousness and solidarity. Perhaps most important to understanding market women's political agendas and behavior is that, in their own view, their activities at home and in the workplace are not separated from one another, as contributors to this collection confirm. Their political actions are shaped by concerns about both home and workplace and take place in both domains. As Stephen observes from her study of women's participation in social movements in Latin America, "Feminism as well as dominant cultural ideologies about women's proper place in the home and family influenced the public discourses and individual interpre-

tations of the goals, strategies and results of these movements" (1997, 3). Although particular events in the workplace might compel women to act,
their actions are deeply motivated by concerns about housing, medical care,
and the welfare of their children. Stephen finds that "public" and "private"
spheres are wholly interconnected and that power is exercised by women
whose practical and strategic gender interests necessarily merge. Likewise,
she argues that to assume that women would enter the "public" political
arena, driven by concerns that involved "private" mothering, misses the fact
that "mothering has always been both public and private. While hegemonic
interpretations of women's proper behavior may confine mothering to the
domestic realm, there is no guarantee that women themselves see mothering
as a solely private activity" (1997, 273–74).

THE POLITICS OF SPACE AND TIME

The design and management of space and time constitute two critical vari-
ables that bear on market women's ability to accommodate particular kinds
of economic activities, social relations, cultural practices, and political action.[10] Many women turn to vending because it *is* a flexible occupation that
dovetails well with existing cultural rhythms of daily life. Market activities,
by their nature, operate within and across physical space, linking distinct geographical and cultural regions. Market women at all levels traverse those
spaces through time. The places where women live and the people with
whom they interact thus play important roles in traders' ability to establish
themselves, become successful vendors, and organize politically. Governments also recognize space and time as important resources to be controlled
for purposes of obtaining revenues, accommodating interest groups, and reflecting images of order or progress they hope to create for themselves.

Because so many market women are heads of their households and share
residential neighborhoods with other market women, a consonance develops between their work experiences as vendors and their living experiences
in their neighborhoods. These experiences lead them to organize around issues concerning both family and work and to use strategies they develop in
both domains. On the one hand, they begin to discern common patterns
in the behavior of the government toward them, whether at home or at

work. On the other hand, they develop coordinated political strategies among themselves to make their work easier and to defend themselves economically.

Market women rely on an array of networks that emerge from living in the same neighborhoods and sometimes from sharing the same rural origins. Participating in neighborhood associations, religious groups, and credit associations, and sharing gossip and economic burdens create a supportive environment for women newly come to the city and make it easier for them to establish themselves as vendors. These neighborhoods where vendors live constitute safe spaces in which face-to-face contact is the norm and can serve as a buffer in an alien environment. Market women pattern their political actions on these networks (see Alexander and Alexander; Babb; Clark; Milgram, this volume). In the workplace, they activate these networks to cooperate in child care, warn of the arrival of tax collectors, share information, relieve each other for rest periods, and help each other when tragedy strikes.

The coincidence of matrifocality among women who work in markets is remarkably high (see Alexander and Alexander; Marti, this volume). Many women vendors are widows, divorcees, or separated from husbands. In all of these cases, women perform extraeconomic functions in both their markets and their neighborhoods: they act as informal political leaders and as cultural brokers, easing communication about prices, trading, and alien belief systems for other market women. Their success in these endeavors results in part from their locus outside formal political hierarchies. Sacks calls such women "centerwomen" and describes them as

> individuals who initiate and sustain informal workplace social networks and who are often keystones of family and kinship networks as well. They tend to initiate activities that maintain group cohesiveness. People expect them to know the events, opinions, and needs of those in the network, and to use that information for their shared well-being. They tend to keep centerwomen well-informed about what is happening on personal, family, and work-related issues. As a result, centerwomen are likely to know everyone's business, not least because people seek them out to discuss it. (1989, 89)

It is easy to see how these informal and flexible networks, activated on a daily basis, provide the blueprint for women's organizing of social movements and the loose coalitions these movements frequently engender. However, this mode of political organizing is fragile. If the position of a centerwoman is jeopardized or she withdraws (or is forced to withdraw) from her activities, then the entire network is put at risk.

Market women also organize into guilds and, sometimes, if they are more permanently established, into unions. The latter are often less effective tools of political mobilization than both social movements and informal networks because the leadership positions are frequently dominated by a male hierarchy (Gill 1994; Seligmann 1989, 1998, forthcoming; Babb 1989).[11] The difficulty of doing political organizing through unions is compounded by the differences that divide market women. It is far easier for women vendors who occupy permanent market sites to organize and mobilize than it is for women who are itinerant or marginal vendors.

RACE, ETHNICITY, AND POLITICAL ACTION
AMONG MARKET WOMEN

The social sites that market women occupy, often bridging class, ethnic, and racial divides and challenging existing gender ideologies, can create considerable social tensions. These tensions are frequently evident in the ways that ideologies of ethnicity are wielded by market women themselves as well as directed against them by different sectors of society. For example, many markets are informally divided according to racial/ethnic criteria that are powerful markers of social differentiation. Those considered "whites" conduct exchange with other whites in the formal markets, while "nonwhites" tend to be the vendors in informal markets who conduct their exchange with a mix of whites and nonwhites. As Babb indicates in her contribution to this volume, it is most often women of lesser status who sell to others of more privileged ethnic and class standing in informal markets.[12] In some cases, more indirect exchanges do take place in which it might appear that the women interacting are of similar status, since higher-class women send their servants to do their marketing for them (see Alexander and Alexander, this volume).

One might venture to ask whether market women, situated as they are economically and socially, challenge the "symbolics of blood" and "scientific naturalism" that are the building blocks of nations. Elites who seek to ensure purity of blood by controlling women's sexuality, and then use that very biological argument as the rationale for determining categories of domination/inclusion and subordination/exclusion in the enterprise of preserving the nation, have a hard time with women of the marketplace. These women's blood, gender, color, values, and economic practices remain ambiguous.[13] That elite frustration is reflected in the intensity with which government officials target market women and repress their modest political aspirations.

The tensions between market women, especially those working in urban markets, and their rural kin are another source of political conflict. The contributors to this volume offer many examples of how market women obtain the goods they sell from rural villagers and kin, the kinds of mutual support systems they develop, and the ways they encourage political mobilization that includes their rural kin. However, rural kin may feel exploited and demeaned by their upwardly mobile and citified relatives, and they are keenly aware that market women orient their interests primarily toward improving their own working conditions and reducing taxes, rather than investing in long-lasting political offensives and alliances. As Platt points out, middlemen and -women have always been expected to take a profit (1992, 138). The real questions are what kind of a profit, how that profit is taken, and what kinds of social reciprocity accompany the economic exchange. These considerations play a significant role in encouraging or disrupting political solidarity between market women and their rural kin.

TARGETING MARKET WOMEN: DISCOURSES OF DEVELOPMENT AND NATIONAL POLICIES

The contributors to this volume pay special attention to how global forces and national economic and political policies impinge upon market women's work. In particular, they trace how state policies and the globalization of the economy shape women's participation in the market. They also consider the impact that women's economic and political activities—including their participation in guilds, unions, social movements, protests, and more hidden kinds of subversive measures—have on state policy, on the attitudes of different sectors of society toward female vendors, and on the dynamics of the market itself.

Huseby-Darvas (this volume) shows how market women from Cserépfalu in Hungary are affected by the ways that state policies clash with household economic models, the gendered division of labor, and generational values. In late socialist Hungary, because families could not meet their needs through agricultural and factory work alone, almost all the women from the village earned a supplemental income by gathering and selling snowflowers and producing and marketing embroidery. Both of these activities were officially illicit because they were not controlled by the state. Although state officials, and men in general, frowned upon the women's activities, the women did quite well for themselves economically. With the transition to capitalism, younger Hungarians have embraced a culture of consumerism. These same women now find themselves increasingly dependent on the income from their marketing activities to support their children, a commitment reinforced by a Protestant work ethic integral to their ethnic identity. At the same time that the women have felt driven to support their children's desire for material goods, their children and younger women view their mothers' activities as "premodern" and shameful.

Clearly women occupy a number of spaces where they "exercise purposeful behavior (agency)," but as Diskin cautions, we also need to recognize "the asymmetry and powerlessness to which they are subject" (1995, 170–71). Although market women may mobilize to gain access to particular resources or to challenge particular ideologies, they are considerably constrained in organizing politically because the market is rarely a permanent physical work space and because the economic hierarchy of trade divides them. They are further inhibited by police/army repression; the state's exercise of patron-clientelism; its capacity to label many forms of women's protest and rebellion as "crimes," thereby limiting their support from potential allies (Harrison 1991); socially institutionalized racism; and the physical realities of working a "double day" (Bunster and Chaney 1985).

Governments have spent a great deal of energy on spatially containing or carefully and strategically courting women who market their wares unofficially. These governmental efforts are motivated by economic, political, and cultural concerns. The presence of these unruly traders selling on sidewalks and in storefronts, without paying licenses and taxes, evokes images of disorder, of development gone awry, and of market failure. The sprawling urban barrios and sidewalks congested with women hawking wares, their children sitting beside them, bespeak the failure of development and government control. These traders labor according to their own flexible schedules, share tasks and sociability with fellow traders, and seemingly operate according to mysterious economic principles. Such traders buy and sell perhaps, but they do not adhere to fixed prices or to neoclassical calculations of how to make a profit. In short, informal marketing is a messy business, particularly discomfiting to those espousing principles of bureaucratic rationality. The economic activities of these women—underselling established entrepreneurs and demonstrating a remarkable flexibility in their ability to vanish and reappear—often ironically represent one essence of capitalism— cutthroat and desperate competition. The intensity of competition among traders and the saturation of informal markets is directly linked to processes of deindustrialization or weak industrialization, the effects of structural adjustment programs, and the social dislocation that these processes precipitate (see Babb; Lessinger, this volume).

National economic policies, often implemented as a result of international pressure, may have unexpected effects on the position and activities of market women. Clark (this volume) shows how structural adjustment policies, because they have led to a deregulation of trade and less state control over the economy, paradoxically have increased the control that women have over their marketing activities, the terms of trade, and the way they provision their stalls. Nevertheless, these policies have also undermined their customer base and, because of the higher unemployment among men, made it less possible for women to draw on income and lineage wealth from their brothers and uncles.

Alexander and Alexander (this volume) offer an unusual case of how economic modernization has impeded women's autonomy. Traditionally, Javanese society constrained women's political and social power, but did not restrict their economic control in the pasar. Economic changes that have replaced the pasar with national and multinational firms have made it far more difficult for women to assert their economic autonomy through petty trade (see Kapchan, this volume). Furthermore, Java's Official Women's Movement has developed a platform that subordinates women's economic activities to those of their husbands, such that Javanese women traders now refer to their work as "helping father." Economic modernization plans, urban planning, and privatization—a constituent element of structural adjustment policies—all have a material face as informal markets are razed and malls and supermarkets take their place in so many parts of the world. These actions narrow market women's economic options, their ability to mount any political resistance, and their sense of public identity (see Babb, this volume).

Under political and economic pressures, market women tend to direct their attacks at the state or at each other, since unlike other parts of the urban working class they have no employers who can be singled out as the source of exploitation. Although the state may indeed be responsible for some of the political injustice they are the brunt of, national and global circuits of capital and gender ideologies also intervene in the kind of exploitation they experience.

Several of the authors (see Clark; Lessinger) question the assumptions that have guided the discourse and policies of development agencies, nongovernmental organizations, and governments, which hail self-employed women in the informal economy as future harbingers of economic development. The authors in this volume stress instead the forces of underdevelopment that propel women into the informal economy and point out the difficulties that women face as they attempt to meet the demands of their households within the intense competition of the marketplace and the inherent limitations of the informal sector.

Women's participation in mutual self-help organizations and social movements, of the kind described in several of the chapters here, may lead women to become aware of the obstacles they face from power structures and to engage in active struggle and confrontation, but unless these organizations or movements are strong and widespread, the failure that often results may actually demoralize participants and threaten the existence of the organization itself. Self-employed women, including market women, who have had these experiences, may then determine that it is best to operate at a level that does not involve direct confrontation (Kalpagam 1994, 281).

The most recent efforts of international agencies to tap into the political capital of mutual self-help organizations have led to a proliferation of women's organizations. In Kenya, for example, 16,000 women's organizations exist and operate (House-Midamba 1995). Although women may genuinely be empowered by their participation in these organizations, one cannot over-look the fact that the very multiplicity of these organizations exacerbates the distinctions among unions, organized labor, and the many differentiated grassroots organizations, thus splintering solidarity and coordination even as their members face many of the same problems.

Finally, and perhaps most often ignored, the extension of "self-help developmental ideologies" to female "microentrepreneurs" can itself become one of women's problems. Rather than genuinely enhancing women's welfare and transforming the structural conditions that perpetuate their participation in the least remunerative activities, such ideologies often lead to women's existence in a "permanent state of vulnerability" with economic stagnation occurring at a microlevel that "this kind of tinkering won't resolve" (Kalpagam 1994, 237; Lessinger, this volume). As Kalpagam notes, such female empowerment schemes that target women entrepreneurs "have to be accepted on pragmatic grounds and rejected on ideological grounds" (1994, 237). Market women are empowered by their participation in social movements of all sorts, but their participation may only have a limited effect on transforming class, caste, and gender relations. In many cases, international lending agencies have adopted the notion of "empowerment" to serve their own interests. What may have been intended as an "anticapitalist critique" is skillfully and easily used as a persuasive element "in the justification of a system which is as likely to disempower people as it is to empower them" (Stirrat 1992, 212).

CONNECTIONS AND CLEAVAGES: MARKET WOMEN AND INFORMAL ECONOMIES

Both government policies and the dynamics of global forces affect how scholars and policymakers view the relationship between formal and informal sectors. Although earlier research tended to stress a dichotomy between formal and informal economies, more recent inquiries have shown the interdependence and interconnections between so-called formal and informal activities and have called into question the usefulness of dividing the economy in this fashion.[14] Many scholars and economic policymakers alike have viewed informal activities as somehow "transitory," a process necessary to urbanization and industrialization. However, as Gudeman remarks, this view is largely the consequence of "where state institutions focus" (1992, 287). In Gudeman's view, state institutions "attend primarily to corporate organizations, and this leaves to one side a vast number of people who, to sustain themselves, must undertake 'informal' activities. The informal economy is a market-organised system that lies outside the margins of state morality as encoded in rules and institutions, hence its liminal and sometimes illegal status" (1992, 287). There *are* aspects of the informal economy that make it different from what is called the formal economy. Informal income-generating activities may be unregulated by society's institutions "in a legal and social environment where similar activities are regulated" (Castells and Portes 1989, 12). However, in other ways the formal and informal economies are similar to each other. Some scholars argue that informal exchange complements and even grows because of the dynamics that the structure of formal exchange may itself have helped to create—such as a reserve supply of labor and the downskilling of all kinds of jobs (Mahler 1995, 9; Lomnitz 1988, 43; see Sassen 1988, 1991). Where permanent markets are promoted by government officials but delimited in terms of which ethnic or gender group can participate in them, informal markets will also proliferate (see Kapchan; Clark, this volume).

Thinking in global terms, one could say that informal activities, especially women's marketing, are in many but not all cases, the result of the gradual outflanking of nation-bound capitalism. As global economic systems come to predominate, composed of large trading blocs, the informalization of the economy also increases. These informal networks constitute what K. Hart calls "mid level structures" that serve as "reference points in a chaotic, frightening world" (1992, 223). Individual isolation and the inability to predict economic outcomes force people to rely heavily on economic informality and on associations that will provide them with needed local knowledge (Gudeman 1992; K. Hart 1992; Alexander and Alexander, this volume). Furthermore, structural adjustment policies, although they may cause a surge in economic growth, lead to greater social and income polarization between wealthier and poorer populations. The consequence of these economic dynamics, together with gender ideologies that create segmented labor markets, is that more women turn to market vending for purposes of survival and poorer members of society find they can only afford what is sold by informal market women (see Lessinger, this volume).

Policymakers and aid agencies tout the potential for the informal economy, hand in hand with structural adjustment policies, to generate economic health and growth, even though it may be poverty and lack of control that propel many women into the already-saturated informal market (see Babb; Clark; Lessinger this volume). Kalpagam (1994) makes a compelling case that international lending agencies and many nongovernmental organizations seek to use the informal sector as their primary rationalization for not confronting the more serious structural impediments to development. For example, Kalpagam cites a USAID document that first condemns government intervention and praises laissez-faire capitalism, reflected in the pioneering spirit of members of the informal sector, in particular, women (1994, 276–77). The document continues by recommending that governments search "for mechanisms that allow the creativity of the urban poor to be tapped and promoted." A. W. Clausen, former president of the World Bank, in a critique of government subsidies and socialization of costs, also reports that development "has been achieved where governments have recognized that in order to harness the individual and collective talents of the people, in urban and rural sectors alike, there must be means for *people to help themselves*" (Kalpagam 1994, 276–77; Kalpagam's emphasis).

In this brave new world, market women are among the "managers of contradictions," a fact that has not been lost on governments and international lending agencies.[15] Market women experience remarkable stress trying to juggle their multiple roles and relationships as economic, political, and cultural mediators. As Stephen notes, the divisions between formal and informal sectors "are largely fictional in terms of actual people," in that members of households work at multiple activities and rely on any number of strategies to make a living (1997, 9). What *is* true is that "the invocation of the word, 'informal' to label part of the economy . . . does have an important political function. . . . The 'informal' economy serves primarily as a symbolic (rather than actual) counterpoint to the 'formal' economy which is read as male, public, and legitimate."

RESEARCH FRAMEWORKS

The contributors to this volume have relied on a number of frameworks and methods as points of departure in conducting their research. Their common emphasis on issues of identity, as these interact with political and economic dynamics, means that each author has been challenged to do research which takes account of the present and past as well as of relationships and processes that are not necessarily empirically discernible and yet have an impact on market women. The contributors have also had to demonstrate how these relationships and processes are constructed culturally. To do this successfully, most authors have stressed institutions that "have a structure that continues beyond the lives of the individuals who are involved in them at any particular time" (Lamphere 1992, 4). Hence, family, economic, and political institutions, in their history, organization, ideologies, and policies, order the relationships and processes described here. Because these domains are not bounded, however, the individuals who operate within them actually gain the creativity, skill, and courage to challenge constraints and to seize advantages that present themselves, using the material from one domain and deploying it in another in a dialectical fashion. Market women who move from household to market and perhaps between three or four geographic sites where their suppliers or clients are located carry with them a remarkable corpus of cultural knowledge and practices from multiple domains. It is this aspect of their being that perhaps makes them a unique subject of research. They offer heuristic models for understanding the dynamics that shape women's work and lives. Because of the mobility of market women, researchers must be innovative in how they approach their subject matter. This volume gives a good, but certainly not an exhaustive, sample of the kinds of methods that are appropriate for this purpose. Marti's use of archival sources is not common in work on market women, yet it is exceedingly important and is a direction that can be fruitfully pursued in future research. By reviewing the archival record, one gains a sense of how different publics and governments have viewed women's work in markets historically; through the voices of market women and their intermediaries, one learns how market women presented themselves to the public and used public institutions.

Alexander and Alexander, Clark, Lessinger, and Milgram find that by tracing key concepts and values, as they are elaborated in the household and workplace, as well as through state policy and discourse, significant insights are possible into the position of market women and the kinds of considerations that shape their identities. Their chapters also provide historical depth, showing how the deployment of key concepts and values are affected, even radically altered, by changing political regimes and economic policies. They bring to the foreground the ways that women mediate social contradictions.

Huseby-Darvas's chapter on rural market women in Hungary, while containing some patterns in common with the other chapters, stands alone because it is the sole case in which market women are working in a national economy that has undergone a dramatic transformation from socialism to capitalism. Huseby-Darvas specifies which conditions changed for market women as they moved from selling in a state-controlled socialist economy to selling in a capitalist one with no state control. New kinds of conflicts emerged between generations, among women, and between men and women as a culture of modernity and rampant consumerism became the norm, and the market women came to be perceived by their children and younger women as "throwbacks" to a socialist past. The effects of national economic regimes on market women's identities is an important methodological direction that needs to be built on in future research.

Sikkink and Kapchan place more attention on commodities, on the exchange process itself, and on how consumers have an impact on the construction of women's identities in the workplace, a direction initially laid out by the groundbreaking work of Appadurai (1986). The discourse of exchange in the Moroccan suq has political implications and suggests the importance of verbal artistry in the creation of both identity and economic role. Kapchan argues that women have carved out a substantial niche for themselves in new economic and physical landscapes by their use of particular discursive techniques. They distinguish their oratory and bargaining from that of male vendors in the marketplace and, slowly, have been able to transform their traditional sphere of authority.

Sikkink summarizes the way women are regarded in rural Bolivian households—as bearers of tradition. As vendors, however, they enter the domain of shrewd entrepreneurs, dominated by partially Europeanized women called *cholas*. Nevertheless, because there is a growing demand for herbal remedies on the part of tourists and urban dwellers in Bolivia, these vendors must present themselves as ultratraditional indigenous women to be successful. They may not necessarily advocate alternative medicine, but they are astute enough to recognize a niche market and to take advantage of it. Although some of them are able to shift back and forth between multiple identities, others find themselves "trapped" in a time warp, forced to root themselves in an identity in which they are not necessarily at home.

A final framework informs those chapters that emerge from the tradition of political economy but now attend to the cultural as well. Drawing on her own research on women in Peru as a basis for comparison, Babb comments on the chapters that comprise this volume in order to assess the present state of work on market women. Babb, along with the majority of the contributors to the volume, worked for many years using a political economy framework. Structure took precedence over agency and the invisible hand of the economy became visible in gender, class, and ethnic conflicts, uneven development or underdevelopment, and in the ideologies that informed policy. Most of the contributors still think that these structures have a tremendous impact on why women sell in markets, where they are situated in markets, and the outcome of their struggles, particularly as structural adjustment policies erode the lower classes' ability to survive economically. The commitment to making explicit the consequences of unequal power relations is reflected in the chapters that follow, as the authors describe the multiple ways in which market women struggle daily to make a living and gain justice, whether in the household or in the workplace. The contributors' scholarly frameworks have changed most in their recognition that market women have available to them greater kinds and numbers of resources to aid them in their struggles, and that these resources are often effective precisely because they are culturally grounded.

PART I

Gender Ideologies, Household Models, and Market Dynamics

Women selling pottery, blankets, and dolls outside the Mercado Alcalde, Guadalajara, Mexico, circa 1898–1902. Source: Señor Juan Victor Arauz's private collection of nineteenth-century photographs, Guadalajara, Mexico.

CHAPTER ONE

Nineteenth-Century Views of Women's Participation in Mexico's Markets

JUDITH MARTI

ABSTRACT: *At the end of the nineteenth century when Mexico was swept into the modern era, street vendors, many of them women, were still ubiquitous in large cities. They provided basic staples for the wealthy, yet they were the mainstay of the poor. Writers of the period presented conflicting portrayals of women vendors—as idyllic, exotic, primitive, or despicable. But how did vendors view themselves, as women and as traders? Petitions to city hall give voice to women otherwise silenced in the historical record by virtue of their illiteracy. Here, widowed vendors used prevailing ideology to their economic advantage, presenting themselves as vulnerable females responsible for dependent children. But from these documents one can also infer they were shrewd, knowledgeable, and, it appears, effective strategists. What underlying motives influenced the representation of self? Was the image calculated to bring about favorable rulings, or does it conform to and perpetuate nineteenth-century Mexican stereotypes? To what extent was it meant to influence city hall, and to what extent does it reflect prevailing ideology?*[1]

A researcher investigating public market and street-vending activity in Mexico City and Guadalajara during the nineteenth century would have to attribute a substantial role to women's participation. But who were these women, and what role did they play in society? From a variety of sources—complaints to city hall (*ayuntamiento*), records of fees paid by street and market vendors, health inspector reports, photographs, illustrations, newspaper articles, and travelers' accounts—one can construct a window on the world of nineteenth-century women vendors.

Who bought goods from women vendors? Photographs show women market buyers and sellers in front of the Mercado Alcalde in the dress of the indigenous poor, *rebozos* (shawls) covering their heads and shoulders. But since it is not possible to distinguish between the housekeeper in a wealthy household and the homemaker from a poor neighborhood, one cannot conclude that only the poor bought in public markets (CA, Mercado Alcalde, c. 1898–1902). From travelers' accounts one learns that the wealthy also bought basic necessities in markets, and from newspaper editorials, that the poor depended on public markets and street vendors for most of their goods.

What goods were sold by women vendors in the public markets and streets? In the source materials, one finds evidence for the sale of pottery as well as a number of other products. Pottery vendors figure in the official lists of fees paid to the city for permission to sell in Plaza Alcalde. Photographs of the Mercado Alcalde show women vendors sitting beside stacks of pottery piled on blankets outside the market (AHMG, caja 1234, paq. 152, leg. 61, 1883; CA, Mercado Alcalde, c. 1898–1900).

Who were these nineteenth-century Mexican women vendors? Sources present conflicting images. One discovers from various sources that the vendors were usually poor, mostly indigenous, illiterate, responsible for children and other dependents, and, often, without a male counterpart. But newspapers presented conflicting images, regardless of gender. Vendors were depicted, on the one hand, as a stain on the image of the modern city of Guadalajara and, on the other hand, as merchants who made important economic contributions to that same city. Mexican and foreign writers of popular literature of the time also present conflicting images. Indigenous vendors are portrayed variously as ideal, picturesque, primitive, even despicable.

American novelist Stephen Crane writes romantically of the young vendors on the Viga Canal who sold wares from canoes: "Indian girls with bare brown arms hold up flowers for sale, flowers of flaming colors made into wreaths and bouquets" (1973, 434). But when he turns into "the narrow street leading away from the canal" he is appalled by the sight of "decrepit vendors of all kinds, [who] raised unheeded cries" (1973, 434).

Petitions that women vendors made to the Guadalajara city government present other kinds of contradictions. In these petitions, women vendors portrayed themselves as vulnerable, helpless, and dependent, at the same time that they showed themselves to be shrewd, knowledgeable, and effective strategists. What can one learn about these nineteenth-century Guadalajara women vendors—how they were viewed and, especially, how they viewed themselves—from the conflicts and contradictions of the historical record? Before one can approach that question, these women vendors should be located in the context of a rapidly growing urban setting of contrasts— of rich and poor, French café pastries and a street vendor's sweets.

NINETEENTH-CENTURY GUADALAJARA: CITY OF CONTRASTS

During the thirty-plus years of Porfirio Diaz's dictatorship (1877–1910), Mexico was ushered into the modern world. Foreign capital fueled technological advances and the development of industry and agriculture. Railroads transported coffee, sugar, tobacco, oil, gold, silver, and manufactured goods to newly constructed ports and then abroad. Agribusiness replaced subsistence agriculture, and thousands of peasants forced off their lands flocked to Mexico's industrializing cities (Coatsworth 1981; Haber 1989; Johns 1997; F. Katz 1981; Knight 1998; Meyer, Sherman, and Deeds 1998). Guadalajara saw a dramatic rise in population with the influx of rural peasants seeking factory jobs and foreigners with capital investment seeking tax breaks. With the advent of industrialization, the face of Mexico's second largest city changed dramatically. Disparity grew between rich and poor, the latter an exploited workforce on whom industrialists and wealthy merchants depended (Muriá Rouret 1983). Although the wealthy now bought luxury goods in elegant shops, the subsistence of Mexico's second largest city remained dependent upon traditional methods of distribution. In Guadalajara, public markets flourished, supplying all classes with basic necessities, and the call of street vendors continued unabated.

By 1900, Guadalajara had a population exceeding 100,000. Its population growth from 1877 to 1910 was tremendous, by some estimates an increase of 84 percent. By 1900, it had reached 101,208; in 1910 it stood at 119,468 (INEGI 1985; see Marti 1990, for other sources and a discussion of the problems related to using census materials).

French and American colonies grew, spurred by a favorable climate for foreign investment (Gallo Pérez 1986; Muriá Rouret 1983). Requests poured in from foreign firms interested in establishing businesses in Guadalajara. In 1900, Charles J. Whimple wrote of his interest in establishing a cookie factory for making cookies of wheat, rice, and corn and inquired about a tax exemption. Others asked about what industries already existed, the local power structure, and, always, what tax incentives they could expect (AHJ, Industria y Comercio, Fomento, F-9-900/GUA-23/AHJ and various).

By the end of the nineteenth century, as Guadalajara was swept into the modern era, engineering and architectural changes were transforming the city. The central streets of the capital were paved, and a sewage system and potable water cost the city almost four and one-half million pesos. The rich could now enjoy indoor plumbing. In 1882, the principal square was illuminated for the first time, by incandescent light with a generator of 20 horsepower. By 1907, electric trolleys were replacing trolleys drawn by mules. Rail and telegraph linked Guadalajara to Mexico City, and subscriptions for the telephone could be had for 3 pesos monthly for a line of 1 kilometer or less.

The upper class looked to Europe and the United States for style and status, and parts of Guadalajara took on the appearance of a European city. Bronze and marble neoclassical sculptures, ordered from U.S. catalogs and coveted in France and Italy, decorated plazas, parks, and public buildings. Government buildings were refurbished and a new congressional wing added. The beautiful neoclassical Teatro Degollado was finally completed and the Biblioteca Pública del Estado built.

The wealthy now lived in European-style mansions. The house commonly known as the "Casa de los Perros" (House of the Dogs) for its two canine statues, which dates from this period, boasts a stone facade, Corinthian columns, and stained-glass windows that illuminate the ballroom.

While public works catered to the rich, the ranks of the poor swelled, populating a portion of the city bereft of modern technology. The city was divided into two parts, "occidental" (west) and "oriental" (east), separated by the San Juan de Dios River. The former was lit with electricity, the latter with oil lamps; the one, a series of uniform blocks and paved streets, the other, groups of irregular blocks and "a poor reputation" (De Szyszlo, quoted in Gallo Pérez 1986, 18; Gallo Pérez 1986; Muriá 1982; Muriá Rouret 1983). The Plaza de Armas, Guadalajara's principal square, reflected these contrasts in both culture and class. During the Porfiriato (the rule of Porfirio Diaz), the square was transformed from an open Spanish square with fountain, market, and public trough for mules to an elegant French square complete with a kiosk from Paris (Muriá Rouret 1983). The neoclassical statues, Cuatro Estaciones (Four Stations), which still stand in the corners of the Plaza today, were ordered by catalog from the J. W. Fiske firm in New York. And the ornate kiosk, site of band concerts, came from the Fundación de Arte Du Val d'Osne, Paris. On Thursday and Sunday evenings, from six to nine, the military band played pieces from Lohengrin and Tanhausser, Liszt rhapsodies and Beethoven overtures (Muriá 1982, 41). Gibbon's description of these serenades underscores the division of classes, segregated within the space of a square: "The gentlemen congregate to form a crowd in the center, the middle classes stroll on the sidewalks and the masses revolve around the periphery enjoying the music" (Gallo Pérez 1986, 18).

Modernization had come at the cost, however, of a growing gap between the rich and the poor. A factory worker in Guadalajara in 1910 earned 50 centavos a day, enough to pay for rent and a meal of corn, beans, and potatoes that could be spiced with chile or sweetened with sugar, leaving perhaps 7 centavos for all other expenses (AHJ, Gobernación "Lista de precios para 1910," s.f. 1910, cited in Muriá 1982, 159). The wealthy, meanwhile, were served French- and American-style pastries that cost 35 centavos apiece at Guadalajara's famous cantinas, such as the La Fama Italiana. Or they dined out for 3 pesos—the amount of a factory worker's weekly wages—in the fancy Chinese Wong-Tong Restaurant. Fifty centavos, a worker's wages for a day, bought a bottle of Spanish or French wine to accompany the repast (Muriá 1981).

San Francisco Street was lined with French establishments selling fashionable cloth and hats, while dry goods and hardware stores were owned by German merchants (Gallo Pérez 1986). The wealthy bought clothes at Señor Casadevant's La Ciudad de París and hats at La Sombrerería Tardán, as well as imported sweets at the Pastelería Lións. Imported perfumes and pharmaceuticals could be bought at several fine stores, including Orendain, Cosas de Viejos, and a branch of the Gran Droguería de Lázaro Perez e Hijo, which received new shipments each month from Dresden, Hamburg, Leipzig, London, New York, and Philadelphia (Muriá 1982).

In Guadalajara, public markets continued to be an important mainstay of the city, and street vendors selling goods could be found on every corner. Although the wealthy most found to their liking imported goods, upper-class women still sent their housekeepers to the markets (Brocklehurst 1883), while the lower classes depended on the markets for almost all their needs. According to one newspaper editorial, any decline in market and street vendor activity would have had a negative impact on the poor (BPE, *La Gaceta de Guadalajara*, May 11, 1902).

Market vendors sold basic goods like grains, meats, vegetables, and fruits at the three principal markets—Mercado Alcalde, Mercado Corona, and Mercado Libertad (San Juan de Dios)—and the thirteen or more markets located in portals and plazas throughout the city. Mercado Libertad was know for its ices, Mercado Alcalde for pottery, Mercado San Juan de Dios for tamales (various sources, see Marti 1990).

Street vendors were ubiquitous. They sold on street corners, in plazas and public gardens, under portals, beside railroad tracks, outside churches and public buildings, and from the shelters of doorways. Fashionable San Francisco Street was lined with mestizo boys selling refreshments, ice cream, and sweets in the shade of the portals. In the Plaza de Armas, groups of vendors sold sugarcane, peanuts, and tequila next to the kiosk where the band played. Vendors sold *aguas frescas* (flavored waters) in the main park, La Alameda, and fruit in the Jardín de Santo Domingo. Students could buy fried foods from vendors in the Plazuela de la Universidad. In the streets, vendors hawked fish, tortillas, pottery, newspapers, and milk. They went from house to house carrying their goods in baskets and on their backs, pushing carts, and pulling mules (various sources, see Marti 1990). Street vendors were so plentiful that a local newspaper complained about the lack of structures to house them (BPE, *La Gaceta de Guadalajara*, May 11, 1902).

NEWSPAPERS: THE VENDOR — IMPEDIMENT OR CONTRIBUTOR?

In late-nineteenth-century Mexico, as a traditional way of life gave way to modern advances, vendors were seen alternatively as an embarrassment and impediment to change, or as an important component of the economy, supporting thousands of the city's laboring poor.

Newspaper editorials often used the issue of vending to support or criticize local government. The debate between two Guadalajara newspapers, *Diario* and *La Patria*, is illustrative. These newspapers argued over the advantages and disadvantages of hosting festivals. Fairs traditionally attracted large numbers of vendors and customers. *La Patria* painted a picture of vendors and the customers they attracted as members of the least-important class (*la clase ínfima del pueblo*), in essence, the class that doesn't count, *charritos*, or cowboys, a term that refers to men, equated with rusticism, lacking in culture, who spend money on cockfights rather than commerce. Thus not only did vendors and their unsavory customers not benefit the city, but they were also a stain on the city's image. The newspaper blamed government for allowing this activity with their command to "be happy, buy, sell." If a "higher class of people" (such as themselves) were involved in running the festival—and I think one can read into this statement, benefited from the profits—then the newspaper would have been willing to back the local government and its festivals.

An opposite view was given by the *Diario*. It argued for *more* feast days in order to increase commerce for the city and to "give more business to those selling goods." The newspaper clearly argued for the expansion of vending activity and backed city government that supported vendors (BPE, *El Correo de Jalisco* 16 July 1, 1895). Hence two images of vendors were presented in the city's papers—that of the uncouth rustic and of the respected merchant. Clearly, their debate on street vending masked deeper concerns—support of or opposition to the government in power and, more important, who had control over revenues accrued from street fairs.

POPULAR LITERATURE: VENDOR AS IDYLLIC, VENDOR AS EXOTIC, VENDOR AS DESPICABLE

Whereas newspapers often presented conflicting images of vendors to serve political ends, the popular literature consumed by Mexican and foreign elites depicted vendors, especially women vendors, in romanticized accounts of travel in exotic lands. Such accounts portrayed the women either as bathed in a quaint or even mysterious light, or as dark and forbidding, products of a corrupting environment.

Ignacio Manuel Altamirano, "a pure-blooded Aztec Indian," was held in great esteem in Mexico as a literary and political figure (Johnson 1961, ix). He authored books, founded journals, and served as attorney general of the Supreme Court and consul general to Spain and Paris. In *Christmas in the Mountains* (*La navidad en las montañas*), Altamirano paints a romantic picture of the idealized rural indigenous peasant. He writes of an "old man, poorly dressed, and of small stature, but in whose countenance . . . could be discovered all the evidences of the pure, indigenous race, there glowed something which inspired profound respect" (1961, 48). He contrasts life in the countryside with the corrupting influence of the "opulent cities [with their] society agitated by terrible passions" (1961, 66). He develops this contrast further in his descriptions of street vendors. On Christmas eve in an idyllic country village, he takes a stroll around the square, attracted by the cries of vendors "of fritters and cakes made of honey and sugared chestnuts" (1961, 29). This, in contrast to the traveling vendors who hawk booklets that are printed in Mexico City and sell corruption, "verses which are customarily quite bad and even obscene" (1961, 43–44).

While Altamirano romanticizes the indigenous and rural, uncorrupted by the conquering race, García Cubas, well-known geographer and political demographer of late-nineteenth-century Mexico, idealizes the Europeanized Mexican of pure Spanish blood. In his book *The Republic of Mexico in 1876*, he decries foreign writers who classify the "Mexican nation among the redskins" (1876, 15). Mexico, he writes, is peopled by a white race indistinguishable from Europeans in education, dress, language, and customs.

García Cubas uses descriptions of vendors to put forth an argument for the virtues of a Europeanized, modern Mexico and to put distance between the white ruling elites and a declining, primitive indigenous population whose past glory is just that.

On the one hand, the Europeanized mestizos (a mixture of Indian and Spanish) who "in their habits and education follow the white . . . ," make up the ranks of artisans and peddlers. The mestizo "possesses many excellent qualities: he is quick and discreet, industrious, intelligent, faithful in his master's service, hospitable and attentive" (García Cubas 1876, 16, 19–20). On the other hand, indigenous people, with their "habits and inveterate customs," are "diametrically opposed to those of the white and mixed races" (García Cubas 1876, 61). García Cubas finds some Indians to admire, the few who still live in a "pure state" in isolated mountainous regions. However, in the cities the Indian is in his most degraded state, a "forbidding type" (1876, 96). "The [Indian] race . . . is extremely debased and prostrated in the vicinities of the large cities. It is here that those types of repugnance are observed, covered with rags and frequently intoxicated, carrying their loads on their backs and returning to their miserable huts, after selling their articles at a vile price" (García Cubas 1876, 67).

Foreign travelers to late-nineteenth-century Mexico seem to have been drawn to scenes of market and street vendors. Two American writers, Charles Macomb Flandrau and Stephen Crane, and the English traveler, Thomas Brocklehurst, are known for their sympathetic and romantic depictions of Mexico's indigenous peoples.

Flandrau spent several years living on his brother's coffee plantation, Santa Margarita, in eastern Mexico. His account of these years, *Viva Mexico*, is considered a classic, "the giant among . . . travel accounts." (Gardiner 1964, xvi). Flandrau finds the "Europeanized, cosmopolitan" Mexicans that García Cubas holds up as an ideal "distressingly nice and similar . . . the world over, [with] money, education, the habit of society and little else" (1964, 130–31). His admiration goes rather to the Indian servant, who in her clean, starched outfit, gracefully serves tea, and is "perfectly self-possessed" (1964, 212). Mexico, for Flandrau, is indigenous—"always pictorial and always dramatic," exotic, somewhat comic, and at times incomprehensible. From his balcony he observes the street below, with its constant bustle of people, and "an Indian woman with apparently a whole poultry farm half concealed upon her person. She calls up to ask if I would like to buy a chicken. Why on earth should a young man on a balcony of a hotel bedroom like to buy a chicken?"

Like Flaudrau, Brocklehurst paints a picture of a romanticized, exotic Mexico. And like Flandrau, he finds the image of the woman chicken vendor to be irresistible. "Indian women stretched on mats indolently watch their wares . . . Indian maidens with great coops of chickens on their backs, and a dozen live fowl hanging with their heads downwards from their waistbelts jostle past you" (Brocklehurst 1883, 52–54).

Early in 1895, Stephen Crane, best known for the classic, *The Red Badge of Courage*, traveled to the American West and Mexico to write a series of special features for the newspaper syndicate, Bacheller, Johnson & Bacheller. The syndicate had distributed his novel as a serial and now "planned to capitalize on that success by paying Crane's bills as he wrote his way along a lightening tour through the West and South, down to central Mexico" (J. Katz 1970, ix). Both the novel and the sketches of Mexico City were published in 1895.

In "City of Mexico," Crane presents conflicting images of the women fruit vendors who plied their wares at train stations. His descriptions can be picturesque—"the bare feet of the women pattered to and fro along the row of car windows. Their cajoling voices were always soft and musical" (Crane 1973, 452). And they can be satirical—Indian women vendors "walked along the line of cars and held up baskets of fruit toward the windows. Their broad, stolid faces were suddenly lit with a new commercial glow at the arrival of this trainful of victims" (Crane 1973, 451). The conflicting portrayals of women vendors can perhaps be explained by Crane's theory of poverty that blamed society for the conditions of its poor, the environment for their ignoble life, theories he expanded on in "The Mexican Lower Classes." Illustrated in *Maggie: A Girl of the Streets*, Crane contrasts the innocent who, at least for a moment, could bloom in a wretched environment, with the majority of the poor for whom a sordid life brought out the worst of human traits (Crane 1967). Crane's representations are not without criticism. Mariani, for one, criticizes Crane's representations of the poor in *Maggie: A Girl of the Streets* and "The Mexican Lower Classes" because they "[depend] on the maintenance of the privileged, higher position of a reader/spectator" (Mariani 1992, 72).

PETITIONS TO CITY HALL:
CONFLICTING AND CONTRADICTORY IMAGES

Conflicts and contradictions are themes that run throughout the chapters in this volume. Whether women vendors are constructing conflicting roles (Sikkink, this volume), or resolving conflicts in roles imposed upon them by prevailing ideologies (Kapchan; Lessinger; Clark, this volume), they struggle to define or redefine roles to their economic advantage.

Likewise, nineteenth-century Mexican market women used the prevailing ideology of the times to their advantage when petitioning city hall. Their petitions invoked an ideology that required females to be homemakers, not decision makers. These women vendors presented themselves as widows, thrust into the role of head of household, forced to work in the public sector. By presenting themselves as vulnerable females responsible for dependent children, they declared themselves deserving of the city government's protection and demanded that the government be responsible for their welfare.

Mostly illiterate and poor, these women did not keep diaries as upperclass women were wont to do. Nor did they write letters to friends and relatives. Yet, one finds traces of their voices in the form of official communications with the local government, in petitions and correspondence to city hall petitioning for aid, redress, and so forth, often compelled by economic pressures.

One form of communication with the government was by petition. Petitions were formal requests made to the city council. Each petition had to be accompanied by a stamp, a form of a city tax. The petition was first considered by a committee that made its recommendation to the president of the city council, which made a ruling that was then communicated back to the petitioner. Given this lengthy process, for vendors it was only the hope of some economic relief or gain that could warrant the expenses of scribe and stamp.

The petitions filed by women vendors with city government for lower taxes and exemptions from burdensome fees provide clues to how the petitioners viewed themselves as women and as traders. But here, one is faced with the same problem all public documents present—the underlying motives that influence the representation of self. As I will discuss, these petitions are not free of contradictions either.

In letters of complaint to the city hall, market and street vendors presented themselves as making the same economic contributions and deserving of the same respect as their wealthier merchant counterparts. In petitions to the city hall, market and street vendors, both women and men, referred to themselves as *comerciantes* (merchants). Vendors who sold beans and corn, rebozos and sandals, or traded used furniture and tin pots in the public markets and streets represented themselves with the same term used by respected middle-class merchants who sold imported American medicines, French wines, Swiss watches, and German sausages in elegant wood-paneled shops.

In Mexico City, market vendors selling cloth in the Mercado 2 de Abril called their *puestos* (market stalls) *comercios de ropa* (clothing stores) (AHCM, Gobierno del Distrito, Mercados, tomo 2, vol. 1728, 1910). Street vendors selling cloth from the streets adjacent to the Mercado de San Juan referred to themselves as *comerciantes de telas* (cloth merchants) (AHCM, Gobierno del Distrito, Mercados, tomo 2, vol. 1728, 1910). In Guadalajara, market vendors often referred to themselves as *comerciantes establecidos* (established merchants) (AHJ, Gobernación, n/c, caja 1910).

PETITIONS TO CITY HALL: THE WIDOWED VENDOR SPEAKS

As members of the lower class, women vendors petitioning city hall might have referred to themselves as respected merchants, but their petitions contain other conflicting and contradictory images as well. Striving to make sense of these various representations and portrayals leads to intriguing questions and paths for future research. Nevertheless, if one reads their pleas for lowered fees, one finds they also presented themselves as poor, vulnerable, and helpless.

Sra. Guadalupe Pérez, Sra. Paula Navarrete, and Sra. María Eleuteria Gómez are representative of the numerous widowed women vendors who petitioned the government of Guadalajara for a reduction in fees. They represented themselves, as did so many other vendors, as weak, and they offered conflicting evidence in their petitions that they were decision makers. Their petitions reveal the differences in circumstances and outcomes found among women vendors' petitions. Finally, through their petitions, one can hear the voices of women vendors who were usually silenced in the historical record because of their illiteracy and poverty.

THE TRADITIONAL VIEW OF WOMEN

In common with most widowed women vendors, these three women vendors portrayed themselves as poor, vulnerable, and helpless. Bereft of male protection and financial support, with primary responsibility for their children and home, they begged city hall to be sympathetic to their plight. Ironically, the absence of a male partner or husband still permitted the stereotypical nineteenth-century view of women as homemakers and men as decision makers and breadwinners to be upheld.

In her 1877 petition, Sra. Pérez explains:

> As a result of the death of my husband, D. Ignacio Castellanos, in June of last year after a lengthy illness, the resources that we possessed were used up in order to take care of the needs of his family. After his death, I lacked the necessary means to run the small commercial shop where we do business . . . and as a result was not able to make the payment which we owed to that institution for the taxes of the mentioned business.

Sra. Pérez begs city hall to be merciful: "I plead that city hall listen to my arguments and please absolve me from my past debts and future taxes on my small commercial shop. . . . I am asking for goodwill and mercy" (AHMG, Mercados, exp. 1914, 1877).

Good will, mercy, and compassion are standard endings to the requests, for both men and women. But pleading from a feminine role appears to be gender related. Men were as likely to ask for justice as mercy, and when they did plead for mercy it was because they "declare it is necessary" (for example, AHMG, Mercados, exp. 3, Libro de Correspondencia, 1916).

Like Sra. Pérez, one learns of the existence of Sra. Paula Navarrete, a street musician, only when her poverty prompted her to write—or rather, to have written, since Sra. Navarrete was illiterate—a plaintive appeal in 1898 to city hall: "I do not know how to sign, thus Sr. Chávez will sign my request." Here one learns that Sra. Navarrete's vending license also carried a man's name,

that of Sr. Pedro Mejorada, one of the men who brought out the pipe organs to play. Gerónimo Chávez penned a note to the bottom of the petition
that reads: "I wish to inform this illustrious institution that even though the
licenses given by the municipal treasury office are granted to Sr. Pedro Mejorada, the pipe organs that are brought out by these men to play belong to
the petitioner, Sra. Paula Navarrete. This has been verified by Sr. Mejorada
Mindrero."

In her letter, Sra. Navarrete begs city hall to lower her municipal tax
to 1 peso a month, or, better still, to exempt her from it altogether, as her
monthly income does not exceed 8 pesos a month, and this is not enough to
meet her needs. She is a widow, "of legal age and from this city [Guadala-
jara]." She writes:

> I have three small children who are in their tender infancy and whom I am
> responsible for feeding daily. I have no other income than what I make
> from my small business of two pipe organs that my deceased husband, Bar-
> tolo Robles, left to me two years ago. And this, as I said before, is not even
> enough to buy the basic necessities for myself and my children.

Sra. Navarrete argues that she has suffered financially since the death of her
husband, upon whom she depended. And she continues to suffer because of
her dependence on the men she pays to carry the pipe organs out to the
street. Often, she complains, they disappear, either because they do not want
to work or because they are incarcerated, sometimes for fifteen days (she does
not say why they are arrested and sent to jail). During those times she makes
no money. Further, Sra. Navarrete presents herself as self-sacrificing, patient,
and obedient, ". . . up to today, I have made many sacrifices so that I could
pay my fees." And she is imploring: "I appeal for mercy and beg you not
to proceed with malice." Although letter-writing etiquette for nineteenth-
century Mexico requires formal, humble language, especially to the authorities, even by these standards, Sra. Navarrete's pleas stand out (AHMG, caja
1244, paq. 162, exp. 163, 1889).

Sra. María Eleuteria Gómez inherited two stands in the Market Plaza Alcalde from her deceased husband. Her daughter, Angela Santa Cruz, penned
her letters, because Gómez was illiterate. In her petition, she pleads with the
city government to lower her taxes. Recently widowed, she explains that she

is responsible for a family of five that she has to support. She works in the shop by herself, with only one servant to help, and the money she makes is not enough to raise a family. The concluding statement by her daughter— "She begs your pardon because she does not know how to write"—furthers the image of her as a woman at the mercy of the courts (AHMG, Mercados, exp. 11, 1893).

In their petitions, these women vendors reflect and perpetuate the nine-teenth-century stereotype of subservient, dependent, vulnerable, and some-what passive female behavior. In the conclusion I will question how accu-rately this stereotype reflected late-nineteenth-century Mexican society.

PETITIONS TO CITY HALL: EVIDENCE OF
WOMEN AS DECISION MAKERS

Yet another view of women vendors emerges from these petitions. From the same documents one can infer that women vendors were shrewd, knowl-edgeable, and, in some cases, effective strategists. Elsewhere I have argued that women played important and dynamic roles in the marketplace—that they were decision makers, risk takers, adept at petitioning city hall, and even had some impact on government policy (Marti 1993, 1994a, 1994b). Sra. Navarrete, Sra. Pérez, and Sra. Gómez fit this description.

Sra. Pérez knew her way around the bureaucratic system. She knew how to back up her plea effectively with the clout of people who could influence city hall. Appended to her petition is a document that certifies her impover-ished state:

> The underwriters of this letter certify that it is evident that Sra. Doña Guadalupe Pérez is extremely poor and she has no capital since the amount she gains from her small business is insignificant. We have drawn up this document in Guadalajara, 19th of May, 1877, for Sra. Pérez. Signed, J. de J. Baeza and José G. González.

Srs. Baeza and González were no ordinary citizens. One learns who they were and of their influence in obtaining a favorable ruling for Sra. Pérez from a third government document—a committee's official recommendation made to city hall. This document first outlines Sra. Pérez's position, as stated in her petition, requesting that she be absolved from paying the 6 pesos and 7.5 centavos she owes for her shop. "In order to justify her current insolvency," reads the document, "she has enclosed a written certificate signed by two distinguished persons, the Deputy, José G. González and the General Inspector of Police, J. de J. Baeza." In this case, the law did not allow for leniency. This is so stated in the committee's recommendations: "The committee believes that in strict observance of the law, we cannot possibly make any exemptions." Nonetheless, the committee still argues for a favorable ruling:

> How could [city hall] carry out the demand for the payment of the tax if the person does not have the means to pay it? According to the certificate I mentioned, Sra. Pérez finds it impossible to fulfill her obligation which is making the mentioned payment even if we give her additional time to pay it. In consideration of Srs. González and Baeza, I conclude with the following suggestions: Absolve the debtor from the money she owes. That is my opinion for the illustrious body (city hall). (AHMG, Mercados, exp. 1914, 1877)

The recommendation for a favorable ruling flew in the face of stated law and relied heavily on the recommendations of these two important figures. Sra. Pérez's strategy worked.

Sra. Navarrete also presented another, more dynamic side. First is her tone. In her petition she is vocal in her criticism of city hall. "The fee that was assessed to me, by the Municipal Treasury Office of this city, I find to be very absurd." She also showed knowledge of and adeptness at working through the intricacies of government bureaucracy. She hired a scribe, most likely Sr. Chávez, adhered the proper stamps, and mobilized her arguments. Like Sra. Pérez, she knew to back up her pleas with documentation: twice in the petition she refers to material that corroborates her statements, writing "enclosed find Judicial Justification." In Sra. Navarrete's case, however, the corroborating evidence does not have the clout marshaled by Sra. Pérez. The committee's official government recommendation acknowledges Sra. Navarrete's need: "She has requested exemption from paying the tax or that the fee be lowered due to her impoverished condition and the need to feed her children." But poverty is not enough: "I believe that the exemption should not be approved because the poor should also pay whatever contribution is within the limits of their scarce funds. Neither should we proceed to reduce the tax since the fee is already at the minimum amount established by the budget" (AHMG, caja 1244, paq. 162, exp. 163, 1889).

An inspector dispatched to investigate Sra. Gómez's case reported that she was, as she asserted, a widow with a large family. However, he found her condition to be much better than she claimed. Her stand was one of the best placed in the market, in good condition, and, further, she sold much more than she admitted. Sra. Gómez, it appears, was more successful than she portrayed herself to be—and more savvy. Sra. Gómez did not rely solely on the city's sympathy for a widow's vulnerable position in the hope of obtaining a favorable ruling. To sway the council, she drew on the political rhetoric of the day that portrayed Guadalajara as a modern and progressive city with *establecimientos de beneficencias* (orphanages and the like) and elucidated her contribution to the city's progress. She writes that she delivers meat to these establishments each day, 5 to 7 pesos worth, even though the monies are still owed her. She asks the council to take into consideration her "good works" and grant her a lowered tax so that she will have enough to raise her family (AHMG, Mercados, exp. 11, 1893).

Most vendors petitioning city government were poor. This one learns from the reports of city inspectors dispatched to investigate each case and file a report with recommendations to the city council. But not all vendors were as poor as they claimed, and rulings were not always in their favor, regardless of their poverty. Circumstances and outcomes differed. These three cases are illustrative. While inspectors reported that two of the women vendors were indeed poor, the third vendor, in fact, was in a much better position than she claimed. Further, in one case, poverty was not sufficient to gain a favorable ruling, and in another, lack of poverty did not preclude one. (Elsewhere I infer that implicit government policies help to explain the rulings the city council reaches [see Marti 1994a].)

CONCLUSION

From petitions to city hall, one is given a rare opportunity to hear the voices of women vendors otherwise silenced in the historical record by virtue of their illiteracy. What can an analysis of petitions filed with the city government reveal about who these women market and street vendors were? What can one make of the contradictory images they present and, described by others, how they perceived themselves?

From a comparison of the three documents presented here, one sees the possibility of three levels of analysis. There is some indication of the women's social status. Sra. Navarrete hired a scribe, and Sra. Gómez's daughter was pressed into service because Gómez was illiterate. Both their petitions state this. One can also be assured that Sra. Pérez penned her own petition. Her signature is in the same handwriting as the petition. If she were illiterate and someone else had signed for her, it would have been so indicated in the document. Further, the weight of the signatures to the appended document, those of Srs. González and Baeza, indicate a higher social status. One can also infer their strengths—knowledge and use of city government bureaucracy and of shrewd and calculated arguments.

However, when contemporary researchers look at these documents for clues to self-identity and self-representation, they must keep in mind that these are public, not private, papers. Letters to kin or friends or private diaries may reflect the writer's true feelings, but these petitions are written with an objective in mind.

In petitions to the municipal government, these women represented themselves as weak and dependent. Is the image of the helpless woman calculated only to bring about a favorable ruling? Or does this image, which conforms to and perpetuates nineteenth-century Mexican stereotypes, accurately portray the person behind the words? And whose words is one reading? Whose voice is plaintive and whose assertive? Hers or the scribe's? Yet, scribe or no, literate or not, the same question remains: To what extent are these words meant to influence, to what extent do they reflect?

Here, I have posed questions, because the historical record does not readily reveal clear answers. Perhaps by continuing to compare and evaluate these various sources one may be able to arrive at a better glimpse of who these vendors were and how they saw themselves.

Bu Bariyah, a copperware trader, Prembun, Central Java, Indonesia. Photo credit: Paul Alexander.

CHAPTER TWO

Markets as Gendered Domains:
The Javanese *Pasar*

JENNIFER ALEXANDER AND PAUL ALEXANDER

ABSTRACT: *Despite its economic importance and the large numbers of persons involved, Javanese commerce has been given little attention in general analyses of Javanese culture and society. These analyses often proceed as if the economy were limited to wet-rice agriculture and the society structured solely by agrarian production relations. An important reason for this neglect, both now and in the past, is that marketplaces are gendered domains, and many aspects of behavior in the pasar are incompatible with conventional understandings of Javanese society and culture. These include: an egalitarian mode of conduct; little concern with linguistic and behavioral nuances; considerable emphasis on economic autonomy; a prominent and explicit economic role for women; and relatively easy social relationships with Indonesian Chinese. While not neglecting structural questions, the focus of this chapter is on the ways in which women traders negotiate their multiple, and sometimes contradictory, roles to make a living within the stressful and highly competitive domain of the pasar.*[1]

Classical accounts of the Javanese rural economy represent the Javanese people as traditionally minded, subsistence-orientated, wet-rice agriculturalists who prefer to share resources rather than compete for them. Protected from the ravages of capitalism by the colonial state, the traditional Javanese village survived 150 years of colonial rule by intensifying traditional agricultural practices rather than developing new crops, new cultivation techniques, or new markets. The flow of money into the villages after 1830, and the government's development policies after 1900, had opened the possibility of a market economy, but the Javanese did not seize the opportunities. Instead, freed from war, pestilence, and famine by an ultimately beneficial colonial regime, they allowed their population to grow too rapidly and thus condemned their descendants to poverty. "Easygoing" and "generous," or alternatively, "passive" and "incapable of hard work," the Javanese were clearly no match for the "cunning and sharp-dealing" Chinese, or the "rational" and "honest" (if "somewhat stolid") Dutch (Gonggrijp 1925, 391). There were differences of opinion regarding whether the root cause was the abundant natural resources of Java or the communal nature of Javanese society, but it was generally agreed that Javanese lacked commercial aptitude. In this narrative it was not until the late 1920s, when the rural population finally outgrew agricultural capacity, that significant numbers of Javanese sought employment in trade and industry.

It is now increasingly obvious that what was once widely understood as the "traditional Javanese economy" is in reality only a sector of it. Investigations of the first two decades of the nineteenth century, before the Dutch established political and economic control over the entire island, reveal an expanding indigenous Javanese economy (see, for example, Boomgaard 1989; Carey 1986; G. R. Knight 1982). The population was growing rapidly and there was a considerable pool of wage labor; increasing areas of land were being planted in both staple and cash crops; extensive petty commodity production was based on the processing of locally produced raw materials, and indigenous trading networks distributed these products locally and to other regions. But as the colonial state extended its control to the interior of Java, the space available to indigenous commerce rapidly shrank. The elimination of the major precolonial industry (the cultivation, spinning, and weaving of cotton) is the prime documented example, although, rather ironically, the flood of cheap imported cloth provided the opportunity for a massive expansion of the "traditional" Javanese industry of batik-printed textiles (Boomgaard 1989).

Rather than a protracted period of defensive involution, the nineteenth century is more aptly described as a period of deindustrialization and decommercialization. During the last decades of the century, the economy became increasingly stratified along ethnic lines. The Dutch controlled large-scale agricultural production and processing and the sale of these products in European markets. They also monopolized the import of European manufactured commodities such as cloth. The Chinese provided supervisors and skilled workers in export agriculture, bulked peasant crops for interregional trade and export to other Asian countries, and wholesaled the imported and manufactured commodities that the Javanese required. The major Javanese role in this Euro-centered model of the colonial economy was to provide labor for the cultivation and processing of export crops and to reproduce themselves, mainly by rice farming.

As we have argued at some length elsewhere (Alexander and Alexander 1991a), this ethnically stratified economy was not an inevitable result of "natural" ethnic talents or desires. Nor does it indicate that the village economy was successfully quarantined from market forces: on the contrary, during the nineteenth century the village economy was radically altered by extensive state interventions that forced Javanese households into finance, land, labor, and commodity markets, while simultaneously reducing their autonomy to act efficiently in such markets. The colonial state introduced new systems of land tenure, "supervised" the leasing of land to sugar companies, and, through its control of irrigation, governed what crops could be grown on the remaining village land. State officials regulated local trade and nonagricultural production, setting prices for the staple commodities, especially rice and labor. Relatively heavy taxation required all households to obtain cash at set times in the year, and government pawnshops had a complete, and extremely profitable, monopoly on legal village-level credit. Whatever the motives for these state interventions, they could not insulate rural Javanese from market relationships; even if they had wished to do so, only a minority of the growing numbers of rural Javanese households could have survived from subsistence production. Java was, and is, remarkable for the small size of both the average and the modal farm. However, as in other peasant societies where the bulk of the land is controlled by a few, as many as 30 percent of rural households were functionally landless by 1900. At least by the 1920s, but almost certainly well before, all village households relied on the market for some of their necessities some of the time, and a sizeable percentage were almost totally dependent on it.

One reason for their persistent failure to understand the significance of market relationships for Javanese households was that even the well-intentioned colonial officials (like many of their successors) regarded the male head of the household as the primary breadwinner and therefore saw his preferred occupation (rice farming) as the only significant source of the household's income. Although they recognized that many Javanese had occupations other than farming, these were deprecated with the term "sidelines" (*nevenbedrijf*); or if they were mainly carried out by women, simply ignored. Thus the first comprehensive investigation of the rural economy, conducted in 1903, concluded that indigenous Javanese trading and commodity production was "insignificant" (Hasselman 1914, 115; cf. van Ginkel 1926, 1:179), on the basis of census reports which indicated that trading and manufacturing were the primary occupations for less than 2 percent of Javanese men. Similarly, descriptions of Javanese marketplaces repeatedly highlight a few small communities of "professional" traders: the dried-fish merchants of Semarang, the goldsmiths of Kotagede, the hatmakers of Tangerang, the batik traders of Solo, the tobacco traders of Magelang and Madura, and the money-lending Kalang. In attributing a separate ethnic identity to these otherwise Javanese communities, and in further identifying them as especially pious Muslims whose favorable attitudes toward money and commerce resulted from their experience of the pilgrimage to Mecca, such texts imply that the market was an alien intrusion with no legitimate place in the authentic Javanese community. These assumptions were later reproduced in the well-known anthropological distinction between *santri* and *abangan* (or, more politely, *kejawen*) variants of Javanese culture (C. Geertz 1960; Hefner 1985, 3–4). In this formulation, the abangan are characterized as nominal Muslims with syncretic religious practices and whose primary commitment is to traditional values of kinship and community. The minority of santri are seen as more pious Muslims whose religion provides both an incentive to accumulate funds for the pilgrimage and the values of thrift, diligence, and honesty, which are supposedly associated with successful entrepreneurs.

But the colonial accounts do leave sufficient space for an alternative reading, one suggesting that the communities of traders which appear repeatedly in the colonial reports were notable precisely because they were small, but very visible, minorities in the marketplaces where they worked. They were strikingly visible, first because they were men and, second, because they traded in commodities produced by non-Javanese or in a different region of Java.

Then, as now, most traders in these rural marketplaces were, in fact, women dealing in commodities locally produced by Javanese for consumption by Javanese. One reanalysis of the 1905 data, which gives appropriate weight to the economic activities of women and to the large residual categories in the tables, concludes that less than 70 percent of rural households were primarily engaged in agriculture, a figure which changed little in the ensuing half century (B. White 1991). An examination of the detailed figures for one district in a densely populated region suggests much higher percentages for individual household members: 29 percent of men and 70 percent of women were primarily involved in nonfarm employment (Alexander and Alexander 1991c). In 1905 when the Javanese population was about 25 million, there were 2,800 official marketplaces, or *pasar*, an unknown number of smaller untaxed marketplaces, and at least 28,000 village stores (*warung*); a high density of sales points to a supposedly subsistence economy. Except for cloth and kerosene, however, the commodities traded at these sites were both produced and consumed by Javanese. For a colonial government primarily interested in Javanese labor and the sectors of the agricultural economy they thought reproduced that labor, such activities were indeed insignificant.

While the local traders were dealing in locally produced commodities, echoes in the government statistics indicate that not all of them were dealing in minuscule quantities. Although overshadowed by the 372 million guilders (approximately U.S.$120,000,000) worth of sugar exported by the Dutch-owned companies, exports of "native" crops, including tea, coffee, cassava products, kapok, and vegetable oils, from Java were worth more than fl. 100,000,000 in 1928. It is true that export, wholesaling, and factory processing of these crops was dominated by Chinese, but village-level trading and processing was a Javanese preserve and some enterprises were quite large: 870 firms with more than five employees (20 percent of the total) were owned by indigenes (Fernando and Bulbeck 1992, 254–59).

The general prominence of women in Javanese society and especially the large number of female market traders had certainly caught the eye of many early observers. Raffles asserted that "women alone attend the markets and conduct all the business of buying and selling" (1817, 1:353), while van Deventer described the Javanese woman as "a petty trader to the marrow of her bones . . . [whose] talent 'in taking care of the pence' in buying and selling is, for its kind, unparalleled" (1904, 98). But, as Gouda points out, while Javanese women's capabilities for hard work in the fields or in the marketplace were occasionally acknowledged by colonial writers, this was usually in concert with attributions of Javanese poverty to a loose family life in which men failed to provide for their families and women failed in their domestic and maternal responsibilities (1993, 14). Trade and petty commodity production could be characterized as insignificant precisely because they were mainly occupations of women: within the colonial discourse on the Javanese economy the pasar was a highly gendered domain located outside the boundaries of the authentic Javanese community.

THE PASAR

While there are obviously important historical and regional variations, it is possible to sketch the rudiments of a "Javanese" economic culture that constitutes a range of social practices as the pasar (used in the sense of market rather than marketplace and encompassing financial and labor, as well as simple commodity, markets). Our approach to understanding this institution is based on a conceptualization of the market as three analytically distinct systems—a system of commodity exchanges, a system of social relationships, and a system of culturally grounded trading practices—which we gloss as "trade," "traders," and "trading" (Alexander 1987).

METHODS

This conceptualization of the market determined a style of fieldwork that required a constant tacking between two broad levels of research: the market as a collectivity (a system), and the individual transactions which constitute it. The market system is geographically dispersed and involves thousands of commodities changing hands in millions of transactions each day. Research into this system inevitably requires relatively coarse-grained fieldwork including reading statistics and collecting a few of one's own, interviewing experts ranging from traders and truck drivers to market officials and bankers, and asking critical questions of the archival sources. But understanding individual transactions requires a different sort of fieldwork: Jennifer Alexander spent hours each day in a marketplace, talking with traders, watching transactions, and when her fluency in colloquial Javanese and her knowledge of trading practices were deemed sufficient, sometimes minding a stall. Information gained through one process informed our research at the other level, but our main method of linking the two broad levels of research was to follow individual commodities along networks of trading partnerships: traveling with a cloth trader when she purchased supplies, for example, and later visiting both her supplier and other traders who used the same supplier. This personal acquaintance with parties on both sides of regular transactions was especially important in obtaining accurate information on highly confidential topics such as prices and credit.

TRADE

Considered from the perspective of trade, investigated as a system of commodity exchanges, or better, as "the trajectory or flow of a single item, thing, service and so on as it passes from hand to hand, from place to place" (Dilley 1992, 9), the most important features of Javanese rural markets were the wide variety of unstandardized commodities, the great range in the value of individual transactions, the large number of selling points, and the enormous numbers of traders. These factors combine to produce highly segmented markets: the pasar is less a single market than an amalgam of numerous, widely different, small markets. Differences between these "submarkets" range from the scale of the typical transaction and of the enterprises involved, through entry conditions, to trading conventions including the class and gender of the participants. The major ordering principle of this diversity is spatial: particular "submarkets" are "localized."

This can be illustrated by looking briefly at one factor: gender. In the Central Javanese town where our research was concentrated in the 1980s, the normal population of 4,500 probably tripled on the twice-weekly market days. The vast majority of customers were women, as were 90 percent of the 400 traders in the daily market and 70 percent of the 2,000 traders participating in the periodic market held twice a week. Women dominated the sale of vegetables, meat, fish, fruit, prepared food, and drinks. These were also the commodities that provided work for the greatest number of small traders. Men ran the livestock and seedling markets, and more than the usual proportion dealt in manufactured goods (including clothing and shoes) and handicrafts. Women sold traditional medicines; men or male/female partners sold manufactured remedies. Overall there was a higher percentage of males among the larger-scale traders, but most of the biggest-volume traders were women. However, commodities and services retailed in shops situated outside the marketplaces proper (the more expensive manufactured goods, gold, photography, and photocopying) were sold mainly by men and, as is discussed in the last section, were part of a separate circuit of exchange. Thus, although women dominated the marketplaces as a whole, there were strong clusters of male traders dealing in particular commodities for which a higher proportion of the customers were also men.

Traders come from all social classes. In one rural village, 18 percent of elite women, 24 percent of middle peasant women, and 33 percent of poor peasant women described themselves as traders, although this was seldom their sole occupation, and similar figures have been obtained in other village surveys (Stoler 1977). As with any other economic activity, trading reflects the class structure of Javanese society. A cloth trader with stock approaching Rp. 1,000,000 (about U.S.$3,000 and twenty years' income for a laborer in 1980) has little in common with a cloth seller whose stock is worth Rp. 20,000. The first woman works shorter hours in different marketplaces, obtains far greater profits, and deals with different customers. As with traders, so too with customers; wealthier rural women are infrequent visitors to the pasar, because they purchase most commodities from shops and send their servants to buy foodstuffs. One consequence is that transactions within the pasar usually involve participants of the same class and gender.

TRADERS

Traders—our shorthand term for the usual anthropological perspective—portrays the market as a social system, describing the types of traders and the relationships that link them into complex trading networks. Although scores of terms can be used to differentiate between particular types of traders (in itself evidence of highly segmented markets) Javanese distinguish two main categories of traders: *juragan* and *bakul*. Juragan are "wholesalers" and are often men or Indonesian Chinese, although there are large numbers of women juragan and most juragan are Javanese. Bakul are predominantly women, dealing with varying success with a wide range of agricultural and manufactured commodities. While some juragan had formerly been bakul, considerable external sources of finance were needed to establish a business as a juragan.

It is unusual for bakul to cooperate to run a single enterprise—even spouses trading in the same commodities normally operate independent businesses—but bakul often cooperate in arranging transport, "lend" particular items of stock to one another, or combine funds to purchase a large quantity of produce. Each of these transactions is discrete, although the same bakul tend to cooperate repeatedly with one another and are often linked by a dense web of very small loans used to meet daily expenses (Dewey 1962). These practices should not be attributed to altruism. Bakul trading in the same commodity do not directly compete with one another, because structural features of the markets that inhibit the spread of accurate price information locate competition between an individual trader and an individual customer, rather than between traders.

Juragan, however, often combine into "partnerships." These sometimes take the form of a single business using common funds, but more commonly involve the relatively permanent trading relationships with juragan in other regions discussed below. In the 1980s a reasonably successful juragan buying vegetables locally for sale elsewhere had at least Rp. 5,000,000 in trading finance and a daily turnover of five times this amount. Such juragan had three or four agents buying on commission and perhaps a dozen bakul as regular suppliers, but they bought from a large number of producer-vendors as well. Juragan have numerous avenues for the disposal of their purchases, but the bulk is shipped by truck to juragan in other regions. Often such juragan visit to make their purchases (and to check on supply conditions), but it is common for goods to be sent first and prices negotiated later. It is also common for large-scale buyers to pay a considerable advance (*persekot*) at the beginning of the season. For reasons discussed in detail elsewhere (Alexander and Alexander 1991b) price is not the major consideration in such deals: a constant, large turnover is more critical. Juragan also sell to bakul for resale. At the other end of the marketing system, juragan enterprises serve a bulk-breaking function, especially for locally processed commodities such as dried chilies or timber and for agricultural produce shipped in from outside the region. Manufactured goods produced in large urban plants, in contrast, are normally wholesaled through shops in the small towns, a good proportion of which are owned by Indonesian Chinese.

Although a successful bakul might have stock worth Rp. 1,000,000, as much as a small juragan, most bakul have less than Rp. 30,000 in stock and many, even less than Rp. 5,000. Bakul operating in the marketplace are "middlemen" in the (more or less!) strict sense of the term: they buy all of the goods they sell. The main exceptions are very small-scale sellers of food prepared by themselves and bakul selling fruit and vegetables who make their purchases in their own village or buy from producer-vendors elsewhere. Bargaining is fierce for all purchases other than staples, and most payments are in cash or short-term credit.

Many apparently discrete and transitory transactions within the pasar take place in the context of long-established dyadic relationships. Although they are described by the participants as "partnerships," such relationships combine several levels of traders or producers into a complex financial system in which the debtor at one level becomes the creditor of other, smaller-scale traders. This serves a critical economic function of cheaply and efficiently distributing scarce financial resources through the marketing and production system as a whole. In view of the widespread tendency to see such economic partnerships as grounded in prior social relationships (Plattner 1985) it should be emphasized that, in this case at least, trading partners are seldom kinsmen or neighbors and partnerships often cross ethnic boundaries. While the relationships are usually cordial, the partnerships are essentially instrumental.

Although there are a large number of indigenous terms, there are broadly two types of institutionalized relationships between Javanese traders: *langganan tetep* and *ngalap-nyaur*. A literal translation of langganan tetep is "regular customer," but among traders the term refers to a reciprocal debt relationship that, stripped to its essentials, is a set line of credit. The creditor advances goods up to the fixed limit, and the debt must be repaid in full at Lebaran, the major Islamic holiday at the end of the fasting month of Ramadan. In most cases the credit line is then extended for the next year. The trader normally pays cash for her fortnightly or monthly purchases (although often a fortnight in arrears) so that the total debt does not exceed the fixed limit, but short-term credit outside this limit may occasionally be granted.

For the debtor the greatest advantage of the langganan tetep relationship is the provision of interest-free credit, which enables her to obtain far more stock than her own finances would permit, but she also has opportunities to replenish stock at "discount" rates and gets accurate knowledge of a benchmark price against which other potential transactions can be evaluated. For the supplier, langganan tetep are advantageous because they ensure a regular cash flow and a reliable outlet for goods, while the viability of her debtor's business can be monitored through the regular purchases.

The ngalap-nyaur relationship characteristic of much petty trade is essentially based on the principle of taking possession of the goods and paying for them after resale. In a strict sense ngalap-nyaur is the provision of extremely short-term credit: goods are distributed in the morning and paid for about noon after the marketplace closes for the day. In periods of slow sales, all or some of the goods may be returned in lieu of payment. Although often described as commission selling, ngalap-nyaur differs in that a price is agreed between supplier and trader and the bakul then sells for whatever she can obtain. In practice, credit arrangements the bakul describe as ngalap-nyaur only approximate this description, often involving longer periods of credit than three or four hours. In a well-established relationship a debt accumulates over the course of a year because the bakul sometimes pays less than the full amount due, but as with langganan tetep, the debtor must be able to clear the tally at Lebaran.

These trading relationships are gradually established over a considerable period, and successful traders require not only the bargaining and general market skills that produce reasonable returns, but also the personal skills to establish and maintain cordial relationships, particularly in the case of ngalap-nyaur and particularly in slow seasons when traders have difficulty paying in full and on time. From the traders' point of view the critical difference between ngalap-nyaur and langganan tetep is the constraints they impose on the scale of their businesses: langganan tetep are essential to maintain a high turnover, and traders unable to establish such relationships must work far harder and longer, for a far lower income. The division between the few large bakul using langganan tetep and the mass of traders whose stock is acquired through ngalap-nyaur is thus not primarily a matter of individual differences in commercial acumen: it is a class-based division. Although a well-established trader using langganan tetep may in fact have relatively little of her personal wealth tied up in her enterprise, she must have ready access to considerable sums, both to initiate such credit relationships in the first place and later to demonstrate that she is able to pay on demand (Alexander 1987). Trading thus provides few possibilities of social mobility, for it is only women from households that are relatively wealthy who can establish the langganan relationships that underwrite the most profitable trading strategies.

TRADING

The pasar can thus be seen as a gendered social domain that is the main locus for particular types of social relationships, but it is also an arena of economic competition. To understand how this competition is conducted, we need to conceptualize the pasar both as a culturally grounded, structured flow of information, and as a contested system of meanings. In other words, we need to investigate the trading practices used by bakul to make a living.

As in other "bazaar" economies (C. Geertz 1978), accurate information, particularly price information, is the scarcest commodity in Javanese marketplaces. Because commodities are not standardized and are variable in supply, because prices are seldom marked on the product or stall, and because soft-voiced bargaining is the usual means of negotiating a deal, prices vary considerably from transaction to transaction. We have argued at some length elsewhere (for example, J. Alexander 1986; P. Alexander 1992) against the conventional interpretation of this lack of public knowledge about prices as a form of "market failure": as a deleterious consequence of an underdeveloped economic infrastructure ameliorated by the cultivation of personal relationships among traders (Plattner 1985). On the contrary, in the pasar as in other markets, it is precisely this unequal distribution of accurate price information that makes it possible for traders to profit from their superior knowledge. From a trader's point of view, inequalities in access to information are certainly not "imperfections," and the established trading partnerships described above are, in part, intended to further restrict the general flow of information. Although it is difficult to demonstrate it conclusively, the main reason why trading as a juragan is more profitable than trading as a bakul is not simply the greater turnover or the scale of their businesses; they also profit from the superior price information they obtain from occupying a strategic point in the marketing system. Juragan can anticipate price changes about a day before most bakul, and they acknowledge that it is the "windfall profits" they derive from the use of this information, rather than the "average markups" in most transactions, which provide most of their profits.

Another way to make this point is to emphasize that earning a reasonable living in the pasar has little in common with levying a toll on goods which pass by: it is not a matter of occupying a position in the marketing structure and redistributing goods after adding a markup. It is true that in most sectors of the pasar it is possible to buy goods, add some minor processing (perhaps only changing the selling unit), and resell them at a small markup. The very poorest traders, such as cigarette and snack sellers, do precisely this; as do the medium-scale retailers of staples, village shopkeepers, and moneylenders. But making a reasonable living from such methods requires both extensive finance and a strategic position in the marketing structure: to adopt such trading practices, a bakul must either become a juragan or move outside the pasar system to become a shop owner in town. Consequently, most successful bakul employ a much more active trading strategy, attempting to maximize the return on each transaction by buying as cheaply as possible and selling for as much as the market will bear. This style of trading involves long periods of waiting broken by brief flurries of intensely concentrated activity: often only one or two genuine customers an hour. Although Javanese are generally regarded (and, more importantly, regard themselves) as reserved and restrained in their manner, the marketplace itself is positively valued as *rame* (noisy, crowded). For that reason it is often thronged with people, many of whom have no intention of making a purchase.

The success of a bakul dealing in potentially profitable commodities depends on two commercial skills: her ability to negotiate prices when buying and selling, and her ability to maintain the reputation of being able to pay on demand. As the latter depends in large degree on the former, it is not surprising that bakul emphasize bargaining skills (including the ability to judge quality) as the key to success. Buyers aim in the bargaining process to obtain a price toward the bottom of the current price range. Sellers describe such prices as *bak-bok*, implying (usually falsely) that they themselves have bought at that price, and their aim is to obtain a "good addition" (*bati apik*), preferably selling above the current price range. Bargaining therefore comprises two stages: testing each other's knowledge of the current price range (*ngen-yang*) and negotiating a particular price for a particular commodity (*nyang-nyangan*). When bakul speak of their occupation as mainly requiring the virtues of patience (*kesabaran*) and a willingness to take pains (*terlaten*), they are thinking of the second stage and putting themselves in the position of a buyer. A clever buyer (*nek tuku kok ulet*), and it must be emphasized that bakul are as dependent on their buying skills as on their selling skills, must be persistent, almost passive, repeating her bids over and over again, only raising them by very small amounts at very long intervals. Her intention is to convince the seller that she knows the current price range and will pay no more. When bakul stress that the ideal bakul is also vivacious and friendly (*grapyak sumeh*), they place more emphasis on the first stage but also switch the focus to the seller. Talking continuously, bakul try and strike up a friendly conversation with every potential customer, attracting them to their stall, answering their questions, and fueling their desire for a particular item. A bakul might well ostentatiously demonstrate her generosity if one of the numerous beggars approaches her stall at this time. In both cases the characteristics suggested for a good trader are virtues more likely to be attributed to women rather than to men, who are more commonly praised for exhibiting reserve and dignity.

In fact, successful male traders behave in much the same ways as successful female traders. Indeed, watching a skillful trader strew a stall with swathes of cloth and (chattering nonstop and sometimes nonsensically) first steer a customer toward a particular length and then entice, cajole, or even bully her into paying as much as possible for it, suggests that other, perhaps less culturally valued, qualities are equally important for success. While each completed transaction is usually followed by a gracious exchange of compliments and the seller tries to convince the customer that she has bought cleverly, protracted bargaining often becomes noisy, assertive, and rambunctious, even acrimonious and aggressive. We were frequently told that pious Muslims charged reasonable prices and were more circumspect in their claims (and almost as frequently told just the opposite), but we seldom saw informants act on these precepts. Although bakul frequently assert their honesty, it is commonly recognized that both buyer and seller will make unreliable assertions as they bluff and counterbluff. Javanese asked by strangers how much they paid for the new goods they are carrying seem automatically to quote a lower price; apparently for fear of being thought foolish for paying too much. It appears that paying a high price is seen as a lack of skill by the buyer as much as, or even more so, than cheating by the seller; certainly the numerous folktales concerning villagers' experiences in marketplaces are ambivalent on the matter.

So although the marketplace is positively valued for its bustle, it also has a number of negative characteristics. Much of the behavior of a successful trader would be regarded as vulgar (*kasar*) if repeated in other contexts, and, not surprisingly given the description above, it is easy for customers to pay far too much. Both characteristics make the pasar seem dangerous to many men, as well as to wealthier women who are not traders themselves. Higher-status persons, both men and women, certainly fear getting into a shouting match with an aggressive bakul, which would compromise their dignity. They can, however, easily avoid the possibility by offering an ample price on a "take it or leave it basis." While the wealthy do not bargain down to the last rupiah, and some give generously to the unfortunate, they do not appear to pay significantly more than anyone else. In fact persons of less status with less wealth have other fears that are more difficult to avoid: the considerable stress of having to buy things they need but cannot afford. Even bakul, while generally positive about their occupation compared to the others open to them, acknowledge that it can be a stressful and exhausting way to earn an income.

IS TRADING WOMEN'S WORK?

The high percentage of female traders and the apparently "feminine" characteristics of some of their trading practices, raise the interesting possibility that Javanese market cultures are gendered: that gender roles, in kejawen Javanese society at least, were "preadapted" to authorize substantial participation in market relationships by women. Certainly when placed in an (at least implicit) comparative perspective, kejawen Javanese society has few of the features that restrict and constrain the economic activities of women elsewhere. Indeed (and rather ironically given the frequent attribution of entrepreneurship to especially pious Islamic communities) the restrictions appear to be far stronger in the santri variant of Javanese culture (Mather 1983). In rural society there is little direct economic discrimination against women. For example, although daughters usually inherit a smaller share of their parents' meager land than sons, women hold property (including land) in their own right before and after marriage. Upon divorce, they are entitled to their own property as well as a share of the household's wealth. Women, including married women, are not overly restricted in their movements as long as they return home each evening, work well into pregnancy, and normally resume work very soon after childbirth. As cooking and other routine household tasks are not highly valued in Javanese culture, and children are often cared for by others, household responsibilities do not much inhibit a commercial career. Women are barred from few jobs, and the agricultural tasks conventionally performed by females can relatively easily be slotted in with the requirements of the marketplace. Despite a tendency to see the high proportion of young women in the labor forces of modern factories as a recent development (see, for example, Wolf 1992), large numbers of women worked in the nineteenth-century factories (G. R. Knight 1982; Saptari 1991). The majority of women has more than one job, and this pattern of female employment is part of a rather unusual rural occupational structure in which most households, as well as a high proportion of individual household members, have multiple sources of income.

Typical family and household relationships also facilitate female entry into commerce. In her definitive study, Hildred Geertz (1961) described the Javanese family as matrifocal, contrasting the warm emotional links between mother and children (especially daughters) with the formal, almost avoidance, relationships between father and sons. Although fathers are treated with respect, sons often try to avoid interaction with their fathers and seldom work with them for long. The perpetuation of family relationships thus centers on the mother: for example, daughters but not sons often return to the household after divorce (which was formerly common), girls often learn commercial skills from their mothers or mothers' sisters, and absent children channel financial contributions to the household through their mothers. While to a contemporary observer the absence of clearly demarcated lines of power and the emphasis on individual autonomy might seem more striking than the matrifocal elements, the Javanese family certainly lacks the patriarchal and patrilineal emphasis which apparently facilitates the lifelong subordination of sons to fathers in some other Asian societies. In common with other Austronesian societies, gender differences are not strongly marked in Java and power is not primarily identified with economic control (Errington 1990, 5).

Moreover, in contrast to other Southeast Asians (on this, see, for example, Szanton 1972) Javanese traders seldom speak of a need to quarantine family relationships from economic transactions. One reason may be that in heavily populated Java only a minuscule proportion of potential customers (even for a village shopkeeper) are kinsmen. Another is that kinship is perhaps a less salient mode of social classification, and there is no sharp distinction between kinsmen outside the household and other persons, especially neighbors. But given their long familiarity with market relationships, it should not be surprising that Javanese easily differentiate social and economic exchanges.

The barriers to female participation are, however, much stronger in other areas of social life; women have considerable economic autonomy, but they are politically and socially subordinate to men. Although hierarchical social relationships appear to be more culturally marked among the elites (Hatley

1990, 181), village women are certainly expected to defer to men, in language and demeanor, publicly and privately, and most women most of the time meet this expectation. Women's formal political and religious activities are severely restricted: men are the recognized heads of households, and they hold most official religious and political positions. Women also suffer legal disabilities; for example, although the divorce laws do not discriminate against women, women find it more difficult to initiate divorce proceedings. Furthermore, in those sectors of the economy which, now and in the past, are subject to state regulation, women face overt discrimination: colonial governments set minimum-wage rates for women at two-thirds those of men, and while the government-set rates are no longer gender specific, women are clustered in the lowest-paid jobs (Saptari 1995, 48). It is important not to underestimate these restrictions, and they certainly caution against inferring social status from economic autonomy, but these social, legal, and political constraints have not impinged strongly on the economic activities of women within the pasar. Traders emphasized how much they valued the freedom from social restrictions made possible by their occupation. They do increase the difficulties faced by women who are trying to move outside the pasar system.

The relationship between Javanese notions of appropriate feminine behavior and female economic participation has been cast more strongly by some who have argued that there are features of kejawen Javanese culture that positively advantage women over men in pursuing a commercial career. Most of these "advantages" are seen to turn on the hierarchical nature of Javanese culture in which the superior status of males is predicated on their ability to maintain control of their emotions and desires. For example, Siegel's comprehensive account of what he calls "the domestication of money" argues that although money is a potential threat to hierarchy, it can be assimilated to hierarchy by treating it as a token of respect from subordinate to superior; as a gift or even "a sacrifice" (1986, 163–202). A proper "man's authority instills sufficient respect/fear in his wife to keep her attentive to his wants, which he need never express" (Keeler 1987, 55). Monetary transactions are potentially stressful for men because they place them in situations in which their claims to status might be questioned and because their use of money for purchases signals that they have not conquered their desires. They are therefore content not only to "hand over their money to their wives"

(Siegel 1986, 200), but also to assign all commercial transactions to her. This is appropriate because "a woman makes fewer claims to ascetic detachment from material concerns, and she need not feel shame at being the centre of a scene" (Keeler 1987, 54). For men conscious of their dignity, female success in commercial activities, far from being a threat to male authority, simply confirms their weaknesses. Other men, less status conscious perhaps, put it more positively: *sing wadon nek golek duwit ulet* ("the wife's good at making money").

As most of the largest Javanese commercial enterprises outside the pasar are in fact owned and run by men, a rather less totalizing account of the gender marking of money, along the lines of Brenner's discussion of the differing roles of women in the merchant and the noble families of Solo, could be instructive (1991, 78–92). Or rather more attention could be given to the consequences of such cultural notions for social action in specific contexts. One female manager, for example, said that she preferred to negotiate with men because women aggressively used their emotional and bargaining skills to gain the upper hand, but she thought women office staff were too often languid (*lamban*) whereas males were full of enthusiasm. There is little doubt, however, that a view of commerce (and not only petty commerce) as an appropriate domain for women is widely held by Javanese men and women, and this, at least, legitimates female commercial activities in ways not possible in societies where commerce is seen as man's work.

This argument might be pushed a little further by looking briefly at changes over the last three decades of "New Order" government. There seems little doubt that the development policies of the postcolonial state in combination with general economic growth have rapidly increased well-paid employment for many women. There appear to be few barriers against the employment of women university and upper-high-school graduates in government and private firms; nor are women restricted to lower-level positions. Compared to Australia, a considerably higher proportion of middle- and upper-level managers in Indonesia seem to be women, and certainly a significant proportion (12 percent) of the very richest indigenous businessmen are in fact businesswomen (Raillon 1991, 108–9).

But outside the elites and the rapidly expanding middle classes, the economic position of women relative to men, and particularly women's ability to act independently in economic matters, is probably deteriorating. The most important reasons are structural changes in the economy that are eliminating what we have called the pasar economy and replacing it with a "modern" structure of national and multinational firms. Women dominate the pasar, and only some of those displaced can expect to find equally profitable employment elsewhere. Female economic autonomy also seems increasingly at odds with the cultural values epitomized by state policies. Whether the values are more appropriately termed "traditional" or "reinvented" is open to debate, but the policies ostensibly based on these values do appear concerned to "reinforce patriarchal stereotypes by circumscribing women's social and political roles more rigidly along gender-specific lines" (Gouda 1993, 22). The five principles of the official women's movement (PKK), for example, promote the ideal woman as a faithful supporter of her husband and as primarily concerned with rearing her children to be healthy, useful members of society. New marriage laws provide some protection for middle-class wives after divorce, but at the cost of less economic autonomy for women within marriage and more difficulty in ending unsatisfactory relationships. Housework, or at least some aspects of it, is becoming valorized and, at least by implication, a good woman has little or no time to provide material support for her family. In this cultural context it is not surprising that women running their own substantial businesses describe their activities, without an obvious smile, as *rewangi bapake* ("helping father"). In conjunction with other forms of state intervention, especially the family-planning program, these developments are herding the middle ranks of Javanese society toward nuclear families constituted by "modern" family roles. The economic consequences of these cultural changes are by no means obvious, however, and they do not always run in the expected direction. They can, for example, lead to more open and direct economic cooperation between spouses than was common earlier: households in which one or both spouses are civil servants often establish a joint business to use the subsidized credit that is a major benefit of this type of employment.

THE END OF THE PASAR

The rapid growth of the Indonesian economy during the past decade has given many people higher, if still far from adequate, incomes, but lower proportions are able to live from agriculture, and there are increasing numbers of unemployed educated youth of both genders. Economists argue that rural trade and small industry has played an important part in enabling Javanese to cope with these changes, particularly by providing "residual" employment, especially for women (Booth and Sundrum 1988). Economists term such employment "residual" because they believe, wrongly, that little capital is required, there are few regulatory barriers to entry, and trading activities can fit into domestic responsibilities. Although aware that such occupations cannot reasonably be called "sidelines" because most participants have been engaged "full-time" for several years, modern policymakers, echoing their colonial predecessors, are mainly impressed by the ability of marketplaces to soak up labor.

But irrespective of whether it provides "residual" or more productive employment, the pasar system is being rapidly and sharply squeezed by changes in the wider economy. One of the most important is the replacement of locally produced goods by the products of urban factories. Ten years ago the most profitable commodities for market traders were probably handmade copperware and batik cloth. Both these commodities are now disappearing from rural markets (although some reappear in elite-oriented craft shops). Copperware cannot compete with cheaper factory-produced goods of aluminum, stainless steel, and plastic, and the skilled artisans are growing old. The cheaper types of batik were initially replaced by machine-printed textiles with batik motifs, which in turn are being superseded by factory-made clothing. Indeed the displacement of locally made goods by urban manufactures is occurring throughout the economy. Local cigarettes and soft drinks disappeared a decade ago; palm oil is replacing coconut oil for cooking; locally made lamps and cooking utensils are difficult to sell, and cheap wooden furniture faces increasing competition from plastic and formica. Since in almost all cases the factory-made product is cheaper and of better quality, in addition to appearing more "modern," the demise of the local product is inevitable.

In addition urban manufacturers are becoming better attuned to the marketing needs of lower-income, rural customers and are packaging their goods in smaller quantities, thus eliminating bulk breaking. In many cases they are bypassing the marketplaces altogether, wholesaling their products to retail shops in the small towns. Such shops are in turn becoming more specialized in the sale and service of a particular line of goods. Whereas a decade ago the shops could be sharply differentiated from the pasar by their location, the commodities they sold, and their clientele, and probably handled less than 5 percent of goods consumed by rural households, the differences are now far less marked. Almost every product other than fresh food can be bought for a similar price in shops, many of them located in newly built marketplaces. Factories use their own traveling employees (earlier almost exclusively men but increasingly women as well) to supply retailers from factory-owned vans. In the case of agricultural products, better transport (if not yet better roads) make it possible for juragan to purchase truckloads at the farm gate, thus eliminating one or two levels of bulking traders, most of whom were women. In addition government-owned cooperatives, again employing mainly men, are eliminating private traders, who were often women, in rice and other cash crops.

Not only is the sale of many commodities moving outside the marketplace, but also the character of the marketplaces themselves is rapidly changing. During the last five years, many local governments have replaced the often ramshackle local marketplaces with modern new markets incorporating more sanitary conditions. Construction and financing of these new marketplaces has been entrusted to contractors who have then recovered their costs, their profits, and a contribution to the government from market rents. Most traders from the old marketplaces cannot afford such fees and are reluctant to move; but the former marketplaces are being redeveloped and the police are less tolerant of roadside selling. The new markets are usually on the edges of town near the bus station and operate every day so the distinction between periodic and daily markets no longer means much, while the high fixed costs increase both the optimum scale of the business and the returns, keeping the numbers of traders down. Traders in a particular commodity within a marketplace get their stocks from a limited number of suppliers, which provides less opportunity to benefit from restricted price information. Posted prices (*rega standar*) are becoming increasingly common, which puts traders in direct competition with one another, while bargaining is limited to negotiating a discount, which removes the possibility of "windfall" profits. Suppliers insist on more "modern" credit arrangements: payment in full every fourteen days requires traders to finance a higher proportion of their stock themselves.

By contrast, the income from a successful business is much higher than before.

Many of these changes are consequences of rapid economic growth and industrialization, together with changing social attitudes toward the sale and purchase of goods. They can hardly be reversed. But their implications for the "pasar system" are profound. No doubt the large numbers of very small traders who have taken up this employment because they have few opportunities for other work will continue. But their opportunities of making even a meager income by bulking, bulk breaking, or using specialized market information are diminishing. The position of medium-scale traders (those bakul currently drawing a daily income exceeding the average rural wage) also seems precarious. The self-employed trader operating with limited financial resources in a highly segmented market is being displaced by large-scale wholesaler and retailer operations using paid labor. As the majority of small and medium traders are women, the loss of this employment will have radical effects on their incomes and thus their position in their households.

While pasar will certainly persist in Java, the "pasar system" and its associated economic culture will not. The skills that enabled juragan and bakul to earn a living are no longer relevant because the structure of the economy is changing. Bargaining is less central to trading success, when most traders have much the same goods purchased at much the same price. Incomes become more closely related to turnover, which in turn is a function of the level of finance. Higher fixed costs raise barriers to entry and thus reduce the numbers, but also greatly increase turnover and profit. Traders must learn to calculate markups, keep at least rudimentary accounts, obtain licenses, pay taxes, and employ staff. Traders must discard their entrepreneurial garb to put on a manager's suit, and their ability to do so depends more upon their class position than their personal or social characteristics. Not surprisingly those who have established businesses dealing in factory products are younger and better educated than the pasar traders and often come from the richer rural families. Not incidentally, a higher proportion are men, and thus the new marketplaces are no longer gendered domains.

PART II

Fields of Power

Shantammal, a plantain leaf vendor, Pannagal Park Market, Madras City, India, 1985. Photo credit: Johanna Lessinger.

CHAPTER THREE

Inside, Outside, and Selling on the Road: Women's Market Trading in South India

JOHANNA LESSINGER

ABSTRACT: *This chapter examines the lives of female produce retailers in Chennai (formerly Madras), a major Indian city, to demonstrate the contradictions inherent in their work. Market employment is essential to household survival for poor urban families and is one of the few options for poor women within a gender-segmented labor force. However, trading forces women out of the household and into a public arena of social interaction with strangers, which contravenes cultural norms of gender behavior still upheld by the city's working classes. To preserve moral legitimacy, women traders invoke ideals of sacrificial motherhood and rely on a technique of public chaperonage. Nevertheless women remain marginalized within the retail marketing system. Nongovernmental organizations (NGOs) and development projects in India that seek to insert women into petty trade as a form of income generation have failed to confront local norms of gender separation or the structure of the labor market itself as they affect women's agency as workers.*

In most of urban India, petty retail traders are visible in city marketplaces and roadside shopping areas, selling produce such as vegetables, herbs, fruit and flowers, betel leaves, banana or dry lotus leaves used as plates, and certain kinds of snacks. Their work is essential to densely settled urban populations dependent upon daily markets for much of their food.

As one of the few occupations not wholly defined by gender, Indian retail trading in cities is carried out by both sexes, and female vendors are scattered throughout most of the country's retail markets. Nevertheless, these women traders are in some sense culturally invisible. India, a country with widespread poverty but relatively low rates of female labor-force participation, has no urban traditions that treat petty trade as a female specialty. People do not see trading as something women are uniquely equipped to do, nor do they envision the marketplace as a center of female activity.

My own research in Chennai (formerly Madras),[1] the major South Indian city and capital of Tamilnadu state, suggests that women traders remain economically somewhat marginal and personally subordinate to the men around them, whether fellow traders or family members. Their ability to work is hedged with the kind of invisible constraints that affect the majority of Indian women. In Chennai marketplaces male traders have a vivid presence. They predominate numerically, dealing in the same kinds of commodities as the women alongside them and therefore actually competing with women for similar economic niches. If Chennai retail traders have any kind of public identity, then it is in these mixed-sex groups, which are often viewed as highly visible representatives of the urban working poor.

The social invisibility of women in Chennai marketplaces occurs despite the fact that South Indian Hindu and Christian women are accorded greater physical mobility, ritual recognition, self-expression, and public respect than women in many parts of North India. Various explanations for this North-South cultural divide point to the lesser impact of Islam on South Indian cultural development (so that institutions such as *purdah*[2] did not develop fully), the matrilateral bias in South India's Dravidian kinship systems, marriage patterns which allow married women to remain in close contact with natal kin, and the importance of female labor in traditional rice agriculture. Nevertheless, patriarchy remains strong in the South. Despite the higher rates of female labor-force participation in Tamilnadu (26.5 percent in 1981, compared to 19.8 percent nationally) and in South India generally, women are still handicapped by social constraints and entrenched customs of gender separation. This pattern is visible in the lives of women traders in Chennai.

To those familiar with the kind of retail trading carried on in Africa, Southeast Asia, or Latin America, women's lack of prominence in the marketplaces of Chennai and of India in general is striking and startling, particularly in light of the endemic poverty which might be expected to force a great many women into petty trade. Among the themes of this volume are the kinds of social identities women market traders utilize or construct in the course of their work, the ways these identities involve the mediation of social categories, and the embedding of identities in larger social structures and processes. I argue that Chennai's market women inhabit intensely gendered identities structured by more encompassing hierarchies of gender and class. The pressures of economic and social change have generated cultural debate within Tamil society about where the lines should be drawn, but the hierarchies themselves remain in force.

The question of women's trade is further embedded in a highly gender-segmented labor market. As MacEwen Scott and her colleagues remind us, local custom and history play an important role in creating the gender segregation of labor markets (1994). In Chennai, female traders manage, with considerable agility, to straddle the social categories of domestic woman / employed man, of good (inside) / bad (outside) woman, but are unable to surmount the larger categories of a gender-segmented labor market and an underlying patriarchal ideology that defines men and women as different orders of being, with differential access to public space.

Local ideals of gender separation and the strongly felt identification of women with the private, inner space of household and family have different manifestations at different class and income levels. Thus, urban middle- and upper-class women in Chennai, while supporting the ideals of women's innate domesticity, are beginning to abandon the kind of homebound life they historically embraced, in favor of education, work, and leisure activities that take them part way into the public sphere. Both the urban working class and the rural poor, in contrast, remain culturally conservative about the role of women. The overwhelming preference is for women to remain at home, and families still derive prestige from women's continued dependence.

At the same time, enormous economic pressures on the urban poor impel many Chennai women into the workforce, and, as Vera-Sanso points out, the ideologies of female seclusion and female dependence are modified by economic necessity (1995). Female market trading in the city is thus embedded within a larger context of class stratification, economic change, and shifting urban social values, in which questions of women's employment and the symbolic value of gender separation are central.

These conflicts around women's trading and informal sector work generally pose a challenge to Indian NGOs and, indirectly, to the Indian state, which tends to deal with women's issues and women's poverty primarily via voluntary organizations. In the development schemes that NGOs have been left to devise for India, petty trade is something of a centerpiece. Planners and NGOs argue that moving women into informal sector employment, and particularly into petty commodity production and petty trade, offers the most practical solution to India's widespread household poverty and low male wages. Some also optimistically see employment and control over money as a remedy for the female subordination for which India is known.

There are numerous harsh political and economic critiques that can be leveled against such "income-generating" development schemes (see, for instance, Kalpagam 1994, 220–40). Most seriously, such schemes tend to leave existing social inequalities intact, simply pushing women into an already overcrowded, poorly paid, and exploitative informal sector, rather than pursuing real structural change that might give regular wage work and viable pay to both women and men.[3] The gendered structure of the labor market is something that many development advocates have neglected to challenge (in other than purely rhetorical terms). Nor do planners and NGOs always tackle the underlying cultural assumptions about women's (non)place in the public sphere that further impinge upon women's ability to become fully effective and autonomous wage earners. Furthermore, these kinds of development schemes ignore the male-female competition for jobs within an overcrowded informal sector, which actually exacerbates ideologies of female subordination and exclusion from the workplace.

WORK AND THE PUBLIC SPHERE

In India local gender ideologies parallel older feminist analyses of a public versus a private sphere. Throughout the country, morally laden distinctions between "home," the center of female activities and values, and "the world," the realm of male activity and value, are articulated—and not just by a high-caste elite. In Tamil culture, these concepts are expressed in terms of "inside" (*uLLe* or *akkam*) and "outside" (*veLLiye* or *puram*) persons and spaces. Ideally, a Tamil woman is largely inside—not precisely secluded or in the kind of purdah characteristic of much of North India but rarely visible outside her home or neighborhood and closely identified with nurturing, family-oriented moral values. Tamils say that a truly virtuous woman never steps over her husband's threshold from one year to the next. Home is where her innate chastity and spiritual purity flourish (Reynolds 1980). "Outside" is full of spiritual and physical dangers for women. In this realm of the ideal, it is clearly difficult for a woman to do paid work for others while retaining her full range of moral prestige.

Despite the ideals, in practice many thousands of Tamil women (like women in other parts of India) do go "outside" to work. Vera-Sanso (1995) has argued that concepts of *maanam* (reputation), are constructed situationally among the Chennai poor, so that families judged by the community to be in real need are spared censure for sending women to work; in contrast, gossip and ostracism threaten working women and their families when they are judged not to need the extra income. I would argue, however, that even when female employment is considered acceptable in particular families, those families will pay a price for women's earnings in the form of lessened family prestige and increased internal tensions.[4] The issue is rarely fully resolved. Certainly thousands of poor Tamil women still confine themselves to unpaid work within the family or household in order to uphold women's normative role, despite their financial need.

In Chennai, as in India generally, female paid employment carries strong negative class as well as moral connotations, since it implies both extreme family poverty and an uncomfortable subordination of the woman worker to nonfamily members. The exception to this social rule occurs when the work itself happens to offer autonomy or high pay, as it increasingly does for the many elite women who have entered the professions in the last thirty years, building on several generations of college education for women of their class. Women doctors, teachers, managers, or high-ranking civil servants may largely overcome the stigma of "going out of the house" provided that they adhere to certain standards of propriety. Today many urban middle-class Chennai families who define themselves as "modern" are beginning to countenance clerical and other forms of "clean" (that is, nonmanual) work for women, provided it can be done far from the public eye inside offices, banks, classrooms, or shops. Although never wholly free from social ambiguities, these women's jobs and incomes tend to increase family honor.[5]

However, most working-class adults in Chennai hearken back to their rural origins and associate female employment with the exhausting, poorly paid agricultural labor that a great many poor and low-caste village women, without land of their own, perform out of necessity on other people's farms and in others' homes (see, for instance, Viramma, Racine, and Racine 1997). This kind of work, although it certainly establishes a precedent for female urban employment, also stigmatizes that employment. Trading, even as it escapes the degradation and subordination implied by performing services for others, shares some of agricultural work's "low" attributes, since market selling involves manual labor, is not particularly well-paid, and is carried out in a highly public arena where men and women, strangers and "known persons" necessarily mix. Thus the woman trader is exposed to the public gaze and to possible sexual danger. Women's trade, like other forms of informal sector work, damages family honor by demonstrating in a very public way that a family's men are unable to provide for its women (see a North Indian parallel in Mies's 1982 study of lace makers). Unlike other parts of the world, where marketing may offer women a route to some wealth and influence, in South India the social constraints on women's trading, even as they attempt to sidestep the negative implications of their work, damage their ability to earn substantial incomes (see Lessinger 1986, 1989).

Working-class Tamil men and women tend to share these negative views of female employment; however, women are more flexible about reinterpreting rules in order to continue working (see, for instance, Seizer 1997). In doing so, Tamil women often invoke and subtly reinterpret a particular piece of the culturally sanctioned female ideal: the self-sacrificing mother identified by Egnore [Trawick] (1980; Trawick 1990), the woman who will do anything to preserve her children and her household intact. Chennai market women thus stress the sacrifices they have made in taking up petty trade, and the importance of their work for family well-being, viewing their work as an extension of mothering and social reproduction. Men subscribe to the same set of ideas—female self-sacrifice in the face of great poverty—when they deploy the labor power of their households' women into petty trade. Yet men (sometimes the same men) seem quite ready to revert to the general proposition that good women belong at home, dependent on their menfolk. The other tactic used by women is what I have called elsewhere "public chaperonage," in which women use the very public nature of employment and the presence of others to guarantee their virtue in the workplace (Lessinger 1986).

Market women in Chennai negotiate these contradictions, rooted in patriarchal ideologies of sexuality, female dependence, and family honor with considerable skill and are able to carve out physical and social space and a validating ideology by which to carry on their occupation. Nevertheless, the contradictions surrounding women who move outside, beyond the direct control of men, remain unresolved.

If women's work itself carries class connotations, there is another way in which market trading in Chennai provides a specifically class-marked identity, which women share with men. Petty market traders—members of a highly visible urban occupational category—are seen locally as emblematic representatives of the urban working poor precisely because marketplaces are such central and public institutions. As such, traders of both sexes are wooed by politicians for public expressions of political support and are promised protection from the rapacity of the police and the unjust demands of landlords in privately owned markets (see Lessinger 1985, 1988). In these situations, whether demonstrating against police harassment, displaying political party colors, or voting as a bloc for a helpful politician, market women in Chennai participate, but do not do so independently as women. They leave organizing and leadership of such endeavors to the male traders in their midst, suggesting that even these women who have some economic autonomy nevertheless still see themselves primarily as wives and mothers who are sojourning, temporarily, in the male world of work and politics.

Interestingly, caste plays little economic role in shaping the work lives of produce traders, or indeed, of most of Chennai's working poor, and is specifically not a part of their work identities. Bremen, writing about the 1970s, sees caste as an important social category by which the urban poor lay claim to scarce employment (1989, 268) and Chennai workers may well use caste ties (among other connections) to find work. However, by the 1970s a great many urban occupations in the city, particularly in the informal sector, had opened up to a wide variety of castes. After fifty years of massive rural to urban migration, the Chennai labor market has become sufficiently divorced from rural traditions that most occupations are no longer caste-specific, while the labor market is too large and diverse to allow caste monopolies to extend far, despite lingering prejudice against those of lower caste. Nor do most of the city's working poor live in single-caste residential enclaves.[6] Instead, for large numbers of urban working-class people, caste has retreated to the private realm of personal interaction, marriage networks, ritual obligations, and village relationships.

People of virtually every Hindu caste group, as well as Muslims and Christians, are found selling in Chennai's produce markets. The majority of retail vendors are from middle-ranked agricultural castes such as Gounders, Naickers, and Nairs, groups which are numerous and politically dominant in the rural districts surrounding Chennai. Nevertheless former artisan and service castes and former Untouchables are also present as retailers, along with a tiny number of downwardly mobile Brahmins. Market retailers' most important survival networks include their bilateral kindred, their current neighbors (who may be of different castes) and, particularly for new migrants, fellow migrants from the same village or district (who may likewise be of a different caste). Those who have been in a marketplace a long time also turn for help to fellow vendors. Political patronage flows from local political bosses, who form a diverse group (see Lessinger 1988). Some of this downplaying of caste identity in Chennai is undoubtedly the result of years of anti-Brahmin and anticaste agitation and feeling in Tamilnadu (see Hardgrave 1965; Irschick 1969), which have made it impolite and often impolitic to stress caste affiliation in public settings.

Political symbolism aside, the majority of market traders in Chennai are genuinely impoverished, although most will insist (quite accurately) that they are better off than villagers. This poverty, stemming from the lack of influential social contacts, education, or marketable skills (see Kalpagam 1994; Bremen 1989) in a rapidly changing job market, forms an important backdrop to women's decisions to work as traders. Despite the growth of India's middle classes, employed in a modern sector of new industries and services and enjoying the fruits of a booming consumer culture, much of India's urban working class has been bypassed by recent industrialization. The country's present efforts to integrate itself into a global economy actually make their situation worse.[7] Industrialization since the 1980s has privileged multinational firms and indigenous high-tech, financial, export, and tourist industries, along with a highly educated, Western-oriented workforce. Without the education and contacts to get a foothold in this modernizing world, much of Chennai's working-class population still experiences daily survival as a struggle. Their lives are made more difficult because Chennai, like other large Indian cities, is woefully overcrowded, suffers from a decline in public services, and has been rocked by inflation, which has eroded wages and increased the cost of basic commodities. This has intensified in the 1990s thanks to the "structural adjustment" mandated by debt repayment schedules set out by international lending agencies.

POVERTY AND TRUE WOMANHOOD

For many of the city's poor families, finding a room or small thatched hut to rent is a major preoccupation in a city swollen to an estimated size of eight million in the 1980s by wave after wave of rural migration. Women worry about being able to buy enough rice, salt, chilies, tea, and cooking fuel to ensure the day's one basic meal. People feel lucky if they can afford some of the extras of life—a more varied and nutritious diet, new clothes, school supplies for children, money for ritual and kinship obligations, special dishes on holidays, an occasional outing to the beach or to a movie (see Kalpagam 1994, 193–228, for a description of the lives of the most destitute). The family that needs to marry a daughter or niece, to pay for lengthy illnesses, or to hold death rituals for an adult family member can be pushed into debt and destitution. (See also Noponen 1991, on male-female wage contributions and household debt in working-class Madras.)

Meanwhile urban migration and economic pressures have also eroded marriage and extended family ties, so that growing numbers of women find themselves responsible for supporting children, younger siblings, or elderly parents without male help. Other women lucky enough to still have resident husbands, or to live with brothers, sons, or sons-in-law willing to absorb them into their households, nevertheless face the problem of widespread male unemployment or underemployment.[8] This situation makes even the most responsible men unreliable sources of financial support and decreases the amount of help a married woman can expect from her own kindred. Chennai is a city with numerous industries and administrative offices, colleges and universities, a port, the country's second largest film industry, and vast service and informal sectors. Nevertheless, there is still a drastic shortage of steady jobs (as opposed to casual labor). Even formal sector jobs in large factories are being converted into "temporary" jobs. Here, as in the rest of the informal sector, wage levels remain very low.

There was, by the 1990s, a widespread perception among the poor that inflation had so eroded income levels that men could not hope to be the sole family breadwinners enshrined in cultural ideals. Poor women all over the city now insist that "these days, it takes more than one income to run the household." They add, "Even when he [the man of the house] works, we cannot manage." Yet what Helen Safa, writing about the Hispanic Caribbean, has termed "the myth of the male breadwinner" (1995) persists in Chennai as well. While the burden of supporting the city's poor families is steadily shifted onto poor women, as it has been in so many other modernizing societies, Tamilnadu and India as a whole continue to uphold the ideal of the family patriarch, who earns a family wage and supports dependent women.

In this precarious situation, employment of any kind is scarce and precious; a great many Chennai working-class women, as well as all men, must fling themselves into the daily struggle to survive. All over the city, poor women are vocal in their anxiety to find ways to earn something, despite Tamil cultural norms, which insist that virtually any paid employment is degrading and dangerous for women.

WHAT CAN WOMEN DO?

Cultural barriers confronting individual women are only part of the problem in defining their chances to work. A severely gender-segmented labor market, bolstered by traditional gender ideology, limits the kinds of paid work women can find in Chennai. Large areas of employment, particularly in the formal sector, are simply closed to women. Even the informal sector labor market, where about 94 percent of Indian women workers cluster, has traditionally reserved the steadiest jobs and the best wages for men (see

MacEwan Scott 1991; Núñez 1993, for comments on this phenomenon as a worldwide trend). I would argue that in this competition for scarce work, a labor market already characterized by segmentation along gender lines becomes further segregated because, in a situation of scarcity and competition, ideologies of female subordination flourish.

In Chennai, petty market trading represents one of the jobs more easily accessible to either sex, requiring for entry only small amounts of capital and no skills beyond shrewdness and stamina. As a consequence, both men and women gravitate toward marketing, although women as a group are less successful in this profession than men.

Some labor market gender barriers do shift or fall. In the 1980s and 1990s certain previously male-dominated occupations such as clerical work and shop clerk work in "modern" offices and stores underwent rapid expansion and began to open to young women who had a high school or college education and a ladylike, middle-class demeanor—assuming, of course, that their families would permit them to work at all. Women's malleable "natures" and lower wage demands, along with a huge reservoir of educated girls anxious to work, undoubtedly have something to do with the opening of some sections of the job market to women. By the late 1980s a growing number of export garment, leather, plastics, or electronics factories in the city also employed working-class and lower-middle-class women alongside men, valuing the women as particularly cheap, docile, and disposable labor. There have even been breaches in some bastions of male supremacy. In the face of national outrage about police rape, urban police forces around the country have begun to hire women constables. In the early 1990s, a voluntary agency began to try to set up women as motor rickshaw drivers.[9] Still, in Chennai, there are too few jobs for too many job seekers. In the competition, women, with less education and fewer marketable skills, tend to lose out.

Among those market women interviewed who had prior employment before taking up trading, most had been domestic servants or had worked as coolies (day laborers) or construction workers. Those who were recent rural migrants had often done village agricultural labor as members of female work gangs hired to transplant and weed rice, or as members of family groups hired to transport, thresh, and winnow grain at harvest time. In virtually all these jobs, women's wages are far lower—usually half to two-thirds those of men's. Other market women had once been unpaid family workers producing pottery or textiles. As artisanal production has died out in Tamilnadu, a great many of these household-based occupations, which permitted women to contribute to family income while remaining at home, have vanished. Still other women vendors had put in stints as pieceworkers, rolling cheap cigarettes, gluing cardboard boxes, or stuffing mattresses with cotton, in the small backyard factories that still dot the city.

Every woman trader offered economic reasons for her decision to begin marketing, and virtually all rated the work as better—in terms of dignity, working conditions, and financial returns—than agricultural or domestic work (see Lessinger 1985). Women mentioned the fact that in the market they now had no employers to harry and humiliate them—a fact that automatically improved the status of the self-employed market vendor in her own eyes. Some noted that although marketing was manual work, it was never as exhausting as carrying enormous head loads in the hot sun. Nor was it as monotonous as sitting cramped in a dark room amid tobacco dust, rolling cigarettes at a frantic pace to earn a few pennies per hundred cigarettes. Nevertheless, all women wished they could earn more, and many pointed out that they faced more barriers in becoming successful traders than did the men around them. The barrier most clearly recognized was the refusal of wholesalers to extend more credit to them. Many women also noted indirectly a whole range of social constraints on their physical mobility and social interaction.

Chennai women's remarks about their difficulty in finding employment, as well as their complaints about men's inability to support their families, are borne out by the few available statistics. In Tamilnadu and in India as a whole, there has been a general decline in female labor force participation compared to the early part of the twentieth century. Moreover, in Tamilnadu, urban areas have fewer working women than rural areas, suggesting that there is as yet no demand for female labor in cities comparable to the demand for women's agricultural labor in villages. Thus one in nine urban women is employed, compared to one in three rural women. In Chennai, women's workforce participation was 7.1 percent in 1981, compared to a statewide level of 26.5 percent. Significantly, men's labor force participation, which has fallen since the 1970s, is only 46.4 percent in Chennai (Tamil

Nadu Corporation for Development of Women, Ltd. 1986, 10, 221). It is hard to determine whether the sheer shortage of jobs or the role of restrictive ideology has contributed more to the skewed gender distribution in workforce participation.

SOME SCENES FROM THE MARKET

The physical aspects of the produce markets in Chennai are similar to markets elsewhere in the world. There are "official" marketplaces, consisting of rows of covered sheds sheltering brick or concrete selling platforms separated by aisles. In Chennai most of these marketplaces were erected by the city government or charitable individuals in the late nineteenth or early twentieth centuries; many are now dilapidated despite the daily rents vendors pay. In the busiest of these markets, vendors and their goods may spill over onto the floors of the aisles and fill empty spaces around doorways. In contrast to the official markets, there are "unofficial" street markets formed spontaneously in newer neighborhoods, around newly constructed shopping areas, or on the margins of overcrowded official markets. Vendors pay no rent in the unofficial sites where it is often easiest for newcomers to find selling space, but many traders note that bribes to the police are "like rent." While those selling on platforms in official markets refer to such traders dismissively as "the pavement people," pavement sellers themselves frequently speak of themselves as "selling in the road," a phrase suggesting the sense of exposure and impermanence felt by those who must work in such conditions.

The technical illegality of these markets, where all vendors are nominally guilty of encroachment on the public thoroughfare, keeps informal vendors from establishing permanent structures. Instead most vendors sit without shelter on mats on the ground, and without overnight storage space. The open, unstructured physical appearance of many street markets, so dissimilar to enclosed domestic spaces, may inhibit some women from selling in them. Yet to construct covered stalls in these locales was, in the 1960s and 1970s, to incite the police to make periodic raids in which traders were beaten and arrested, and their goods, equipment, and shelters destroyed. However, in some locations where vendors had organized and reached a fragile accommodation with the police, some of the more successful traders invested in small, semipermanent stalls of bamboo and matting.[10]

Virtually all the traders in all the retail markets, whether official or unofficial, are dependent for their supplies on the city's central wholesale market where all the wholesalers are men. That market, Kottuwal Chavadi, was located until the mid-1990s in Georgetown in the core of the original seventeenth-century Indian settlement north of the British fort.[11] Kottuwal Chavadi market itself was owned by one of the city's oldest temples. The dense wholesale trading activity sprawled beyond the old market's often-extended boundaries into narrow, winding adjacent streets where male produce wholesalers had warehouse-shops. From before dawn until mid-afternoon, the area was almost impassible with seething crowds of retail traders buying supplies, carts and trucks delivering goods, coolies moving bags and bales, ordinary citizens seeking bargains, prowling pickpockets in search of prey, and mounds of fermenting garbage. A male wholesaler once described the area as "one of the circles of hell."

In addition to its overcrowding, cacophony, and filth, the area is also a red-light district catering to truckers, businessmen, and tourists. Particularly after dark, pimps and touts solicit customers from the doorways of seedy rooming houses. All of these factors made the wholesale market a difficult locale for respectable women to enter, although some braved it in daylight. After dark, and in the predawn hours when arriving produce was auctioned off most cheaply, the area was off-limits to anyone who valued her reputation or her safety.

In Chennai retail markets, women are considerably more at home, and often manage to redefine their selling spaces—especially those in enclosed official markets—as part of the private, domestic sphere. Nevertheless, they cannot be said to dominate retail markets. Mapping of individual marketplaces and comparison between different locales show that women make up from one-third to one-half of the vendors in any retail market. Furthermore, they are marginalized both physically and socially. Women working alone (and very old men) cluster in the less desirable selling spots, have the smallest stalls and stocks of goods, tend to sell the lowest-profit items (such as betel leaves, flower garlands, or damaged vegetables), and are most numerous in declining markets that are losing customers and have already been abandoned by more enterprising and socially mobile male vendors. Where a woman trader is found to have a large stock of good quality vegetables and a permanent location in a busy, profitable marketplace, she is also inevitably a woman working in some form of partnership with a husband, brother, son, or son-in-law. In such a partnership, where the man (who may have another job elsewhere) does much of the wholesale buying, arranges the transport of goods, and shares some of the long hours of retail selling, a woman can concentrate on sales, talking to regular customers, and washing and arranging the produce attractively. She may even be able to get home to prepare a meal. Yet the complete absence of women in the ranks of institutional suppliers and secondary wholesalers underlines the way women vendors find it impossible to augment their income by moving upward into the most profitable niches of petty trade.

The social constraints on women traders are apparent in their relatively quiet and restrained demeanor while at work, despite Tamil women's formidable reputation for self-assertion and verbal competence in urban working-class communities. In Chennai it is generally male traders who shout to each other across the stalls, joke loudly, or treat the market as an arena for public performance. The women either act as a quiet, appreciative audience, talk quietly to female friends, or speak in wheedling tones to female customers. There is remarkably little direct interaction between male and female traders selling next to each other. When male and female vendors must speak to each other directly, they use kinship terms—"older brother," "older sister," "aunt," or "grandfather," which denote respect and defuse sexual implications inherent in other kinds of direct address.[12] This reticence and insistence on "respectable" behavior on the part of market women and men suggests that the market environment, despite its domestic ambiance, is sufficiently sexually charged that even within their own marketplaces women continue to feel inhibited. Vendors' creative response is to use kinship terminology to transform the potentially threatening "outside" realm of market, work, and cross-gender relationships into a safer, more protective "inside" realm of ideal familial relationships.

Shantammal and her husband Mani worked side by side in the very prosperous Ponnagal Park market in the upscale neighborhood of T. Nagar in 1973. He sold fruit—an expensive delicacy—while she sold a large selection of the best-quality vegetables. The market itself was technically illegal at that period, but it was about to become legitimate thanks to intricate political negotiations with a local political figure. The wealthy T. Nagar residents clearly wanted a clean, well-stocked produce market and were prepared to tolerate the market's encroachment on a rare local park, which had been one of the neighborhood's 1930s-style amenities. Consequently, the vendors had felt free to build a neat, spacious row of thatched stalls. Shantammal and Mani occupied two of the best of these, at the center of the line of sellers flanking an entrance. They had started out with a single stall, selling just vegetables, but as it did well, and as Mani became a friend and client of the market leader, they branched out into the fruit business and acquired a second selling space—a mark of both prosperity and political influence.

Mani did all the buying of produce at Kottuwal Chavadi, leaving Shantammal to manage both stalls in the morning rush of customers. On his return, she went home to cook the midmorning meal for Mani and the young male servant (whose hiring was another sign of the family's prosperity). Shantammal brought the food, plus an afternoon snack, to be consumed in the relatively spacious, homelike privacy of their stalls. In the hot afternoons they napped there or received visitors. Shantammal kept rudimentary written records of Mani's credit accounts with wholesalers and checked the day's cash tied up in her clothing. Their two sons, still schoolboys, joined them in their stalls in the late afternoon, to rest, play, and do homework after the petrol lamps were lit for evening sales. The young servant helped both Mani and Shantammal during the evening rush, but he remained technically the husband's servant. It would have been too compromising for Shantammal, as a good-looking woman in her thirties, to have hired a young man directly.

Saroda was a more typical, if less prosperous, vendor selling largely unassisted. She occupied the central and most prominent stall in the legal but underpopulated Mandaivalli Market in an older section of southern Chennai. A deserted wife in her thirties with one teenaged son apprenticed to a car mechanic, Saroda was able to maintain her location thanks to the help and protection of her brother Ramu, the thuggish and politically connected market leader. Ramu's own large vegetable stall dominated the far busier illegal market on the street outside. When he was off buying in the wholesale market or away on political business, his young male servant minded the stall. Ramu's plump, pretty, and very young second wife made only occasional appearances in the market to bring Ramu his meals, chatting with him

and fanning him as he ate. Ramu, although he valued these signs of defer-
ence, made it clear that he believed her place was at home at all other times,
under the watchful eye of his mother. Ramu's mother visited the market occasionally, to talk to her son and sometimes to ask his permission to go to
the movies. Ramu would question the old lady solemnly about the propriety of the film she was to see, then hand her the money for her ticket.

Saroda, whose husband had deserted her years ago, chafed at her dependence on her brother and his servant who fetched her vegetables from the
wholesale market. She often felt they deliberately had not brought her a very
good selection. If they forgot her goods or were late in arriving, then she had
nothing fresh to offer and her regular customers moved on to other vendors.
Nevertheless, she shuddered at the idea of going to the wholesale market
herself.

Nearby, the elderly and intensely respectable widow Visalakshmi, whose
only surviving child was a married daughter living on the other side of the
city, bought squashed or old vegetables from Ramu and resold them in small
piles (rather than by weight) to the poorest customers. Sporadic gifts from
her daughter enabled Visalakshmi to rent a sleeping/cooking spot on the ve-
randa of a ramshackle old house nearby. (She was luckier than the pair of old
ladies in another market nearby, who slept in a corner of the market building because they were too poor to pay rent elsewhere.) Visalakshmi's earnings bought her food and kerosene to cook with and sometimes paid her
rent. Nevertheless she was often in debt to local moneylenders. Her profits
were severely limited by a low sales volume and her need to buy from an
intermediary. Respectability and physical weakness kept Visalakshmi away
from the wholesale market.

Both Saroda and Visalakshmi remained inside Mandaivalli market, sharing space with a shifting group of fishermen's wives selling fresh fish and four
or five male mutton butchers whose banter and jokes all the women stu-
diously ignored. Both of them believed they might have been able to sell
more in the illegal market outside, where vendors were much more visible
and able "catch" customers before they reached the inside market. Saroda
admitted she might be able to insert herself into the market outside with her
brother's help. Visalakshmi had no such expectations and said that if she
tried to move outside, nobody in the line of sellers would shift to make room
for her.

Additionally, both women were afraid of police raids on the street market, which had at that period become frequent and intense. Local police constables took regular bribes to leave the vendors alone, but insisted in the aftermath of one dramatic incident that they had been helpless against their superiors' direct orders to dislodge the street market. Police officials, in turn, were under pressure from middle-class residents of the area who complained the outside street market made one of Mandaivalli's main streets dirty and impassible to cars.

In one recent raid on the street sellers, for instance, the soft-spoken Meenakshi had lost two baskets of unstrung flowers, yards of garlands already woven, her small palm-leaf umbrella which kept her stall cool, plus the few coins she had on hand. She and five other male and female vendors had also spent almost twenty-four hours in custody and in court before their release was arranged by Ramu (who had himself neatly evaded arrest). As the wife of a house painter crippled in a fall from scaffolding, Meenakshi, in her midtwenties, was the sole support of her family, which included two young children. Without effective male help to buy and transport goods, she had opted for flower selling rather than the slightly more profitable vegetable selling. Her husband minded her stall on those mornings she went early to Flower Bazaar at the edge of the wholesale area to purchase baskets of loose flowers, and he stayed on in the late morning while she went home to cook the day's main meal and feed the children. Then he returned home to eat. When he finished, she ate and dashed back to the market. If the family managed another meal, then it was prepared after the market closed down for the night around 9 P.M. It is likely that Meenakshi's husband also wove some flower garlands in the privacy of their hut, but this is an intensely feminine activity that many men dislike performing in public.

During the time Meenakshi was in custody after the raid, her husband was frantic with worry, fearing not only that she might be jailed for a prolonged period but that she might have been molested by the police. She was apparently able to calm him down by reminding him that she was never out of the sight of two older women vendors seized at the same time. Her husband, who had tears in his eyes as he praised Meenakshi's heroic efforts to keep the family alive, was in no position to order her to stay home.

GENDER IDEOLOGY IN ACTION

These examples reveal a deep-rooted local ideology of gender difference and gender separation that translates into behaviors circumscribing and curtailing the economic activities of women traders. An ideal Tamil woman's fertility and chastity are powerful forces that flourish most fully within the confines of, and for the benefit of, her own household. Beyond the realm of household and kin, her chastity begins to be bruised and battered, and the moral force of her virtue dissipates through contact with strangers and "the eyes of men" (Egnore [Trawick] 1980; Trawick 1990; Lindholm 1980), since the gaze itself has sexual connotations. The dangers to women's chastity are not simply spiritual. Sexual harassment (known all over India as "Eve teasing") and rape do occur, and they are increasing in urban contexts where lone women are more apt to be considered fair game by men socialized in a society simultaneously patriarchal, puritanical, and gender-segregated.

These ideological constructs are manifested in daily practice in Chennai as a generalized spatial and interactional separation of men and women, even within the household. The Tamil system, subtler and with fewer external markers than those of many parts of North India, allows women to leave their households on some occasions, to walk about with uncovered heads and faces, and to have some legitimated access to public spaces.[13] Yet even this limited freedom is hedged with prohibition. If Tamil women leave their homes for certain approved activities, such as religious or kinship obligations, then they should not use these occasions as a general license to "go roving about here and there" (in the words of a testy elderly man). Preferably, they should be escorted by male relatives or older women.

This system of gender separation, enforced most severely on adolescent and newly married young women whose sexual powers are at their height, is also modified by social class. The idealized form of self-seclusion is fully possible only for the well-to-do, who have servants and extended families complete with elderly aunts or leisured menfolk to act as chaperones or to undertake a household's "outside work" such as shopping, paying bills, or fetching children from school. Today in a metropolis such as Chennai, the ideal is adhered to most closely by those who are both comfortably well-off and culturally traditional. For instance, certain highly orthodox Brahmin families or certain aristocratic Chettiar (rich landowning/merchant) families still make it a mark of pride to keep their women in close seclusion, rarely seen except by their close relatives and their servants. For the rest of the Hindu urban middle and upper class, including the large numbers of Brahmin professionals, these restrictions today carry far less weight. For these classes chastity is increasingly understood as a set of internalized restraints, which a properly reared postadolescent woman will impose upon herself.

Nevertheless, even for the relatively modern, much of the local construction of female virtue still depends on various forms of surveillance. Today bourgeois Chennai women attend school, go to work, shop, visit, attend meetings, and worship on their own (see Caplan 1985), at least during daylight hours. Yet even these women are still enjoined to move purposefully toward a destination, to walk or ride with other women as far as possible, to avoid lingering in the street to talk, to avoid strangers, to be home before dark, and to give a full account of their movements when they get home. (See also Seizer 1997, on the travels of female actresses.)

As one moves down the social scale, strict female seclusion within the household is increasingly modified by the material facts of poverty and nuclear households. Poor women, even those without jobs, must move around their neighborhoods and speak to nonkin if they are to fetch water, do laundry, buy the day's food, find fuel, borrow money, and maintain kinship ties. Working-class women prefer to move in groups if they leave their immediate neighborhoods, but if they must walk or take the bus alone in the daytime, they will. Movement after dark makes companionship imperative. Poor families tend to confine adolescent daughters or young brides to the house quite strictly (and the girls complain bitterly about the tedium of confinement in a one-room dwelling), but an adult woman, responsible for her family's survival, can rarely stay indoors all day. Vera-Sanso (1995) describes the ways in which neighborhoods and kin groups judge a family's economic standing: women without men to provide for them are tacitly permitted greater freedom of movement in order to earn a living and are spared some of the gossip and ostracism which enforce female conformity. `

As these examples suggest, there are social mechanisms that allow women without their own personal chaperones to bend the ideals of female seclusion somewhat and to gain protection from the presence, at critical junctures, of other women or other people in general. This system of "public chaperonage" or "social chaperonage" (Lessinger 1986, 1989) operates best when a woman can arrange to be surrounded by "known people" who can vouch for her good behavior; in the absence of other companions, even a crowd of strangers offers some protection.[14] This strategy suggests that there is a culturally unmarked sphere midway between the public and private which replaces the seclusion of "inside" with the social density of "outside," and turns the public gaze from a threat into a protective surveillance which bears witness to blameless behavior. It seems evident that Tamil women, either those who see themselves as modern or those who, like market women, are too poor to have much choice, have seized on the ambiguities of this sphere in order to pursue activities outside the walls of the home. It is a strategy that offers a measure of freedom but also has its limitations, as the career paths of market women make clear.

MARKETING IN THE PUBLIC EYE

Public chaperonage is interwoven with women's entry into marketing. They begin to work as traders only as adult married women, past the period of greatest spiritual and physical vulnerability when they are still fiercely protected virgins and young wives. They go to work only after they have explicit permission from men or older women in the household. They only sell in marketplaces where they have kin, neighbors, or friends already present. They avoid any unnecessary contact with men and strive to surround each aspect of their work, from buying produce to chatting up regular customers, with the protection of publicity and openness. Nevertheless public chaperonage begins to break down as a protective mechanism beyond the range of a woman's own marketplace and the group of fellow traders who have come to know her and feel responsibility for her. Serious limitations remain on market women's physical and social mobility and their occupational mobility. The women recognize and complain about some of these limits. Others, they take wholly for granted.

In my field research, market women described their first efforts at trading as difficult—not because they had to calculate weights and prices,[15] but because they had to spend the day in public view and to maintain a bold, self-confident demeanor in front of customers inclined to haggle and complain.

Sitammal's husband, a dock worker who experienced long stretches of unemployment, explained how he had to coax and encourage his young wife at
length before she agreed to go into the street market and sell the selection of
vegetables he buys for her from another, larger retailer. She says shyly that
she only agreed when it became clear that their children were often too hungry to sleep. Sitammal's husband comes to the market with her whenever he
has days without work.

Manjula, by contrast, describes "just getting used to it [the conditions of
marketing]"; she went to work with the encouragement of her mother-in-
law. Her husband, a handcart puller, is rarely able to help her. Manjula says
her courage has increased with age and with the realization that nothing very
bad has ever happened to her. Manjula explains her sense of ease within the
market by recalling a dispute over prices with a male customer who had tried
to walk off with a bag of vegetables without paying her fully. Other vendors,
both male and female, immediately came to her defense, first with remon-
strances about the shame of cheating a poor woman, then with threatening
shouts. The customer quickly paid up and fled, and has not been back.

Sitammal's tale of hungry children whose crying sent her into trading is
typical of those told by Chennai market women, who frequently invoked
these culturally approved images of female self-sacrifice and heroic motherhood to suggest that their trading work was a form of suffering, engaged in
as a way to save the family but not as an end in itself, and not as something
women enjoyed. As a result, this discourse about suffering and sacrifice
makes it difficult for women to articulate how or why they get satisfaction
out of their work as traders. Personal autonomy is so contrary to stereotyped
ideals that working-class women, unlike urban middle-class women, rarely
acknowledge it directly as something desired or obtained through work.

One of the forms of suffering many market women invoked was the trip
to the central wholesale market to buy supplies, an arena where public chaperonage has only limited utility. Even when traders travel to Kottuwal Chavadi in groups, the buying process is individualized and subjects women to
a series of insults, irritations, and confrontations that reenforce their sense of
female helplessness and class inferiority.

Running the gauntlet of the crowded, sexually charged Kottuwal Chavadi
area streets, women approached wholesale shops individually to begin to bargain, assertively if not aggressively, with male wholesale suppliers and their

clerks. Many wholesalers or their servants slighted or mocked women retailers because they were lower class and likely to make only small purchases. Women were made to wait before being served until after male customers making large purchases were attended to. Some wholesalers or their clerks addressed the women as "thou" (*nii*) instead of the more formal, respectful "you" (*ningaL*) by which middle-class women are invariably addressed. Others sometimes joked suggestively with women, an act which itself underlines women traders' class inferiority. Additionally, women vendors claimed that they could never get as much credit as male retailers. Unless they could pay cash every week, they were limited in how much they could buy for resale and thus in how far they could expand their businesses.[16]

After making their purchases, market women then had to negotiate the transport of their goods across the city to their own marketplaces. Groups of friends either shared the services of a carter or rickshaw driver, or they tried to wheedle their way onto public buses despite regulations banning cargo. After rush-hour, bus conductors might let market women board with their bundles and baskets, sometimes out of pity but sometimes in order to harass them with crude remarks, pinching, and improper propositions. Women endured this treatment partly because, in a public setting, they knew it could not go much beyond verbal harassment and covert touching, and partly because they were all engaged in a conspiracy of silence about this aspect of their work. Women knew that it would do little good to protest; it might, however, encourage their male relatives to order them to stay home.[17] It was better, they reasoned, to swallow the humiliation and shame, to suffer and keep quiet.

GENDER SEPARATION AND THE FAILURE OF NGOS

Like many other developing countries, India is now home to large numbers of NGOs that operate in settings where the state lacks the will to act. Indian NGOs have been left since the 1970s to tackle, among other intractable problems, both endemic poverty and women's subordination. Because government planners have tacitly abandoned any national strategies to create new sources of formal sector employment to employ the unemployed or to raise wages, NGOs have instead begun to promote women's informal sector employment in particular locales, reasoning that two wages, however low, will nevertheless raise overall household income for the very poor. Precisely because they are not state initiatives, these efforts are bound to have only limited success. Nevertheless, under the rubric "income generation," NGOs have increasingly emphasized insertion of women into petty commodity production and petty trade by providing women with capital to get started and sometimes with minimal training or guidance. The resulting efforts are often spoken of optimistically in terms of "female empowerment."

Although many Indian NGOs have their roots in the Indian women's movement or in leftist movements (Omvedt 1993), most of these organizations do not aspire to social structural changes. Few NGOs directly confront local norms of gender separation or their impact on women's agency as workers. Most NGOs simply accept local forms of labor market segmentation and try to insert their clients into forms of work compatible with local rules of gendered behavior, hoping to find or create, for instance, piecework or petty production that women might carry out in the seclusion of the home (see, for instance, Mies 1982; Mies, Lalitha, and Kumari 1986). Others have emphasized the entry of women into petty entrepreneurship, regardless of the overcrowded and competitive nature of the informal sector. These assumptions and practices have contributed to the ineffectiveness of a number of income-generating schemes aimed at women. Nonetheless, such schemes—so attractive in theory—continue to be proffered and poor women continue to be presented with cows, goats, or sewing machines in efforts to establish them as petty commodity producers or self-employed entrepreneurs.

Some NGOs have noted the kind of exclusion from credit networks that women, including Chennai's market women, experience. In an effort to launch more women into petty trade and petty commodity production, some groups have used their governmental ties to begin to channel small, low-interest bank loans to female producers and traders who would otherwise be unable to get the credit needed to go into business (Everett and Savara 1991). Today a number of voluntary organizations act as intermediaries between poor women and state or national banks, undertaking credit checks, choosing loan recipients, and guaranteeing repayment on behalf of female borrowers previously snubbed by both official and unofficial sources of credit.

Two much-studied women's organizations in different parts of India have been particularly energetic in this effort, using loan schemes as part of larger efforts to organize urban women in the informal sector and to launch poor women as income earners. Both have concentrated particularly on women traders and petty commodity producers, forms of self-employment open to women as well as men. In Ahmedabad, a city in the North Indian state of Gujarat, the Self-Employed Women's Association (SEWA) has since the early 1970s used a variety of imaginative tactics to organize and support poor women as traders, small-scale producers, and wage workers (see Rose 1992; Jhabvala 1992). In Tamilnadu, particularly in Chennai, the Working Women's Forum (WWF), established somewhat later, has used a similar model to organize a narrower range of female petty traders and producers (see Azad 1981).

SEWA has continued to evolve since its founding. It has not only set up loan schemes but encouraged cooperatives for women producers and has helped poor women set up their own banks in which they can begin savings accounts. Where necessary, women have been offered training in skills such as bookkeeping so that they can run their own organizations. SEWA, rooted in Gandhian traditions of nonviolent confrontation and linked to local trade unions, has also been effective in mobilizing Ahmedabad's women produce traders into street protests against police corruption and brutality. After local bureaucrats and shopkeepers, backed by police enforcement, attempted to evict all vegetable sellers from the city's main market, SEWA members used a combination of street protests, lobbying, and lawsuits to reverse the ban (Jhabvala 1992). Over the years SEWA has extended its activities to reach other groups of poor women such as coolies and piece workers, encouraging them to confront exploitative middlemen, to demand higher wages, and to resist bureaucratic oppression (Jhabvala 1992; Rose 1992).

Because SEWA is democratically run and dedicated to promoting self-help among the ranks of poor women, it has managed to provide its members with all-female reference groups outside their immediate families, and its meetings often serve as forums for consciousness-raising on subjects such as wife beating or male alcoholism, which are of great concern to poor women. To a certain extent SEWA has helped to legitimate female employment in the eyes of local working-class communities by demonstrating that working women can get attention and support from the larger society. In this regard SEWA continues to be more sophisticated than other NGOs.

In Chennai the WWF has also launched many women as petty producers and petty traders (see Azad 1981; Noponen 1987, 1991, 1992), but its activities have moved little beyond the provision of loans to those wanting to enter business or expand existing businesses. Despite an organization formed around neighborhood-based borrowers' groups, WWF has been less successful (or perhaps less ambitious) in launching broader forms of mobilization. Observers such as Noponen (1992) suggest this is partly due to WWF's intense focus on making loans and enforcing repayment through collective responsibility of each neighborhood loan group. WWF's organizational ties to the local Congress Party political machine would make a SEWA-style political confrontation with police or local administrators impossible. Furthermore, it is highly unlikely to mobilize traders within particular markets against police, landlords, or bureaucrats. Nor, as Noponen notes (1992), is WWF presently ready to launch mass campaigns among its members on such specific gender issues as dowry, male alcoholism, or domestic violence.

Despite a great deal of commendable work, SEWA and WWF have been rather narrowly focused on the issue of bringing women into the informal sector workforce, particularly as small traders. Neither has been able to contemplate the next step: taking aim against the complex of attitudes which keeps women, once they are actually working, marginalized in the least profitable niches of that work, unlikely to become self-supporting. This suggests that female producers' cooperatives and woman-oriented loan schemes are simply a few of the economic mechanisms in a larger cultural battle that demands to be waged on many fronts.

If women workers are to be placed on an equal footing with men, a first step might be the examination of local cultural norms that severely restrict what women can do to earn money and when and where they can do it. Groups that have already created organizational bases among poor urban women need to lead their members in examining, making explicit, and then challenging—in practical rather than simply rhetorical ways—some of the ideological constraints on women's work which poor Indians have taken for granted all their lives. The final step, of course, is to move beyond the economic status quo represented by the informal sector and to insist that women also have access to formal sector jobs. The historical experience of middle-class women in Chennai suggests that cultural resistance to female employment decreases when the work itself offers autonomy and decent pay. To leave these issues unexamined is simply to reproduce women's economic vulnerability in urban economies marked by increasing poverty and low wage levels. As long as the pettiness of female trading remains an accepted fact, trading will not lead women, or their families, out of dire poverty.

CONCLUSION

Using case material from the large South Indian city of Chennai, this chapter has placed women's lives as retail traders into the larger context of women's and men's employment within the city's gender-segmented labor market at a period of increased stress on working-class livelihoods. The material suggests some of the ways in which patriarchal ideology and practice remain strong despite social and economic changes forcing women into the workforce—sometimes, as in the case of petty retailing, in competition with men.

It is clear that in Chennai, as in the rest of India, women's identities as workers are still entwined with larger contestations about the relationships between gender, extradomestic employment, family honor, and class status. The issue is particularly acute for women traders, both because their work takes place in highly public locales, far from the shelter of household and neighborhood where women "naturally" belong, and because the particular history of petty trade in Chennai places women in a series of morally ambiguous, if not dangerous, situations vis-à-vis wholesalers, transportation workers, and the police.

Chennai working-class women accept, in theory if not always in practice, many of the restrictive gender ideologies that define and confine them, at the same time that they also show skill in manipulating and reinventing some of the rules of behavior. Ideas of self-sacrifice and suffering justify their breaches of social conventions, while techniques of public chaperonage and domesticating public space allow women to work in markets without becoming defined as shameless and bad. Yet these older gender ideologies remain tenacious and popular with women as well as with men precisely because they are also class ideologies. Without immediate hope of larger social changes in India, the urban poor, battered by rural to urban migration and economic displacement, cling to fine distinctions of status and class as markers of respectability and self-respect. Female invisibility and dependence remain powerful status markers. Although women's professional and pink-collar employment has begun to loosen these kinds of restrictions on upper- and middle-class women, poor women's market trading, with its built-in limitations, is not the kind of prestigious, well-paid, permanent job that might break down social prejudices and older gender ideologies among the working-class population.

NGOs dealing with issues of women's poverty in India have given little practical attention to the ways in which patriarchal ideas and practices, in interaction with the characteristics of the informal labor market, severely limit women's earning power. Organizations seem to take the attitude that if poor Indian women wish to earn money, NGOs can shoehorn them into work such as petty trade; poor men, it is assumed, will simply have to accept the workplace competition and household reorganization that ensue. This approach leaves intact in Chennai's working-class communities large reservoirs of male resistance and female ambivalence toward women's employment. Women seek informal sector work if they can find it, but they do not see themselves as permanently committed to the role of wage-earner. Their hesitation is accentuated by the fact that their earnings are small and the work itself lacking in social dignity. As a result both men and women remain convinced that women's employment is an exceptional response to exceptional poverty, rather than something to which all women might aspire. Only the widening of economic niches and economic rewards for women, as is beginning to occur for middle-class and elite women, will genuinely erode these attitudes.

Two mothers earning money by vegetable retailing, Akan, Ghana. Photo credit: Gracia Clark.

CHAPTER FOUR

"Nursing-Mother Work" in Ghana: Power and Frustration in Akan Market Women's Lives

GRACIA CLARK

ABSTRACT: *While honoring the biological aspect of motherhood, Akan gender ideas consider economic support central to the daily experience of mothering. According to Akan complementary matrilineal gender roles, sisters contribute children, and brothers contribute wealth, while husbands reciprocate their wives' domestic services. Mothers value their power to earn income to successfully raise their children and consider the financial, not the domestic, burden of children as limiting their wealth. In life narratives, Kumasi women traders use the concept of nursing-mother work to show the unity and contradiction between child rearing and breadwinning as life projects. Tensions over dwindling real incomes and shifting power balances fuel accusations and ruptures in gender relations within the family, the community, and the nation-state. Conversely, women's shared maternal identification generates solidarity among traders and legitimizes their visible profits in spite of government attacks and continuing austerity measures.*

Feminist and antifeminist analyses of gender often agree in placing motherhood at the center of feminine gender identity, and in placing biological childbirth at the center of motherhood. Even those who acknowledge that the biological process of pregnancy and birth is saturated with and transformed by specific cultural meanings still place this culturally constructed "biology" at the center of motherhood. Disagreement about whether motherhood empowers or disempowers women overall also erupts on both the feminist and antifeminist sides. In feminist models of women's universal subordination, childbirth triggers a sequence of nursing, child minding, and self-effacement that keeps women in the private sphere, easily available for unpaid labor near the home and restrained from income-generating work and the pursuit of personal ambition in the public sphere. In sociobiological models, pregnancy and child rearing make women more vulnerable and dependent on the protection of men, who are more efficient in defense and production.

Positive interpretations of motherhood can be equally biologist and naturalistic. The creative drama of physical reproduction can be presented as a significant source of power even (or especially) in environments that otherwise strictly circumscribe women's agency. In a patriarchal society, a maturing woman's children may constitute the core of her support in household politics. Motherhood may be experienced by individuals as a powerful expression of personal agency and may provide a model and inspiration for further expressions or a compensation for other disappointments.

Feminist analyses of women's political activism also cite the shared experience or identification with motherhood as a common ground of solidarity. Assertions of universal sisterhood now seem naive, but the political mobilization of women in various parts of the world explicitly as mothers undoubtedly forms a notable genre of political organization. It appears in a range of contexts from revolutionary or progressive on through reactionary nationalism, calling on the loyalty of women as mothers of every nation and movement. Ecofeminists, for example, lay claim to the maternal values of survival and protection on a global scale and solicit the allegiance of women to policies of sustainability by asserting a natural basis for these values.

Universalist models from feminism in the United States have been critiqued for excluding the historical experience of U.S. black women, the majority of whom worked outside the home. They also generally neglect to incorporate alternative conceptual frameworks of gender and motherhood from within the United States and other countries. As McCormack and others have noted in diverse cultural contexts, the categories of male and female may be sharply divided and their borders deeply felt, without corresponding to the contrast between public and private to any meaningful extent (MacCormack and Strathern 1980).

African women have figured in all sides of these arguments for many years. They have been brandished as emblems of oppression in missionary descriptions as beasts of burden, in Marxist analyses as slaves of slaves, and in feminist denunciations of genital mutilation, bride price, and the feminization of poverty. Meanwhile, other feminist and Afrocentric writers have romanticized West African dual gender systems as providing autonomy, security, and pride for both men and women. The experience of Asante market women from southern Ghana, which informs this chapter, is susceptible to both positive and negative interpretations. The strong Akan emphasis on fertility can be depicted as loading down women with an inescapable physical burden of many children through their inescapable identity as mothers, compounded with the agricultural or financial burden of feeding them. At the same time, matrilineal Akan society gives mothers public as well as private respect for their fertility. As family elders, they retain direct control of their children and permanent authority over them. They also gain access to property and public office as maternal figures.

WORK AND BIRTH

Akan market women's narratives of their life experiences as mothers and as daughters[1] throw light on how they themselves weigh and reconcile various aspects of gender and parenthood. In this chapter, I argue from their statements that the privileging of biology as the experiential core of motherhood, even a socially constructed biology, is just as culturally specific as the public/private dichotomy. Akan accounts of the daily experience of motherhood give priority to their economic support, even though the biological relationship remains structurally central to their matrilineage organization and the most common term used for the devoted mother clearly acknowledges childbirth as part of that identity.

The Twi phrase most often used to describe or discuss appropriate maternal activities and emotions is *obaatan*. Its literal components *obaa* (woman) and *otan* (fireplace) evoke the image of a woman during her period of home confinement after childbirth, when she and the baby are kept warm by the hearth. A more literal English translation would be "childbearing woman," but this does not convey the intimacy of the original because of its clinical flavor and frequent use for an age category, rather than an individual. The translation with the English phrase "nursing mother" selects an equally common idiom that has a similar biological basis and stereotypical deployment. Besides, Asante in practice use this Twi word most frequently for women clearly past this protective period and precisely about their public activity in working for and defending their children's interests. The phrase nursing mother thus suggests this more extended period of commitment to the child, without losing the colloquial tone or the emotional hook of a biological referent. This phrase was invariably used by English-speaking Asante, including those translating the interview tapes. Asante who did not speak English also implied it nonverbally, by pantomiming a baby held up to the breast to make me understand.

Despite this biological etymology, it is the intensity of purpose, rather than the physical activity, that characterizes the obaatan. Without the capacity to take care of her children financially, a woman's biological power of childbearing cannot be fully realized. Men likewise consider fathering children biologically to be an essential demonstration of fully gendered personhood, both physically and spiritually. Their substantial financial duty to support and educate their children is significantly compromised by contradictory imperatives to accumulate property for personal reputation and for their matrilineage, which does not include their biological children. A proverb often used to define motherhood says, "If I don't eat, she doesn't eat." For Asantes, this phrase encompasses complete identification with the child economically, through shared poverty, and emotionally, through the loss of appetite emblematic of sorrow and anger.

The occasional use of obaatan to describe men underlines its tighter association with emotion than procreation. While by implication fathers may be less likely to show this degree of devotion, and very few cases were discovered, it is not contradictory when they do. One young woman warmly praised her father in front of friends as a very good father, a "real nursing mother" (*obaatan paa*), because he always wanted to know what all of his children (from both his wives) needed and provided it for them immediately. Most impressive for this woman was her father's immediate return from an overseas business trip when he heard she was dangerously ill. In a similar vein, an educated, devout Christian woman invoked "God the nursing mother" in a public prayer, only a few moments later using the more conventional "God the father." This form of address was unusual, but passed without a lifted eyebrow from a large, apparently conservative, mixed audience that then considered Adam and Eve the appropriate starting point for a discussion of proper gender roles.

Discussions of child rearing with Akan men and women confirm that they consider the economic imperative of motherhood much more absolute than the responsibility for physical child care, which can be delegated with comparative ease and confidence. Her children's growing financial needs send an Akan mother into the workforce with all the intensity of her pronatalist values. One woman trader explained earnestly that any normal adult could be trusted to take care of her children. "No one will sit and let a child cry, but no one will work for them like I do." [2] The only case I knew where fostering seriously compromised the maternal bond involved a young prostitute who left her baby daughter with the father's wife while she moved to Abidjan and remained away for many years without sending money or messages. Still, when the daughter eventually got pregnant while in school, she tried living with her returned mother before coming back to the stepmother with her new baby.

The complex interpenetration of the financial and domestic responsibilities of motherhood is not without its tensions for Akan mothers in contemporary Ghana, but it creates a positive identification of motherhood with work different from the conceptual opposition between the two that Eurocentric gender ideals continue to enshrine, however frequently these ideals are contradicted by history and experience. For Akans, this image of the devotedly working mother genders work itself by constructing a distinctive configuration of boundaries between male and female work. Akan gender ideas acknowledge a contradiction between women's work, seen as merging unpaid domestic services with earning income to feed and educate the children, and the accumulation of property, seen as men's privilege and responsibility. Market women's specific range of professional roles both exemplify and cross this border. Mediating this contradiction between survival and accumulation defines women traders' ideological vulnerability and their avenues for both upward and downward mobility.

GENDER AND WEALTH

Proverbial formulations of gender ideals within the Asante matrilineage contrast brothers, who bring wealth to the lineage, with sisters, who bring children. Motherhood and capital accumulation appear as opposites, as substitutes, and as complements in a range of highly gendered contexts. Married men pay twice the per capita contribution of women to lineage assessments for funerals or court cases, for a reason considered obvious: they have more money. When pressed for more elaborate explanations, men and women specify that having children prevents women from saving, by taking unpaid time away from their work and by taking money away from their capital for the children's food, medicine, and schooling.

The presumed primacy of this demand on their time and income locates women differently from men with respect to inheritance and use of lineage property. They can claim access to lineage property to use for raising children, because these children secure the perpetuation of the lineage. Women's rights to live rent-free in housing left by deceased lineage members and to use lineage farmland to grow food take priority over income needs of male lineage members. A man who had inherited houses or land through his lineage would face great pressure to allow female relatives to continue to occupy rooms in the house or farm plots, both of which they could pass on to female descendants for subsistence purposes.

At the same time, women complained that they had less access than male relatives to larger plots of land suitable for commercial farming, to housing used for rental income, and to sums of money large enough for business capital. Under the rather flexible Asante matrilineal inheritance guidelines, the family elders should consider various eligible persons' ability to make good use of the asset when choosing a successor to a deceased person, or when allocating the use of assets available to benefit the lineage as a whole. According to some women who had been passed over for loans or cocoa farms, elders tend to assume that men can take better advantage of commercial or productive assets precisely because they face fewer demands on their time and income. Even assets built up by a woman, which should ideally pass to a female successor, were sometimes considered "men's things."[3] These differentiated inheritance and use rights, along with broader patterns of gender disparity in employment and business, reinforce the pattern of higher average incomes for men.

Women gain access to these higher male incomes legitimately through their brothers and husbands. Brothers should be willing at least to help a sister's children, who are their lineage successors. Appeals for subsistence support are particularly difficult for a brother to refuse and provide an important safety net for divorced women. Marriage normally involves more substantial financial support from the husband, but this comes with significant strings attached in the form of unpaid domestic services. A husband gives his wife or wives a regular daily allowance for cooking (called literally "neck-rope"). This arrangement distinguishes marriage from more informal sexual partnerships, which may also involve gifts of money. The allowance is linked conceptually and pragmatically to a woman's actual provision of meals, warm bathwater, and sexual satisfaction. If a man travels, takes a second wife, or loses interest in the first, his payments are reduced proportionately to his actual consumption of her services. One elderly woman explained that her husband even gave her 50 percent more allowance for Sundays, because he stayed home from work and ate three meals at home, rather than two.

Wealth or income is central to fatherhood as well as motherhood. It is difficult for a man to assert recognized fatherhood, by naming the baby at the naming ceremony, without making at least a symbolic presentation of cloth and of supplies or funds for the mother's rest period after childbirth. In the ordinary poor family, a man's cooking allowance to his wife is the most substantial payment she receives from him, although he may also pay rent if they live together. A father should also contribute to medical expenses, school fees, and other children's needs according to his ability. Unlike cooking allowances, these claims should be honored even after a divorce. Wealthy men can effectively father more children, both by supporting them more fully and by attracting and keeping more wives with their greater capacity to pay regular allowances. Even so, some wealthy men also flagrantly neglect their paternal and marital duties.

Conversely, wealthy women fall under suspicion of neglecting their children or their childbearing potential because of their wealth, not in spite of it. These suspicions surface in a number of ways. Discussions of Christian gender roles, taken seriously by increasing numbers of Kumasi women traders, mentioned the wealthy woman as likely to be neglecting her domestic and emotional duties toward her husband and children in order to spend enough time on business affairs to prosper. Stories about witchcraft often feature conspicuously wealthy traders or businesswomen. Descriptions of common forms of "money magic" include magic charms, such as snakes or wristwatches that turn into snakes at night and vomit enchanted money that always returns to the hands of its owner quickly after it is spent. Like more generalized witches' circles portrayed in Rattray (1927), these charms must be periodically fed on the life force of blood relatives or a woman's own children, causing illness, deaths, or miscarriages. One woman made veiled allusions along those lines about a wealthy neighbor with only two children in the 1970s. In the 1990s, she called the same woman lucky to have miscarried many times and thus avoided the financial burden of many children, making it possible for her to get ahead.

Despite this ambivalence, Akan culture does provide considerable support for women's financial aspirations. As long as a woman raises an appropriate number of children and makes substantial efforts to preserve her marriage, her wealth becomes a further sign of success. A woman's wealth also enriches her lineage and hometown. Brothers and uncles will applaud and reward women who achieve considerable wealth against the odds, and sons will be proud of and grateful to them. Like wealthy men, wealthy women disarm resentment and accusations of witchcraft by conspicuously helping their relatives and communities. On a less exalted level, ordinary mothers (and their relatives and friends) are well aware that their own savings provide essential security for their children's future well-being, in an environment where a father's support is always somewhat uncertain. Even the most devoted father cannot be sure that death, illness, or bankruptcy will not deprive his children of paternal protection.

The irony in this historically specific intersection of gender and class is that wealthy women traders most contradict the gender stereotype, but experience less material role conflicts. Mothers with comfortable incomes can more easily meet the competing demands of maternal care and capital accumulation. The financial needs of their growing children for food, clothing, and schooling do not threaten the stability of their larger trading enterprises. They delegate domestic work more often and more completely than poorer traders, since they can afford to support extra dependents who are older and more competent. Given Asante concepts of maternal bonding, leaving others to handle child care creates few problems, compared to delegating cooking for their husbands (Clark 1989).

Wealth and power differentials within the market hierarchy do create ideological tensions by making the legitimate maternal subsistence goal more or less plausible for women traders at opposite ends of the spectrum. The distinction among richer and poorer traders is not between a capitalist and a subsistence orientation, since all want to accumulate. Most try their utmost to do so, but relatively few succeed. Many more have a realistically low estimation of their individual chances, given their personal and family resources and demands.

MATERNAL CONTRADICTIONS

This widespread frustration defines the contradiction within Akan cultural constructions of motherhood, as both motivating and interfering with work. The dilemma was highlighted by the concept of nursing-mother work (*obaatan adjuma*), used in some of the life histories I recorded in the 1990s. Nursing-mother work has both positive and negative attributes in comparison to other kinds of work. It must be completely reliable, providing "something to eat every day." Women highly value this uninterrupted income, with no risk of losses or delays, because it gives them the power to raise their children successfully regardless of the fortunes or reliability of husbands and relatives. One great-grandmother described her early efforts at cloth trading as unsatisfactory: "I saw that it was not nursing-mother work. Sometimes you had to wait a long time before people bought the cloth. So I decided to sell oranges, because people would buy them every day and you would get something." She explained further that only people with more capital could sell cloth, since they could afford to wait. Another elderly trader pointed out that the concept was relational, not abstract. Any commodity could be your nursing-mother work. "It could be cloth, or yams or soup greens, if it did well for you."

Negative comments about nursing-mother work referred to the lack of accumulation. Higher profit levels often required waiting to complete bigger transactions, or accepting more risk of loss. Men's profits at the same capital level tended to be higher partly because they could often accept more risk, relying on their wives' incomes to cushion their fall. One woman trader who sold weekly to credit customers on the coast put the contrast in their words. When price conditions there gave a buyer windfall profits, the buyer said, "I can't call you my nursing mother any more," as she had when her profits were only steady dribbles sufficient to sustain family life. This supplier, across geographic and ethnic (but not gender) boundaries, could become another adult woman's nursing mother because she always managed to bring her some goods to sell on credit that enabled her to find food to eat.

Even when other women traders did not use the term itself, they explicitly linked the relentless financial drain of providing subsistence for their children to their frustrating inability to get ahead. They might blame inadequate paternal contributions, commenting that "only people with good husbands can get ahead," but what they aimed at was making even higher maternal contributions. Higher capital levels would allow them to provide better educational and other career sponsorship and accumulate property to pass on to their children.

The time-honored Western road to prosperity through education and professional employment presents additional material conflicts with maternity. The rigid schedules of formal work and schooling make child care supervision difficult, and schools and many employers still get rid of pregnant women one way or another despite legal protections. One informant was forced to resign from her bank position in the late 1970s when she became pregnant. Her manager explained that although the law required the bank to provide maternity leave and nursing breaks if she gave birth, she was still not allowed to get pregnant.

The fact that families intervene strenuously when they perceive serious threats to childbearing in other occupations underlines the lack of conflict perceived with trading. Women who delay childbearing to earn advanced degrees or promotions provoke serious reactions from their maternal relatives who fear a young woman will lose interest in childbearing or lose attractiveness to potential fathers. Small completed family size is especially disastrous for matrilineages with only a single fertile woman. One middle-aged woman reported that she grew up in such a position, as the only daughter of the eldest daughter of a notable Kumasi lineage. When in secondary school, she did well in science and expressed a desire to study medicine. Her grandmother at once offered to sign over all her considerable property to her if she quit school and started having children immediately. She eventually compromised with her family's priorities by choosing a shorter academic program, qualifying as a pharmacist rather than a medical doctor, while having six children.

Notably absent from the discourse on nursing-mother work is any mention of domestic work, child care, or actual nursing. Specific occupations or trading activities are not evaluated here in terms of their compatibility with physical child care. The issues of interruptibility and location near the home, that loom so large in anthropological and feminist discussions of motherhood and work, barely surface here (Brown 1970). Market traders did complain of the interruptions young children forced on their market work, but nursing babies tied firmly to their backs were not the problem. Preschoolers could and needed to be left at home more often. The financial pressure that defines "nursing-mother work" continues unabated after a woman completes physical childbearing, when less intimate marital relations and growing daughters combine to relieve domestic work demands considerably (Clark 1989, 1994).

Women did show concern for their children's safety in the workplace, evaluating certain market locations as unsafe that exposed young babies carried on the back to direct sun and rain. Others were unsafe for toddlers because they were located near deep open drains or heavy traffic. By these criteria, women might classify the home itself as an unsafe workplace. Making cooked food at home is usually considered highly compatible with the burden of child care by academic analysts, but not always by Asante women. One elderly trader had been forced to stop selling cooked food as a young mother because the large pots of boiling water presented too much danger when she had many small children at home.

In many ways, market trading as a category is the archetypal nursing-mother work, or at least fits the criteria more than other major employment sectors. For urban traders, it provides a daily income, compared to wages and salaries paid monthly or weekly. Traders who sell local foodstuffs are able to take home surplus food at wholesale cost. Rural women contrasted the annual or seasonal income and harvests they got from farming (especially cocoa, but also most food crops) to the daily or weekly profits from trading that enabled them to buy food as needed. The small amounts most traders earn fit the negative stereotype of low incomes for women/mothers, who supposedly have lower personal status needs than men/fathers. Although about 30 percent of those trading or working in Kumasi Central Market were men, and many of them were at least as poor as the average woman trader, their location and income levels were anomalous in gender terms. A majority of the men traders also came from other ethnic groups, not always sharing Asante gender norms.

SOLIDARITY AS MOTHERS

The ideology of economic maternity provides an important basis for solidarity within and beyond the ranks of traders. In bargaining contexts, the low incomes associated with nursing-mother work can provide a strategic defense against allegations of excessive profits. Shared maternal responsibilities help market women overcome conflicting interests based on wealth, trading role, local politics, and ethnicity to unite into the commodity groups that are the backbone of market organization (Clark 1991). A group comprising all the sellers of smoked fish in Kumasi Central Market, for example, crosses important economic boundaries between the scores of retailers and a handful of wealthy wholesalers. It links those with fixed premises in Kumasi with hawkers circulating in the streets and market pathways and with travelers bringing in fish from many disparate sources. It also bridges ethnic cleavages, since Asante women bring and sell fish from nearby Lake Bosumtwe, Fanti women bring and sell ocean fish from their coastal homeland, and non-Akan men supply sundried fish from the distant northern rivers. Only because wealth does not contradict the maternal imperative can shared maternal identification preserve as much solidarity as it does amidst considerable envy and bitterness.

Linking across these divides is essential for commodity groups to carry out their primary task of settling disputes between traders. Disputes arise most frequently between a trader and her continual bargaining adversaries (her buyers and suppliers up and down the distribution chain) or her closest competitors (her colleagues at the same commercial level). For successful dispute settlement, both sides must be members of the group, acknowledging the authority of its leader and subject to the penalty of expulsion or ostracism. They see no practical possibility of using formal legal channels even to enforce credit claims, let alone norms of commercial relations that would have little standing in court.

Such consensual mutual assistance supports commercial self-interest, rather than contradicting it. Women rely for enterprise survival on their ability to receive credit and extend it when necessary with confidence that group authority will back up their collection efforts. Most credit within Kumasi Central Market passes from supplier to buyer or vice versa. In the case of many farm commodities, credit reverses direction seasonally in response to harvest gluts and dry-season scarcities. Steady customers, either buyers or sellers, need each other's commercial survival to build up their own volume of trade (Clark 1991). While pushing for relative advantage over her customers, a trader wants her own customers to prosper compared to those of her competitors. Just as Alexander reports from Java, such rivalrous interdependence leads traders to share substantial but not complete price information and other valuable assistance (Alexander 1987).

Credit patterns do not link many Kumasi traders into horizontal groups for joint buying or rotating credit. They use the Yoruba word *esusu* for both rotating credit groups and ambulatory bankers, attributing both to the Yoruba traders common in Kumasi before their expulsion in 1969.[4] In rotating credit groups, members pay a daily, weekly, or monthly contribution collected by a leader, often at a meeting. Each member in turn takes the total amount as a lump sum, until all have received it once to complete the cycle. An ambulatory banker, often a young man, collects daily or weekly contributions from many clients and records them in a passbook kept by the client. He can use or invest the deposits until he returns the total to each depositor at the end of the month, or on demand, sometimes keeping one day's contribution as his fee. Many Kumasi traders distrust such bankers, citing known examples of embezzlement. Unlike supplier credit, neither of these practices expands the trader's commercial capital beyond the amount she contributes. Some traders seemed to look down on participants as lacking the self-discipline to save on their own and avoid the fee or the risk. These older women recommended them only for teaching young girls how to save.

Traders who operate at the same commercial level, whether related as commodity group members or simply as market neighbors, compete energetically while preserving a mutually sustaining social context. They exchange many kinds of unpaid help, much like mutual customers do. Neighbors watch each other's goods and children, pass on information about police activity and other dangers, settle disputes informally, and contribute to family funerals. Like fellow group members, they express their commitment to mutual commercial survival (not equal prosperity) by saying, "We are all mothers here, just trying to get something to feed our children."

DEFENSIVE POSITIONS

The maternal identity also gave traders one of their few effective arguments for protection against the central government during a long series of attacks on their activities for causing inflation. Attempts to blame the deteriorating international terms of trade on traders' excessive numbers and profits had begun in colonial times. Nationalist Dr. J. B. Danquah defended traders against British censure in the 1930s as women who were only feeding their children, working long and hard without getting ahead (Danquah 1947). When consulted by the Armed Forces Revolutionary Council (AFRC) regime in the 1970s or the related People's National Defense Council (PNDC) regime in the 1980s, traders defended themselves from charges of selfish profiteering by saying they were forced to work to support their children. Market leaders complained consistently about low incomes compared to rising prices, rising fees for transport and schooling, and the exactions of corrupt corporate managers. They denounced these causes of high prices, which hurt traders as mothers and consumers. In the 1990s, Kumasi men who had witnessed earlier violence against women traders during price control enforcement regretted targeting them, calling them "good mothers" working on through middle age to keep their children in school.

The traders' image as devoted mothers also gives them legitimacy in building solidarity outside the market on the basis of town citizenship or ethnicity. During the 1930s and 1950s, Kumasi yam traders repeatedly appealed to the Asantehene as "mothers of Asante" for support in their commercial rivalry with men from Mali (Clark 1994). Since most traders' groups organize within a particular town or market, they can take up broader community issues, especially the populist or local issues they share with the consumers and producers whose goods they carry. For example, Accra traders joined in protests about violent repression of university student demonstrations on several occasions in 1978 and 1979, as mothers of the students, metaphorically if not literally. Women traders had been active as individuals and groups in the various political parties in the 1950s, around the time of independence.[5]

Market traders figure prominently as geographical mediators and so embody urban/rural tensions. They are the visible representatives of the village in town, in the "villagers' markets" that provide fresh produce supposedly straight from the farmer. In the villages, women from Kumasi and other large towns are the most visible city slickers, facing the farmer with all the sophistication, information, and buying power they command through urban residence and frequent travel. Urban traders themselves manipulate such boundaries to include themselves and exclude others. I heard some individuals increase the urban/rural social distance by exaggerating the mystery and hostility of market leaders and institutions, in order to preserve their monopoly on sales. Many others sought to reduce social distance, cultivating fictive kinship ties and learning local dialects and languages to put villagers at ease.

Supporting local issues reinforces traders' commercial alliance with the local producers and consumers on whom their prosperity depends. Traders from different locales, however, may find their occupational solidarity overwhelmed by such local loyalties. For example, yam traders in cities all over southern Ghana cooperated to renegotiate freight charges with long-distance truck drivers. Chiefs in Techiman, an important market town and yam-producing center, nonetheless got enthusiastic support from Techiman yam traders in 1979 for restricting commercial buying in that district by outsiders, such as Kumasi-based yam traders. This rivalry drew on deep-rooted land and chieftancy disputes over the autonomy of Brong-Ahafo Region and its indigenous Brongs (also Akans) from Asante overlords in or near Kumasi who had sent in settlers even before colonial rule.

Where interethnic tensions run high, traders can provide an accessible flash point or an easy target. In Gonja, north of the Akan area, violence between Gonja rulers and Konkomba immigrants led chiefs to announce in 1994 that they could not guarantee the safety of Kumasi traders buying yams there. They accused such outsiders of financing the rebellion by buying directly from Konkomba farmers and sent Gonja women with yams to sell in Kumasi Central Market, where they were turned away. This gesture was perceived as particularly insulting, although it might also have contained an appeal to gender solidarity, since Konkomba men had already established a rival yam-selling location in a Kumasi truck parking lot.

LIMITS TO MATERNALISM

While the maternal ideology builds solidarity effectively in many contexts, it also places important structural limits on how far traders can openly pursue self-interest and positive advancement. As mothers, they cannot value their own profits above their children's benefit. The association of trading with women as legitimate maternal subsistence work only fits comfortably so long as trading profits in fact remain markedly smaller than in other lines of work. Ghanaian traders have been repeatedly attacked for causing inflation by making too much profit. Neither traders themselves nor their male defenders could directly justify promoting high, solid incomes for women traders, as the expropriation of Lebanese in favor of Ghanaian businessmen openly intended, for example. Instead, they invoked the image of women who were "only" feeding their children, and "good mothers" worked long and hard through middle age and did not get ahead (Clark 1994). As Marti discusses in this volume, for Mexican women traders the absence of other legitimate frameworks for approaching government officials pressures women to retain the option of portraying themselves as vulnerable or helpless, even when this stance contradicts other strategies they might deploy simultaneously for further accumulation.

In fact, market trade was historically constructed as a female activity within a coordinated process that simultaneously marginalized it and restricted upward mobility within it. Before British control was established on the Gold Coast gradually around 1830, and much later in Asante, African men were more prominent traders than women. Chiefly and elite connections wove the market system intimately into politics and finance at the highest levels. British conquest in 1900 broke the chiefly dominance of Asante trade, making it less attractive for men of ambition. At the same time, the rapid spread of cocoa farming offered a much more lucrative option for Asante men, subsidized by their access to farm labor and family foodstuffs from unpaid wives. Women took over trading many important commodities from men in the 1910s and 1920s, until the marketplace itself became thoroughly identified with women (Clark 1994, forthcoming).

Politically active women traders during the period of electoral politics around independence left little legacy of advancement of their shared interests as traders or as women. Party strategies during the 1950s and 1960s suggest that commodity groups did vote as blocs to a significant extent. Candidates affiliated with each major party hotly contested elections for market leadership positions as these came along, under the assumption that each victorious new queen would turn out her members for her party. In contrast to Nigerian women traders in Lagos and other Yoruba towns, market leaders in Kumasi exerted little leverage on market policies through such participation. Nigerian parties wooed established market leaders by promising legalization and expansion of market facilities and reduced taxes (Mba 1982; Barnes 1986; Johnson-Odim and Mba 1997). Ghana offered many appropriate trading issues that traders felt sharply, such as the prevalence of hostile commercial regulations and the acute need for repair of market buildings, but politicians only ever delivered patronage favors for prominent individual traders that undermined group unity.

Political tensions rose in the 1970s and 1980s, as world prices for cocoa declined and prices paid to Ghanaian farmers declined even farther. Rampant inflation eroded real wages and salaries to the point that formal education or vocational training no longer brought its expected reward in predominantly male occupations. The few notably wealthy women traders, primarily located in large cities and selling imported commodities, had always been somewhat anomalous and attracted scandalous public attention and spasmodic government hostility. As common trading incomes visibly approached those in the newer male-identified sectors, more generalized public ideological attacks began to condemn all trading profits as selfish and destructive. The association of cocoa farming and the educated professions with men and of trading with women (even more strongly as images than in statistics) gave these commercial debates a gender content that connected them to growing tensions about changing family relationships.

Direct government interventions meanwhile were intended to reassert control over this runaway part of the economy, reminiscent of the runaway wives of the early colonial period (Robertson 1983). Price controls aimed at directly limiting trading profits dated from World War I; a succession of national governments from 1960 to 1985 extended them more widely and enforced them more frequently (Clark 1988). During the same decades, specific segments and agents of the state regularly participated in illegal trade, sometimes through their wives, girlfriends, or female relatives. Such personal connections weakened enforcement overall, but only while intensifying resentment of and among traders and implications of their immorality.

When J. J. Rawlings returned to power as head of state in 1981, the PNDC intervened in market commerce in a more authoritarian mode than in other informal sector occupations like vehicle repair or building construction. Those two predominantly male occupations were both also centers of controversy, but controls were initiated through negotiations with unions and business associations, the results of which were then respected by government. Without consulting traders, new state-sponsored channels were instituted through the Workers' Brigades and local Committees for the Defense of the Revolution. These were given monopoly status to replace market trading for the distribution of consumer goods and the collection of rural raw and processed foodstuffs. Urban market women were exhorted to return to the farm, where the only remaining truly virtuous Ghanaian mothers undeniably worked hard and earned little feeding the nation.

In contrast to traders in Accra, the capital, Kumasi traders avoided direct confrontations with national or local authorities (Chamlee 1994). Faced with overtly hostile policies like price controls for many years, few traders and no group leaders in Kumasi openly refused to comply. Instead, their resistance remained passive and indirect, although their cumulative actions in continuing to buy and sell when and where they could were critical to enabling alternative unofficial distribution channels to remain open for producers and consumers benefiting little from legal supplies. Price controls kept official prices so low that official supplies dried up both at the farm gate, where farmers could get better prices from surreptitious private traders, and at the customs gate, where foreign exchange at official rates was in short supply. Official measures failed to capture or maintain the circulation of goods, leading to the tacit suspension of their enforcement. Pressure to relax controls came not only from individual state officials, acting as buyers, sellers, and protectors, but also from the Kumasi city government, which depended on the market's survival for major tax revenue and urban food supplies.

NEOCLASSICAL MOTHERS

The ambiguous relationship between the Ghanaian state and traders continues despite a dramatic turnaround in state economic policy after 1984, under the Structural Adjustment Program (SAP). Dismantling price controls under pressure from international donors and lenders has significantly extended the reach of traders' recognized and legitimated autonomy. Deregulation of trade, while far from total, has perhaps benefited formal and international sector enterprises more than local traders. Civic beautification campaigns have now replaced price control campaigns as the justification for demolishing stalls and confiscating goods. These street clearances mainly target traders operating on the fringes of formal markets, or outside them, including numerous men along with women. Still, the free market philosophies promoted by international institutions have undermined many long-standing policies overtly hostile to markets. Traders again insist on their position outside the range of the state, for example, in matters of travel, pricing, and the reassignment of stalls. Some would like to extend their autonomy to greater consultation on market issues like taxes and repairs and to more complete self-regulation of trade.

In other respects, most traders embrace greater integration into community institutions. They have consistently agreed to pay the market taxes and rents that provide a major proportion of local government revenues, although like most citizens they would like to see less taxation and more assistance. At least a few market leaders have accepted positions in local government councils and commissions, as representatives of traders, while many more individual traders have run for local offices. Leaders continue to par-

ticipate enthusiastically in civic festivals linked to the Asante chiefship system, including the recent Silver Jubilee celebrations. Attendance at local funerals, not only those of group members, and the celebration of market rituals such as pouring annual libations for the new yam harvest, remain
important duties of group leaders.

Now that multiparty elections have returned, market leaders refrain from
bringing their commodity groups in behind any one party as a bloc, fearing
a return to the violence that characterized the party rivalries of the 1950s in
Kumasi. They erect a higher ideological wall between the state and the market by declaring that national politics has no place in commodity group operations. Some group leaders refused to announce their personal party allegiance in 1994, while others declared it openly so that any favoritism could
be monitored by all group members. This did not prevent individual leaders and members alike from taking part in recent election campaigns, join-
ing protest marches, or courting governing party leaders according to their
inclinations.

Less obviously, the current national policy climate leads to a growing es-
trangement between the neoclassical goals of structural adjustment and the
traders' own goals. As traders servicing local demand, they depend on the
long-term strength of local consumers and producers for the local market.
The fall in real income levels that has continued and intensified under SAP
has affected them deeply. The continuing direction of available economic resources toward exports of cocoa, gold, and timber that yield income for relatively few also undermines their customer base (Clark and Manuh 1991).
Layoffs in the public and private formal sector have increased competition
for this shrinking or stagnant demand, literally crowding the marketplaces
with new traders as other employment options fail to keep pace.

As "nursing mothers," market women support the broad social-repro-
ductive goals of survival and of the development of human resources. This
subsistence ideology, often sincerely held, has worked against as often as for
traders. It prevents established Kumasi Central Market traders from openly
excluding the flood of new entrants, even men, who have no other means
of support. At the same time, traders have seen little government response
when they invoke these reproductive goals to argue against spiraling school
and medical fees they pay as mothers. Group leaders also solicited government assistance for trading activities on the premise of feeding their chil-

dren, but with little success. In the 1990s, they petitioned the government to provide access to capital assets, such as trucks, buildings, and loans, which they could use to generate this subsistence income. Such programs would have put the government in a position analogous to that of Asante lineage elders, who gave women access to rent-free farmland and housing for the benefit of future generations. No one mentioned accumulation, when so many were conversely liquidating assets, such as used clothes.

Since the late 1980s, growing financial pressures on both men and women have intensified tensions over family budgeting. This has reduced women's ability to draw on male incomes and assets through their lineage and marriage relationships, even as compensation for their continuing unpaid services to children and husbands. The balance of payments within marriage has shifted, leading to hostility on both sides. Older women reported that in their youth, they routinely saved from the cooking allowance even an artisan husband could afford, to buy a headscarf or add to their trading capital. Male incomes no longer provide a family wage, so higher school fees, higher rents, and continuing standards of male personal consumption now stretch paternal investment to the limit.

Women also receive shrinking support from lineage brothers and uncles because these men concentrate their resources on supporting their biological children. The possibility recedes of tapping lineage inheritances, funeral proceeds, or wealthy uncles for loans of trading capital, because hard-pressed men compete for first consideration. Access to rent-free rooms in inherited lineage houses is more restricted, partly because housing in general has become more commercialized into income-generating rentals.

As a last resort, Asante mothers expected that their sons would help support them in their old age and ideally sponsor some younger siblings or build them all a house. Now it is difficult for young adults to even become self-supporting within the constraints of the local economy. Mothers and grandmothers expressed their desperation, faced with the prospect of supporting the younger generations indefinitely. Their reproductive work as mothers, "to replace yourself," could only be completed by providing the world with another fully functioning Asante adult. Quite a few saw only one way out for family survival—placing at least one son or daughter overseas to send money home to the rest—and pointed out houses that had been built with such remittances. These mothers have adopted the international perspective or export orientation of structural adjustment with a fierce twist, one whose long-term demographic and cultural consequences remain to be seen.

SUGGESTIVE CONCLUSIONS

A folktale told in the course of a language lesson epitomized the economic core of motherhood and its economic dilemmas. It was introduced as a story of why chickens have no ears. The central character in this *anansesem* is not the venerable Mr. Ananse the spider, but a "nursing-mother chicken." Like many of these stories, it takes its cue from animal behavior; Asante chickens have a reputation as particularly devoted mothers. I knew several people who placed duck eggs under a chicken to hatch because they said the duck would not be as careful of her own offspring.

Once there was a chicken who was a nursing mother. There was a famine in the land, and she could not find any corn for her children to eat. She heard that the fox had some corn, so she went to ask him for some. He agreed to sell her some, but she had no money to pay for it, so she cut off her ears and gave them to the fox to make soup. He gave her some corn to take home, but before long it was finished and she had to come back. She asked for corn, but he told her she had to give him one of her children's ears to make soup to pay for it. One by one, she had to cut off her children's ears to trade for corn for them to eat, until they were all earless. The fox still refused to give her any corn (doubtless looking forward to more substantial body parts). She lost her temper and flew at the remaining corn with her children. They ate as much as they could, saying, "We have already paid enough for it." That is why a chicken will still eat any corn that she finds, because she has paid for it already.

This mother hen clearly fulfills the economic, not the mammalian, mandate of the nursing mother. Not only in her trading but also in her management of family sacrifice and draconian choices she exemplifies the Akan mother who is successful at keeping her family alive under seemingly impossible conditions. Her situation is eerily reminiscent of contemporary mothers forced to cut back on food, medical attention, and schooling for their children, in a cruel juggling act portrayed as liberating economic choice. Her response, "I have paid for it already," may become increasingly appropriate if mainstream economic and political institutions continue to frustrate and trivialize the "nursing-mother" goals of survival and human growth. Akan gender constructs set up these maternal goals not as opposed to productive energy and ambition, but as the motivations and prerequisites that underpin these values at every step.

For Akan women, the positive and negative aspects of motherhood confront each other within the terrain of income and profit, not at the boundary of paid and unpaid work. While women's biological powers are highly respected, so are their economic powers considered both formidable and gendered. The economic mandate of motherhood has proved a powerful organizational strength among Akan market women. They draw solidarity from their shared intent, rather than from a homogeneity that would have to deny or exclude differences, since their significant internal differentiation actually aids them in accomplishing this goal. At the same time, the ideology of motherhood creates a kind of glass ceiling above which negotiation is difficult. Women's occupational advancement beyond a generous subsistence level loses legitimacy with the explicit displacement of accumulation onto the next generation.

Gender contestation here does not pit production against reproduction, but mediates rival uses of both labor and incomes. This extends gender problematics beyond issues of sexuality and personality throughout every part of the economy. At the household level, budget conflicts are as crucial to negotiating gender as conflicts over sexuality and domestic work. Economic contestations at the local, communal, and global levels are also highly gendered, whether over jobs, capital, legal protection, or public services. Women invoke their ideological leverage as mothers to claim rights to many productive and financial assets, not always successfully. Each level shows not only ideological and material echoes of the others but also concrete intersections with the dynamics of broader or narrower contests.

The pattern of gendered contestation between human resource development and capital accumulation repeats itself in quarrels over cooking allowances, in lineage inheritance discussions, in national budget priorities, and in structural adjustment negotiations. This ultimately sterile opposition is potentially reconciled within Akan gender ideals, since it operates within the boundaries of each gender, as well as between them. As fathers and brothers, Akan men today find their mandate for accumulation as deeply frustrated as their continuing implicit commitment to family survival. This conceptual framework holds out a possible model for successful reconciliation between survival and accumulation in development policy, as partners rather than enemies. It is perhaps their exaggerated separation within the current global context that so frustrates both goals for most men and women.

PART III

Identity, Economy, and Survival in
the Marketplace

Handicraft trader and assistant sanding carved wooden bowls before taking them to sell in urban markets, Banaue, Ifugao, Philippines, 1998. The trader's husband assumes responsibility for child care. Photo credit: B. Lynne Milgram.

CHAPTER FIVE

Situating Handicraft Market Women in Ifugao, Upland Philippines: A Case for Multiplicity

B. LYNNE MILGRAM

ABSTRACT: *The commercialization of artisan production continues to expand as the world market for craft objects grows. Past scholarship argued that with the commodification of rural economies household enterprises such as crafts would be restructured such that women, particularly, would lose their access to the means of production and distribution. Based on research in Banaue, Ifugao Province, northern Philippines, the author argues that women, rather than being marginalized, have built on the historical precedent of their involvement in trade to emerge as the region's foremost craft marketers. She examines the strategies women employ to maintain or diversify their roles in rural crafts and to (re)fashion their identities with commodification. By documenting how different female marketers use different strategies to negotiate their relationships, both gendered and political-economic, with artisans, urban buyers, and fellow traders, the author demonstrates that the main differences that have arisen with commodification are not those between men and women, but rather those among women.*[1]

Patricia Tayad, a weaver, augments her income from cloth production by sewing her weavings into a variety of functional bags she sells to shops in regional markets; Gloryia Balog, formerly a cultivator, now buys unfinished wood carvings she sands and varnishes before she sells them to urban craft shop owners.

Handicraft traders, such as these Ifugao women, are a type of rural, nonagricultural entrepreneur about whom research has begun to emerge during the last ten years (see, for example, J. Alexander 1987; Brenner 1998; Cook and Binford 1990; Rutten 1993; Stephen 1996; Tice 1995). In Banaue, Ifugao Province, northern Philippines, although both men and women market crafts, women form the majority of traders. In this chapter, I focus on this prominent group of female handicraft marketers, examining how shifting economic conditions inform the way they construct their multifaceted identities, which are defined and redefined within specific historic and cultural contexts. Their negotiations with artisans, their dealings with their fellow traders, and the demands and expectations of urban buyers all contribute to the construction of their identities. Their close ties historically to both craft and agricultural production—rice cultivation and ownership of rice fields—also contribute to how they perceive themselves and are perceived by others. By mapping new experiences onto indigenous ideologies, the women marketing Banaue's crafts manifest their identities as both local and global.

In Banaue, as throughout the northern Philippines, rice is the economic and symbolic staple of people's subsistence. Located at an altitude of 1,500 meters, however, Banaue's cool, upland climate means that the majority of households cannot grow enough rice to support themselves through the one-crop annual cycle. Because of the region's rugged mountain landscape, no more arable land is available for cultivators to expand their irrigated rice fields. Thus, artisans, especially weavers, have historically produced crafts, not only for local use but also for barter with other villagers to obtain goods they do not produce themselves. Banaue, moreover, is renowned for its spectacular rice terraces, which extend the full height of the mountainsides. Since the late 1970s, with the partial paving of the National Highway, the only road to Banaue, the region has become more accessible to visitors wanting to view the terraces. This increase in tourism means that crafts, formerly made for local use and regional trade, are now also targeted for commercial sale. Craft production and trade in Banaue has thus emerged as the most viable way for cultivators to earn additional cash to meet household needs. Because the number of tourists visiting Banaue fluctuates seasonally with the wet and dry season, many women, who formerly combined subsistence agriculture with craft making, now apply their skills in production to marketing Banaue's weavings and wood carvings to ensure a more steady source of income.

In research examining the commercialization of rural economies, some studies argue that forces such as expanding markets and tourism dramatically restructure simple commodity enterprises such that women, in particular, lose their access to the means of production and distribution (Boserup 1970; Ehlers 1990; Etienne 1980). They suggest that this is especially true for those in household craft production, since these women often work in return for the lowest rewards in order to combine their work with their reproductive tasks. When new technology is introduced to increase production, for example, it is often men who gain access to this knowledge and to the economic and social advantages it confers (Etienne 1980; Stamp 1989). In other instances, intermediaries may intervene between rural producers and their urban buyers to establish workshops in which they monopolize the supply of materials and distribution networks (Mies 1982; Pineda 1995; Waterbury 1989). In Banaue, however, my findings suggest that the production and trade of weavings and wood carvings is too small to support an intervening level of such intermediaries. These crafts remain low-technology, household enterprises, controlled by independent artisans and marketers. The aforementioned approach, then, does not examine the potential for capital accumulation at the community level nor the agency of individual actors to control local-level changes. Nor does it explore the ability of individuals to refashion their personal roles and identities as they decide the extent of their participation in their commercializing economy.

As Banaue's handicraft business has expanded, women, rather than being marginalized, have emerged as the industry's foremost entrepreneurs. This chapter illustrates how Banaue's female handicraft marketers have used the current transformation in their local economy—the articulation between the so-called precapitalist and capitalist economies—as the pivot around which to craft their own emerging identity as traders. Specifically, these women call themselves *ahinti* (businesswomen) and project themselves, as "economic brokers" (Long 1977, 121), capable of straddling the expectations of both rural artisan-producers and urban buyers. As mediators of the marketplace (Seligmann 1989), they function as the key people who are able to draw from both traditional kin- and community-based connections and Western capitalist business practices to control "crucial sets of relationships [that link] the local economy with the wider regional and national structure" (Long 1977, 121; see also J. Alexander 1987, especially Chap. 5). On the one hand, female handicraft marketers assume a mothering role with artisans by providing them with both their production and consumption needs. On the other hand, they sharpen their image as shrewd and reliable suppliers for urban buyers as they negotiate prices, deadlines, and product designs.

Female marketers, in turn, continue to draw on their simultaneous participation in various interlocking, local activities—reproduction, craft and agricultural production, and trade. In so doing, they are continuously "crossing and recrossing" local borders between different "contexts of identity" (Sikkink, this volume), transforming their skills and knowledge in one sphere for use in another. They negotiate the meaning and morality of marketing and accumulation for themselves by rooting their actions in the dynamics between local-to-regional-to-national contexts.

As women's involvement in the business of marketing handicrafts occurs at various levels, demonstrated in the examples above, I argue as Lynn Sikkink does (this volume), that in Banaue, marketers cannot be categorized or identified as a homogenous population. Rather these traders mold an identity for themselves according to the success of their businesses and their target market—local, regional, or national—which to some degree is determined by the products they sell (that is, weavings or wood carvings). Female marketers emphasize the distinctions and inequalities that arise among themselves based on these criteria. They manipulate their self-image according to the demands of the particular contexts in which they are operating to maximize their position personally and in business. Indeed, the marketers themselves dispel the notion of a singular identity by continuing to practice and publicly take pride in their traditional knowledge and control of production activities, both in agriculture and crafts.

METHODS

During my research in Banaue, Ifugao, I spent as much time as I could with various handicraft marketers. I conducted interviews with them and informally listened to stories in their shops and homes. While we talked, I often helped sand rough wood carvings or wrap orders in preparation for delivery to urban markets. I also contributed my own stories of making and selling crafts based on my experience as a weaver. As long as I could help, I felt that I was not disrupting daily transactions. To follow their businesses, I accompanied marketers on their collecting trips to the villages of artisans and on their selling trips to regional Baguio City and national Manila buyers.

Through these interactions, I had the opportunity to listen to these women's voices. Lynne Phillips perceptively points out that "reciprocity is integral to the construction of knowledge" (1996, 21). Without people's willingness to participate in research, ethnographers cannot learn about their subjects' lives. At the same time, a reader comes to know these people's lives only through the ethnographer's understanding and contextualization of them. To resolve this epistemological dilemma, it is not enough for the author simply to highlight people's voices; he or she must "make explicit their theory of listening," the way in which conversations are "initiated, heard, presented and understood" (Phillips 1996, 21). In this chapter then, I have tried to contextualize the circumstances within which I have framed the voices of female craft marketers. This understanding has shaped how I have portrayed the way female marketers conduct business, face new problems, and forge their emerging identities as new businesswomen in a rapidly changing economy.

THE CONTEXT FOR CRAFT PRODUCTION AND TRADE
IN BANAUE, IFUGAO PROVINCE

The Ifugao live on the eastern side of the Gran Cordillera Central mountain range, which extends through the center of northern Luzon. The term Ifugao identifies the people as well as their province and their language. This chapter focuses on six of Banaue's seventeen villages (*barangays*), known for their crafts. The main economic activities in Banaue, as throughout the

Cordillera, are wet-rice cultivation and raising pigs for ritual and domestic use. Women also grow vegetables for household needs. Since there is only one rice crop per year, as noted above, most harvests provide enough rice to feed a family for only two to six months. With no mixed agricultural production base and no agricultural surplus for commercial sale, cultivators must seek alternatives to earn cash. Building on their history of bartering crafts for products not locally available, artisans currently produce and sell weavings and wood carvings to the growing number of tourists visiting Banaue. In the six barangays considered here, an average of 55 percent of each village's approximately 250 households have at least one member involved in handicraft production or trade.

As the ownership of irrigated rice land and personal reserves of "native" upland rice continue to symbolize wealth and prestige, any surplus of upland rice is never sold. Rather, it is stored for later distribution to family and community members on special ritual occasions. Hence, those involved in handicraft production and trade do not easily abandon their work in rice cultivation. Instead, the production and trade of crafts is integrated with their agricultural activities as cultivators or landowners.

The region of the Gran Cordillera Central resisted Spanish domination for 300 years, from 1565 to 1898. It became part of the Philippine state through negotiation rather than conquest during the American colonial period from 1898 to 1946 (Fry 1983). Early American policy in this region stressed local control over the local economy and resources. Although this policy was later reversed, it set the precedent for the autonomy of the indigenous population (Fry 1983; Jenista 1987). This has meant that many of the socioeconomic and political elements of the local culture have remained dynamic and provide the basis of unique local development. For example, traditional Ifugao religious beliefs, with their extensive pantheon of deities and their ancestral cults, coexist in a setting where, from 1900 and increasingly since the 1950s, most Ifugao have been baptized Roman Catholic. Similarly, Ifugao kinship ties, reckoned equally through one's parents to both lines of blood kin, comprise the foremost network of social relations. The Ifugao derive their identity from their kin group and draw on family members first for assistance in agriculture and craft activities.

The production and trade of crafts by independent artisans and marketers, moreover, coexists with a commercial market economy that was introduced by the American colonial administration in the early 1900s and that has accelerated since the Second World War, particularly since the 1970s with the growth in tourism. For example, in the early American period when Cordillera arts were increasingly featured in U.S. expositions such as the Universal Exposition in St. Louis in 1904 (Ellis 1981, 260; Worcester 1913, 1255) Ifugao wood carvings found a small, but growing market in the field of "souvenirs and collectibles." However, the Second World War and Philippine independence in 1946 dramatically opened the way for the commercialization of rural crafts, especially wood carvings (Aguilar and Miralao 1984, 6–7).

During the Second World War, significant military activity occurred within the mountain region, resulting in widespread destruction of property (Jenista 1987, 267–68). At the cessation of hostilities, with properties devastated, there was no rice crop with which to feed families. The scarcity of local wage work meant that many men left Ifugao to find jobs in the mining and lumbering industries in Baguio City, Benguet Province, to the south. Older carvers explain that during their time in Benguet, when they were not working, they would make wood carvings. These carvings were purchased by American servicemen stationed at military bases throughout Luzon and by Philippine and foreign tourists visiting Baguio City, which was established by the Americans as a summer mountain resort. In the 1950s, an entrepreneur from Banaue opened a retail craft store in Baguio City. His daughter, a prominent official in the Philippine Tourist Bureau at the time of my research, recounts stories of the early growth of her father's successful business. The wood-carving industry became rapidly commercialized throughout the Philippines because of the timely encouragement from the Marcos administration's "export-oriented policy" in the 1970s. With regard to crafts, this policy was selectively aimed at rural industries that were labor intensive, used local raw materials, and commanded a potentially high foreign demand (Pineda 1995; Rutten 1993, 21). In the mid-1980s, products such as wood carvings entered the category of "giftwares" (Bunolna 1995), and were increasingly modified to meet foreign tastes (Aguilar and Miralao 1984, 7).

Although the national and international demand for wood carvings was always higher than that for weaving, cloth production in Banaue underwent its own unique transformation. In response to the increase in regional tour-

ism, Banaue weavers developed a line of commercial or market-driven textiles patterned with a variety of locally inspired designs. These are produced
specifically for sale to visitors shopping in local Banaue craft shops or in the
regional tourist markets in Baguio City.

WOMEN'S HISTORICAL IDENTIFICATION WITH
HANDICRAFT MARKETING

Throughout highland Southeast Asia women are renowned for having a
high degree of gender equality (see, for example, Atkinson, Monnig and
Errington 1990; Cherneff 1982; Jefremovas 1992; Karim 1995; Manderson
1983; Ong 1989). Although Ifugao women ultimately seem to assume responsibility for domestic chores and child care, men in Banaue are very
much involved in domestic activities and, indeed, commonly dominate this
sphere when their wives are successful in business (see also Bacdayan 1977;
Milgram 1997). Women in upland areas are also integrally involved in managing finances, within and outside of the household.[2] Indeed, Banaue has a
history of locally controlled marketing and distribution through local and
regional networks dominated by female traders. Roy Barton's (1919, 1963)
early-twentieth-century research on Ifugao economics, for example, charts
instances in which Ifugao weavers commonly engaged in their own business
transactions, traveling to neighboring municipalities to barter their textiles
for livestock and for vegetables not locally available. My interviews with
weavers in their sixties and seventies confirm this earlier practice. Artisans
relate stories of their trading ventures to the neighboring municipality of
Kiangan, known for its large population of landed elite. These same weavers
transformed their early bartering transactions into cash sales in urban centers during the 1970s and 1980s, as they regularly traveled to Manila to sell
their textiles to noted handicraft dealers. This history of production for exchange is "tied to the ability of current-day marketers to take advantage of
existing marketing networks and skills when tourist and export markets
opened up for their craft products" (Stephen 1996, 382).

Roy Barton (1919) suggests that success in business is part of Ifugao ethnic identity. In meticulous accounts, he outlines how lists of gifts were kept
at rites of passage to enable recipients to determine the value of their return

donation, and how careful records documented the number and type of items traded in a variety of other exchanges. Each transaction emphasized the prestige attached to shrewd economic negotiations. As Ifugao women have always been involved in marketing, in cash or in-kind, the success of their trading relations has thus always played a part in defining their identity.

Within this environment of relative gender equality, Banaue's female marketers have also constructed their self-image with reference to the pride uplanders take in their independence. As noted earlier, Spanish colonial rule spent more than three centuries unsuccessfully trying to conquer the Cordillera through military and missionary efforts. Under subsequent American rule, assimilation and integration of the uplands into the majority lowland culture was never fully attempted (Fry 1983, 232), leaving the people of the Cordillera actively promoting their distinct and individual upland identity. This regional pride in individualism (*kanya kanya*) is expressed economically by Banaue's handicraft marketers, both men and women, who work on their own to develop their personal web of contacts. Female marketers, particularly, have eclectically built on these indigenous socioeconomic systems and values, adapting certain ideas and techniques from external contact and actively resisting others. Elizabeth Bannug, for example, a trader in carvings and weavings, is usually adamant about working on her own. However, because of her close friendship with her neighbor Elsa, a fledging businesswoman, Elizabeth agreed to introduce her neighbor to her Manila buyers only if Elsa consented to always sell products different from those of Elizabeth. Banaue's female craft marketers, then, have forged a public profile for themselves and an identity that emphasizes their self-sufficiency.

Trade channels in Banaue are not monopolized by established classes. Thus, anyone with enough capital can exploit the business opportunities that may come his or her way (Smith 1976, 355), facilitating the shift from producer to marketer. As there is "no ideological restraint on economic upward mobility" (Rutten 1993, 138), the ease of entry into relevant trade channels means that peasants, particularly female artisans, can easily become marketers. Indeed, although both men and women market handicrafts, women, either as sole owners or in husband-and-wife teams, dominate this trade.

Women engage in selling handicrafts at various levels of the market. On Saturdays, at Banaue's weekly market, seven to ten weavers assume their regular positions behind the permanent vegetable stalls to sell yarns. On their blankets, they spread out the commercial yarns they have purchased during the week at factories in Baguio City and Manila. They sell these materials to weavers on a part-time basis to augment their own weaving income. In the Banaue town center, there are nineteen handicraft stores whose sales of hand-woven and -carved products are solely targeted to the local tourist trade. Of these, twelve are owned and operated by women. In the six barangays in which I worked, I have identified thirty-three traders in both weavings and wood carvings who work independently from their homes and whose sales concentrate on regional and national markets; some also operate local retail stores. Of these thirty-three traders, nineteen women and four men are sole operators of their businesses, and ten are husband-and-wife teams. As the marketing of wood carvings has emerged as the larger and more profitable trade, twenty-seven traders now concentrate on selling only carvings. Only four women and one man are full-time traders in weavings, while three women periodically sell woven articles in addition to carvings in response to irregular, small orders. The following discussion focuses on the local to national trading practices of these thirty-three marketers, of whom I have worked closely with twenty.[3]

How a marketer identifies herself within the relations of trade in commercial or market-driven wood carvings and weavings is shaped by both the nature and destination of these products. Both carvings and weavings are relatively cheap products made by rural home production, but channeled to local, regional, national, or export markets. While women are the primary weavers and men dominate in wood carving, some female artisans have started to carve small versions of the most popular types of wood items (see Milgram 1999a, 1998). It is important to note that the products marketed are not gender specific. Although women dominate the trade in weavings, both men and women buy and sell wood carvings.[4] Inequalities in status among marketers do emerge, however, according to the target market of the product. The market for handwoven textiles sold as yardage or sewn into a variety of functional items is limited to local Banaue and regional Baguio City shops (see Milgram 1999b); wood carvings are sold locally and regionally, as well as nationally and internationally. Having made the leap from local to international sales, wood carving is the more profitable handicraft trade and imparts a degree of prestige to the women marketing this craft.

Traders in weavings add a tone of reverence to their voices when discussing the wood-carving marketers' frequent trips to Manila and their familiarity with and knowledge of the city, confirming the latter's identity as members of the new mercantile elite. Marketing handicrafts, especially wood carvings, has the potential to become an important basis for local accumulation, which can, in turn, be transformed into other forms of capital. Indeed, three Banaue wood-carving marketers—two women and one man—were elected to the political office of Banaue municipal councilor in May 1995, no doubt aided by their numerous ties with carvers and by their identification with this prestigious trade.[5]

Local female village or barangay marketers in Banaue dominate the wholesale trade in both weavings and wood carvings and operate as the main risk-taking entrepreneurs. As noted earlier, they identify themselves as businesswomen equipped to trade in a certain range of commodities that provision local, regional, and national markets. Women's involvement in and identification with such marketing, moreover, is part of a historical continuum and not solely the result of the growth of the handicraft trade resulting from the rise in tourism and the continuing popularity of collecting indigenous folk art. Any analysis of the character of women's marketing activities and how this has been incorporated into the way they represent themselves must be framed within a historical context to emphasize that their current identity as craft vendors cannot be seen as static and bounded, but rather as complex and continually shifting in response to both internal and external forces (Lepowsky 1993; Tsing 1993).

THE ORGANIZATION OF HANDICRAFT MARKETING

Whether as a sole owner or as a husband-and-wife team, female handicraft marketers assume responsibility for all financial business matters. They issue cash and in-kind advances to artisans and, when required, negotiate their own loans for both business and personal purposes with local moneylenders or banking cooperatives. They communicate with buyers in Manila and Baguio City, negotiating the terms of the purchase order, the delivery date and extensions, if necessary, as well as traveling to urban centers to follow up on orders and payments. Women marketing both handwoven products and wood carvings personally make the ten-to-twelve-hour trip to either Baguio City or Manila to deliver their orders; depending upon the size of the order, those delivering carvings may be accompanied by their husband or an assistant. In contrast with the activities of female traders in the lowland Philippines, the mobility of Banaue women is not restricted to the local context. Rosanne Rutten (1993, 54, 160; see also Forshee 1996) points out that female marketers of woven hats and mats in Aklan Province are relegated to the role of small, minor traders because custom restricts the distance they may travel from home. In Banaue, however, individual female marketers commonly travel to larger urban centers to sell their local crafts. Indeed, most women tell me that when their husbands make deliveries to Manila on their own, the buyer usually asks, "Where is your wife? I have been negotiating with her." Thus, female traders are both identified with and empowered by their mercantile savvy.

The man in the husband-and-wife team in the wood-carving business is often a carver and his responsibilities revolve around this skill. He finds and purchases the wood, carves the orders, and supervises his assistant carvers. He also organizes the transportation of the wood or rough carvings from the forest to the house where the final carving is done. He works on new designs, repairs the cracks in the wood, and may help with the waxing and buffing finishes applied to the completed carvings. Even in the businesses of the men who are both carvers and sole operators of their marketing enterprises, their wives are usually involved with daily financial matters and may help with finishing the carvings. These women also divide their time between child care and farming. Traders are the linchpin in the marketing of handicrafts and in the industry's cash flow (Rutten 1993, 131). They obtain their stock directly from local artisans and, in turn, sell these directly to urban buyers, without the involvement of intervening brokers. On the buying side, faced with the collection of goods from artisans who live, not together in villages, but individually, scattered over a wide area near their rice fields, traders provide advances in cash and in-kind (or *vale*) in order to gain more control over artisans' products. In so doing, they create personalized credit ties with producers. Often traders take pieces from artisans on consignment, known as *pi-la-u*. The opportunity to obtain goods on consignment allows traders to participate in trade when they are short of capital. On the retail end of the trade chain, marketers sell their goods through their shops if they have a local retail outlet, or independently to their own network of urban buyers in the Baguio City and Manila craft stores (see also Rutten 1993).

Once marketers lay a stronger claim on the products by giving producers advances, the locus of wholesale buying moves from the marketplace to traders' homes and workshops in their individual barangays. Unlike most of the studies of market women whose businesses are located in town marketplaces, in Banaue, the trade in handicrafts has largely bypassed the central market. Depending upon their need, marketers will personally make regular trips into the villages to collect the products they have ordered from artisans. However, on each Saturday, the main collection and market day, traders with craft shops wait at home for producers to deliver their goods when artisans commonly come to town to combine selling with their weekly food shopping.

Most traders do not get advances from their urban buyers, but bear the responsibility for transporting their goods to regional or national markets and for negotiating all payments and contracts themselves. In most instances, Banaue marketers respond to specific orders from their buyers in Baguio City and Manila and must formulate strategies to cope with the fluctuating demand. With handwoven products, there is a definite seasonality to the orders with the slow season corresponding to the rainy and nontourist season from mid-May to December. Generally, the traders dealing in textiles either stop going to Baguio City during this time, or make the trip every month and a half just to keep in contact with their buyers. Only a few of the larger traders who have retail space and ready cash are able to stock weavings and carvings at this time of low demand.

Contained within the framework of informal credit ties, the marketing of handicrafts remains very much a labor-intensive process and one in which the ingenuity of individual marketers is most important to success in business. Positioned between the demands and expectations of urban buyers and of rural artisans, marketers' businesses are vulnerable to interruptions in their cash flow, which may arise from problems with either group. Building on their mediation skills and mobility between rural and urban spheres and between different local contexts of activities, female marketers draw on their flexible identities selectively in the contexts in which they find themselves operating. They emerge as "intermediaries who broker not only economic goods, but also cultural values and political power" (Seligmann 1989, 695).

THE *SUKI* RELATIONSHIP

To facilitate trade and reduce risks, marketers, producers, and buyers throughout the Philippines often develop a *suki* relationship. This is a regular trade relation that involves trust and reciprocal favors such as advances of credit and favorable prices by traders in return for a steady supply of products from producers (Anderson 1969; Dannhaeuser 1983; W. Davis 1973; Rutten 1993). In theory, the aim is to reduce risk in an economic environment that is unpredictable and where few traders operate with written contracts. Negotiations are conducted through informal channels based on trust. Their form is one of personalized relations, marked by "subjective values and extralegal sanctions which encourage individuals to meet obligations to others" (W. Davis 1973, 211). As James Anderson argues, "economic personalism" is so important to Philippine entrepreneurs because it is only by forming "personal networks of obligatory relationships that they can overcome the barriers posed by a lack of trust and a weakness of institutional credit facilities" (1969, 642, 648; see also J. Alexander 1987, especially Chap. 5; Alexander and Alexander 1991b). By developing suki relations with producers, marketers can, in theory, give credit with less risk and be somewhat more certain of the volume of supply of commodities. This consideration is an important one because most traders, in filling orders of urban buyers, need to meet the latter's deadlines in order to uphold their reputation as dependable suppliers.

In the 1990s, however, with the rise in the cost of basic commodities in Banaue, artisans are increasingly defaulting on their credit advances, often spending this money on their family's subsistence needs such as food or medical expenses. My findings reveal that the suki relationship as previously documented cannot be simply regarded as enduring. Rather, it emerges in Banaue as a heterogeneous combination of relationships that must be innovatively managed by marketers to ensure the survival of their businesses.

Female handicraft marketers in Banaue have evolved their own strategies to address the current weaknesses in the suki bond. They continue, as they have always done, to adapt, reinterpret, and transform their identification with and skills in reproductive activities to their business practices. To reduce the risk of artisans' defaulting on their advances in credit, traders have tried to ensure a sense of personal obligation on the part of their suki producers. They have built up their survival networks of suki relationships by developing new personal ties or by activating existing relations of kinship and neighborhood.

In her study of market women in Peru, Florence Babb suggests that female traders are uniquely situated such that their market work and their domestic activities are closely integrated (1989, 43). She argues that "both forms of work are fundamentally reproductive in nature" (1989, 44). Similarly, Gracia Clark (this volume) disputes the dichotomy between motherhood—women's responsibility in and identity solely with the reproductive sphere—and capital accumulation—women's ability to conduct business. She equates market trading in Ghana with "nursing-mother work." In such an understanding, the reproductive sphere merges with the productive sphere as women's daily income from marketing fulfills the need to daily feed and provide for her family. Judith Marti (this volume) also demonstrates how market women in nineteenth-century Mexico have set a historical precedent to dispel this interpretation of the productive/reproductive split. Her documentary sources illustrate how market women in this period manipulated the contradictory positioning of public/private in their petitions to government officials. They presented themselves as dependent, vulnerable, and helpless, while simultaneously proving themselves to be shrewd, knowledgeable, and effective strategists.[6] Similarly, in Banaue, women's income from marketing has always been critical to the survival of their families. Thus, female handicraft vendors' activities, both within and outside of the household, emerge as part of a continuous chain of enterprises in which so-called domestic resources may be directed to "productive" purposes (see also Karim 1995, 28).

Marketers confirm that in order to nurture and maintain the loyalty of their producers, when artisans approach them with requests for help, they feel they have to explore every avenue to "remedy their problems." Artisans most often request cash to pay for medical expenses or for sacrificial animals required for the numerous rituals such as funerals and curing rites. Traders similarly explain that if they do not have the cash on hand to fulfill artisans' requests, then they approach a third party to arrange for a personal loan in cash or in-kind. When marketers know that their wood-carving orders will require their carvers to work away from Banaue for more than a month, the woman of the husband-and-wife trader team ensures that she has sufficient cash or food on hand to distribute to the carvers' wives who inevitably come during this time if they run out of rice. Yet, these are not considered gifts, but rather advances of credit to producers that are, in turn, deducted from the value of future deliveries. Marketers explain that they try to fulfill these requests because they appreciate the precarious position of the artisans. At the same time, they know that they must help producers in order to fulfill the expectations of the suki relationship. In such an arrangement, artisans through repeated advances may find themselves caught in a cyclical pattern of debt and obligation to marketers.

In marketers' efforts, however, to present themselves as nurturers, they put no time limit on when artisans must repay the advance, and indeed, no interest charges are due. Thus, depending upon the strength of the suki bond, artisans have access to interest-free loans for unlimited periods of time. Traders, although they gain the loyalty of the producers, must bear the financial burden of having their capital tied up for long periods of time in outstanding loans that do not accumulate interest. In turn, when marketers have obtained a loan from a third party to supply producers' needs, the interest due on this loan is yet another drain on that trader's resources.

Everyone involved in the handicraft business in Banaue acknowledges the integral role of the suki at every level. Currently, however, due to Banaue's competitive business climate, artisans are moving in and out of their suki relationship with marketers if the opportunity arises for personal advancement. In most cases marketers do not bear a grudge for long and, indeed, will approach artisans who have defaulted on their advances if the latter's services are required for a particular order. Many marketers feel that reemploying the artisan is the only way they can reproduce their benevolent role as the ever-forgiving mother and recover their investment in outstanding loans. Negotiations between producers and their suki buyers often involve a pattern of behavior that Rosanne Rutten perceptively describes as "wooing and flattering" (1993, 148). Such behavior or "performance" in trade relationships is shaped by the specific trade conditions of Banaue's handicraft industry. In wood carving particularly, the number of carvers is decreasing because of out-migration. In efforts to find more profit-earning income, carvers have moved to the lowlands in Ifugao and in neighboring provinces to be closer to new sources of wood. Others have moved to Baguio to work in the city's large wholesale carving industry, while still others have left wood carving altogether. Hence, among marketers, competition for carvers is fierce at the same time that wood is becoming more difficult to find and more expensive to buy.

"Groveling and cajoling" (Rutten 1993, 148) then are very much the norm as traders try to wrest carvings from producers and convince them to honor their suki bonds. Indeed, the threat of artisans withholding their supply of products or selling them to another trader, in fact, constrains traders' opportunism. Susan Angeles, a Banaue marketer who sells both weavings and wood carvings, explains that her role with her carvers shifts between that of mother to that of older sister. She knows that if she scolds carvers for not delivering her order, then she will meet even more resistance, like that of a child pushing the limits of a parent's authority. Thus, like other female traders who similarly describe their relationship to producers, Susan seeks a balance between asserting enough pressure to secure her goods, while still maintaining her reputation for being a generous and nurturing trader who will fulfill carvers' needs. If she sees that a carver is not working steadily on her order, she pleads, "Please have pity on me, you are making me lose my job. Please work on my order so that I will have money to feed and care for my family." When carvers fail to fill their orders, she says that she challenges them on their word like a man: "Aren't you ashamed as a man to lie to me as a woman? When you are sick, you come to me and we find a remedy; when you need money you come to me and we find rice." Employing a mothering rhetoric, she explains that when she is approached by carvers requesting alcohol (drinking is a serious problem among some Ifugao men), she cooks food for the artisans instead of giving them gin, saying, "How can you fulfill your agreement to work for me if you are drunk . . . and besides, your wife will blame me when you fall over. Then we will both be upset and without your services." She talks to the carvers calmly and encourages them to return to her the following day to discuss their work and their needs.

Similarly, Jean Cabbigon, another trader who feels that she is responsible for the well-being of the carvers and their families who work for her, fashions her identity after this protective role. She supplies the carvers with everything they will need when working in the forest closer to the source of wood. She assembles their food, plates, pots, eating utensils as well as sheets of plastic from which they construct a shed as a protective shelter. She will also supply their bedding if needed. In some instances, to ensure delivery and let the carvers work closer to their families, she has transported the wood to her house and has had the carvers work in her backyard where she can check their daily progress. She explains that "once I have provided for all their needs, how can I not get upset when the carvers do not deliver my items." In such situations she complains that artisans have betrayed her trust and careful efforts as well as "stocking my money." In her description of the lowland Philippine trade of mats and hats, Rosanne Rutten similarly notes that the suki relationship "suggests an obligation of loyalty, and denotes the real feeling of betrayal that one party experiences when the other does not live up to this obligation" (1993, 148). In addition to nurturing, the mothering rhetoric and behavior employed by marketers such as Jean and Susan serve as powerful managerial and control techniques these women use to maximize their economic transactions.

ACCUMULATING SOCIAL CAPITAL: TWO CASE STUDIES

Female marketers often apply a subsistence logic to achieve the profit-maximizing logic of capitalist enterprise. This approach strategically informs the way they do business. One female marketer in Banaue, for example, has been particularly successful in addressing the problems she encounters with artisans by firmly portraying herself as a generous and nurturing benefactor. In so doing, she has succeeded in building a prosperous business, while simultaneously accumulating social capital. In his documentation of entrepreneurs in Fiji, Finney argues that "those who are most successful in business continue to operate with one foot in a 'traditional' (albeit changing) economy and one foot in a cash economy" (1973, 107; see also Scaglion 1996). Addressing similar issues, Villia Jefremovas (1985) and Susan Russell (1983) examine the changing economic practices in the weaving and knitting industries in neighboring Cordillera provinces to illustrate how two aspects of rural society—kinship and community ties—are utilized and manipulated by different businesswomen to benefit both their businesses and their personal positions within the community. These entrepreneurs, who manufacture and sell woven and knitted products, have been able to maintain their operations by recruiting labor on the basis of kin and community ties and by representing themselves as generous distributors of goods and sponsors of lavish feasting. Similarly, to maintain their social capital, marketers in Banaue are expected to continue to faithfully fulfill producers' requests and partake in ritual distribution and gift giving to mark the important rites of passage of the artisans with whom they conduct business. The following case study illustrates one marketer's strategies in her relationships with Banaue's artisans.

Jane Pinan, formerly a weaver and small grocery store owner, is now a prominent trader of wood carvings in Banaue. She and her husband, a carver, started their business in 1970, first supplying rough carvings to Baguio City wholesalers and currently selling finished carvings to the more lucrative Manila market. Like other husband-and-wife teams, Jane attends to all financial matters. She laments that her husband will no longer look at the record book of advances to carvers because it "makes his head spin and his heart angry." Drawing on her twenty-five-year business history, Jane has become an influential member of the community. In May 1995, she was reelected for a second three-year term as one of Banaue's eight municipal councilors, receiving substantial support from her numerous business connections. Unlike the conditions for success described by Susan Russell (1987) in Benguet and Villia Jefremovas (1992) in Mountain Province, one's social position in Banaue today does not depend upon one being part of the landed, agricultural elite. Jane's current position in business is the direct result of how she uses her reputation as a fair marketer in the interest of upward mobility. For her regular carvers, Jane will always advance cash or rice, money for medicine, and livestock for family rituals. She explains, "If I want to keep working with the same carvers, I must be there if they need me. . . . Even though they have a credit with me, I must give them medicine and pay their hospital bills if they get sick. Some die and I have already paid their clinic bills. How will I recover this money?" From her former job as owner of a grocery store, Jane has maintained her contacts in the wholesale food business, enabling her to stock rice to advance to the carvers. Her truck, which is empty on the return trip from Manila, is loaded with rice in Solano, the nearest market town. She buys the rice wholesale, but advances it on credit to the carvers just below or equal to the retail price. She explains that the charge above the wholesale price pays for the cost of the gas, but through this gracious gesture she still seems to make a small gain. If she has neither cash nor rice, she simply writes a note for the carver to take to her neighbor's grocery store where he will be able to obtain food on credit. One carver relates that during a meeting with Jane, another carver arrived desperate for money to purchase a pig for an upcoming ritual. Jane sent the carver to a neighbor who raises pigs saying, "Just tell the owner to charge it to me." These goods represent debts and obligations to Jane that continue for years.

By buying most of the carvings that artisans make, regardless of whether or not they have been ordered, Jane gains the allegiance of the artisans, but also she concedes, she gains an overstocked storeroom that ties up her capital for months in this interest-free investment. She remarks aptly, "If you do not have patience, you will not survive in this business."

Jane is unique in the manner in which she has structured her accessibility to artisans. She meets carvers in a small room set aside from the workshop where a table and chairs formally dominate the space. She puts artisans at ease by always beginning her greeting with "Come in, how are you? What do you need?" Carvers get her personal attention; they can have private conversations to discuss either their request for orders or loans, and Jane, if necessary, can privately express her displeasure with them if problems arise. This situation contrasts sharply with the manner in which other traders publicly conduct business either in their shops or in their homes. Traders often take advantage of such a public forum by using the excuse of customer demands or of family responsibilities to make artisans wait hours for attention, to refuse to see them altogether, or to publicly humiliate them over business problems and negotiations. In both approaches, traders seek to control negotiations with artisans, but Jane cloaks her strategies in graciousness.

As part of the new merchant elite, Jane is able to turn particular situations to her advantage. For example, it is well known that she pays the lowest rates for sanding and varnishing rough carvings both to her regular finishers working on-site and to off-site freelance workers. But the opportunity for finishers to obtain continuous work, given the large volume of carvings that she turns over, augmented by easy access to loans, enables Jane to keep finishing prices lower and her profits higher. By fostering her image as a dependable provider, Jane has been able to mitigate some of the problems in Banaue's handicraft industry such as carvers and finishers not completing her orders on time. Her business is expanding, while she is garnering a stock of social capital.

As noted by Carol Smith (1976) and William Roseberry (1988), class relations arise from unequal access not only to the means of production but also to the means of exchange. Indeed, Lynn Stephen describes merchants and artisans as "class-based occupational groups," defined by their access to the distribution of goods (1996, 388). Jane's soft-sell approach to marketing practices demonstrates how exchange relations can be manipulated by dominant parties for their own benefit, not only between marketers and producers but also among marketers. When two marketers vie for products from the same artisan, the one most likely to receive the goods is the marketer such as Jane who is renowned for giving generous advances.

Nonetheless, here, as in the handicraft trade as a whole, the use of community ties has left avenues of resistance open to artisans and thereby forced marketers to redistribute a portion of their surplus to maintain their good working relations. Thus, for Jane, as for other traders, to maintain her position, she must continue to meet the community's social expectations of her. In personalized trade agreements such as these, the importance of a marketer's trading reputation and his or her need to ensure a steady supply of products when required are what usually constrain a trader's opportunism (W. Davis 1973; Russell 1987). This keeps Jane firmly entrenched in a pattern of fulfilling artisans' requests and, when the occasion arises, offering generous donations of food and/or cash at her producers' and neighbors' important ritual occasions.

Other marketers, however, rather than being seen as nurturers, have chosen to distinguish themselves by highlighting their shrewd business accomplishments. In a situation in which producers are dependent upon marketers for both their production and consumption needs, some traders have chosen to manipulate marketing transactions to facilitate their control of distribution networks. As a result, artisans, constrained by financial and resource dependency, have been exploited by some marketers. In flaunting the expectations of the suki bond, these traders have gained reputations as ruthless businesswomen whom artisans reticently approach as a last resort.

In 1993 Elizabeth Bannug, a former weaver, opened a handicraft store using the profit she and her husband made from their grocery business. As well as her trade in wood carvings, Elizabeth also buys weavings, and either sews them herself or has them sewn into bags she sells locally in Banaue through her shop or regionally in Baguio City. Elizabeth has a reputation for always bargaining with producers to get the lowest possible price. As soon as she spots any flaw in a weaving or carving, she goes off on a tirade about how poor the product is and how she will have to reduce her price accordingly. She conducts all her negotiations publicly in her shop and often keeps artisans waiting for hours before giving them her attention. By protecting her knowledge of urban selling prices, she intimidates producers into selling their products at a lower price and from asking for a price increase. Thus, artisans sell to Elizabeth only as a last resort. This occurs more often than producers would like, however, especially in times of low demand when there are so few traders who can afford to buy. Indeed, when passing Elizabeth's shop one day, I saw Carmel, a very good weaver who purposely avoids selling to Elizabeth. She was waiting patiently, but dejectedly for Elizabeth to examine her blanket. When I later spoke to Carmel, she confirmed that it was imperative for her to sell her blanket that day, even for a low price, as it was just before the harvest and she had no rice.

Elizabeth pays her artisans in-kind, not in cash, and this has also generated resentment among producers. The artisans receive food from the grocery store, and more recently, ready-to-wear garments that Elizabeth has started to buy on her return trips from Baguio City. Elizabeth, like Jane, buys the food and garments wholesale, using her connections in the grocery business, but advances these to artisans at retail prices. Thus she gains by bartering for the craft products and by making a profit on the in-kind exchange. Producers are denied the opportunity to choose where to shop and the possibility of obtaining a better purchase price for their groceries, although the facility of shopping at Elizabeth's does save them time. They are repeatedly subjected to public humiliation and have their self-respect undermined. Artisans feel too intimidated to protest to Elizabeth face-to-face, because she has been able to translate her position as a major handicraft trader, reinforced by her ownership of substantial rice fields, into one that is now part of the business elite. As Susan Russell points out about farmers in a similar situation in upland Benguet:

> Status-based restrictions inhibit small, relatively isolated producers from pressing demands or complaints in a straightforward manner, and these inhibitions are increased by the greater knowledge middlemen have about the wider society. . . . The cultural meaning of indebtedness and dependency between people of markedly different statuses insulates middlemen from direct criticism and reinforces their social dominance in the wider community. (1987, 152)

Elizabeth and Jane's practices illustrate the complexity of the relationships between traders and producers. These relationships demonstrate the conflicts and constraints arising from the structure of local power and economic relations that depend on both personal ties and participation in market exchange (Russell 1987, 152). As with men, there is considerable differentiation among female craft traders. Women have made varying choices about how to fashion their identity in the light of the current economic transformations. They employ individual business strategies that often conflict with those of other traders. Although female traders share the problems caused by gender, there is intense competition between them, indicative of the larger trade in crafts. The manner in which female traders choose to conduct their businesses, like that of men, may involve deceit and secrecy and may, as has been noted, depend on comparative advantage over other women. Their trading strategies are often reliant on paying low wages to their female laborers as evidenced by Jane Pinan's practices. Thus female traders are as likely as men to manipulate gender inequalities. Moreover, within Ifugao customary tradition that depends for support on trusted kin, women's trading strategies most often involve alliances with those women who are relatives or close neighbors, to the exclusion of others (see also Mayoux 1995, 27).

The nature of women's trading relationships illustrates that the commercialization of crafts is not a cohesive force, but may result in an unequal distribution of resources among artisans and marketers and among marketers themselves. As the majority of Banaue traders in both carvings and weavings are women, the differences that have developed have been along class rather than gender lines with the distinction made according to one's access to the means of distribution. Although in the end, both Elizabeth Bannug and Jane Pinan control the means of exchange, Jane has achieved an edge by identifying with and being respectful of artisans' needs.

MARKETERS' RELATIONSHIP WITH THEIR URBAN BUYERS

As is true of the relationships between producers and marketers, those between rural craft traders from Banaue and their urban buyers in Baguio City and Manila are constantly undergoing redefinition and renegotiation. Craft marketers from Banaue, including those with local retail outlets, are always looking for new buyers for their products. The main markets for Cordillera crafts are the handicraft shops that cater to visitors in Baguio City's and Manila's tourist shopping areas. Local Banaue marketers actively seek the patronage of these urban buyers. On the one hand, Banaue's female marketers pride themselves on their independence in freely traveling to urban centers and controlling urban business transactions. In their negotiations with buyers in Baguio City and Manila, they identify themselves as embodying the larger, regional Ifugao spirit of individualism, or kanya kanya. On the other hand, the expectations of economic personalism and the potential edge urban buyers have over price control threaten to undercut Banaue marketers' self-image.

Marketers from Banaue may refer to one another as kanya kanya during discussions of their urban selling trips and especially when they have achieved successful transactions in either Manila or Baguio City. Many rural marketers often make their first contacts with urban buyers when the latter travel from Baguio City and Manila to Banaue to take stock of the products available in marketers' homes and shops. Once Banaue traders have filled and delivered their first orders to urban centers, especially Manila, they are more comfortable initiating subsequent trips to the city to pursue new buyers. Banaue marketers simply look through the Manila phonebook under the section on handicrafts, make calls, and set up appointments to display and sell their most competitive products. Although the trip to these cities takes ten to twelve hours driving over partially unpaved, and often single-lane roads, Banaue traders are in no way isolated. Since the mid-1980s, the establishment of daily, direct bus service between Banaue and Baguio City and Manila and the availability of local truck rental, means that large and small marketers think nothing of the distance and often make the return trip in two days.

Most Banaue marketers are reluctant to share the names of their buyers with each other, fearing competition through price undercutting. Horizontal cooperation between traders is limited to sharing transportation to Manila and listening to each other's business stories, but it does not extend to sharing one's network of buyers; once in Manila or Baguio City, marketers work on their own. Although guilds or cooperative organizations would give local marketers more power with respect to urban buyers, such group efforts in both craft production and marketing have not been successfully initiated in Banaue. In the spirit of kanya kanya, Banaue's handicraft business is very much a singular endeavor since each trader develops his or her own personal network of buyers and contacts.[7]

Foremost among the problems between rural Banaue marketers and their urban buyers is the latter's pattern of delaying, sometimes for months, the payment of their balances. Although transactions in Manila are usually recorded on written purchase orders, ultimately, the responsibility to collect their payments rests with individual rural traders. Sales transactions in Baguio City are most often done verbally. Without prompt payment, Banaue marketers cannot pay their producers. Hence, they risk compromising their position as provider and ultimately jeopardize their supply of products.

The efforts of Banaue traders, especially those in wood carvings, to raise prices with Manila buyers is a further issue of contention that threatens to undermine rural marketers' independence. Traders try to maximize their profits by asking the highest price the market will bear the first time they offer new items. They know that once the first order is filled, their unique design is likely to be copied and the reproduction offered for less than the original price (see also Causey 1997; Stromberg-Pellizzi 1993). When orders of carvings are destined for export, Banaue marketers do not have access to the prices that Manila buyers receive. In such cases, when traders ask for a price increase, Manila buyers respond that they cannot give more money because their overseas buyers in Japan or Taiwan or Europe will not pay more. Lacking the knowledge about these selling prices, Banaue marketers lack the power to fight for higher returns, which results in their rather passive acceptance of this explanation. Thus, rural traders often find themselves in a situation where their identity as independent businesswomen is undermined by urban business practices.

In her effort to encourage her urban buyers' prompt payment and repeat business, Susan Angeles applies the same approach to buyers as she does to producers. She gives, as a gift, samples of her new products in which her buyers have expressed interest. If these samples sell well, then she feels she has a better chance of receiving new orders. Similarly, if the buyer does not bargain with her to reduce the amount of the final payment, then Susan will make a symbolic gesture of good faith by rounding off the total due to make a small deduction. Recently, to maintain a buyer's favor, Susan agreed to take back and repair three woven vests which had been damaged by rodents. Since the vests had been sold months ago, this was clearly not her responsibility. Susan felt, however, that to refuse the request would ultimately alienate this buyer as her suki.

The nature of the relationship between rural marketers and their urban buyers illustrates how the former individually impose their own order and interests onto business transactions to fashion their identity out of the often contradictory possibilities they encounter. How Banaue marketers conduct themselves in business is repeatedly reshaped amidst the conflict and constraints they encounter in being both rural and urban traders.

MARKETERS ARE STILL PRODUCERS

As I learned more about the marketing of handicrafts, it became evident that most traders also continue to be involved in artisan production. Marketers draw on their knowledge of craft production in their negotiations with producers and incorporate this knowledge as another facet of their identity. Rather than viewing marketing within the separate sphere of distribution, recent scholarship sees as a unified process the production of goods for exchange, their passage from producer to trader, and the realization of the exchange value of these goods as they pass from trader to consumer (see, for example, Babb 1989; Cook 1986). In her discussion of market women in

Peru, Florence Babb suggests that it is more useful to regard these traders as petty commodity producers and sellers than solely as petty entrepreneurs (1989, 44); this becomes clear when one examines their place "in interlinking modes of production." Babb maintains that no sharp line exists between "work that produces goods and work that circulates them" (1989, 200). Similarly, in his discussion of weaving and brick making in Oaxaca, Mexico, Scott Cook points out that the prevailing tendency to reify the "managerial" function of entrepreneurs as separate from labor, namely, as a "discrete factor of production," obscures the realities of the situation in which traders often combine selling with supervision and production (1986, 77–78). His account of the production and trade of metates illustrates how in the marketplace, traders play an essential role in finishing their products. Thus, in a complex combination of activities, Banaue marketers pride themselves on their individual production skills, and their ability as craftspeople adds physical value to the products they market.

Most traders in Banaue began their careers in the handicraft industry as producers. They have learned the trade from their personal involvement in the labor processes, which they currently maintain. In the marketing of woven products, traders may also act as manufacturers when they sew the weavings into a variety of functional bags, purses, and garments; in wood carving, male traders carve and repair carvings, while female marketers assume the responsibility for varnishing, sanding, and applying the woven basketry embellishment to the rough carvings. Indeed, women control the entire industry in finishing rough wood carvings. Even Jane Pinan, a prominent wood-carving entrepreneur in Banaue, can be seen each evening crouched over a row of carvings applying the final spray lacquer coat. My visits with her were always scheduled for 8:00 P.M., after her day at the Municipal Hall as Banaue councilor and just as she was completing the day's varnishing.

This skill in finishing is essential for wood-carving marketers to master, because it enables them to repair cracks that routinely occur in the carvings after they dry. It also ensures that most of the pieces damaged during shipping to Manila or Baguio City can be repaired on-site rather than being returned to Banaue. Many of the marketers take their finishing materials with them and spend extra time in the cities, patching, sanding, and varnishing the damaged pieces to ensure a complete order. Indeed, sanding and varnishing carvings is one way producers have been able to accumulate enough capital to enable them to combine finishing with part-time marketing. Female craft marketers take pride in their skills in finishing weavings and wood carvings. They add their knowledge of production processes to their marketing initiatives and present themselves in the marketplace as capable of fulfilling both roles.

TRADING AND FARMING

As well as maintaining the skills of handicraft producers, marketers rarely stray far from their preoccupation with agricultural production. As noted above, ownership of irrigated rice land and personal reserves of "native" upland rice continue to be primary measures of wealth throughout the Cordillera. Thus, an informed understanding of how marketers place themselves within the dynamics of Banaue's rural economy requires a consideration of the linkages between the spheres of agriculture and industry. In Banaue, what is the impact of marketing handicrafts upon the trader as agriculturalist? Does the precarious position of Banaue's handicraft traders prevent the abandonment of subsistence agriculture or does having access to land mean that agriculturalists do not have to depend upon marketing?

Consistent with the Cordillera custom of ranked primogeniture, in Ifugao, inheritance of land and goods is bilateral with seniority being the decisive factor. At marriage, women and men inherit equally from both parents with the oldest child, male or female, receiving the larger portion. As women are responsible for the majority of the work in the rice fields and participate in every stage of cultivation—planting, transplanting, weeding, harvesting—female marketers, particularly, continue to nurture their connection with their irrigated rice lands regardless of their income (see Milgram 1999a, 229). Even if traders operate successful businesses, both men and women will still maintain ownership of their land as a visual statement of their status. Those marketers whose handicraft businesses are doing well have the option of using their profits to hire others to work their land for them. Nevertheless, wealthy male and female marketers will make public their control over agricultural lands by usually participating in the harvest, a festive communal activity. They either help harvest the rice themselves or cook the generous midday meal. Indeed, buying or mortgaging additional irrigated rice land is one of the most desirable local investments.[8] Commenting on Jane Pinan as a trader, one carver states that since she has bought rice fields with her business profits, "now she has everything, money and land." It must be emphasized that Banaue's local, upland rice is never for sale. Even if one's fields produce a surplus, the extra rice will be given as a gift to other, less fortunate family members or saved for special rituals. By firmly identifying themselves as conscientious cultivators and as benevolent distributors of their rice surplus, female marketers, especially, reinforce their image as maternal providers. The important cultural value attached to irrigated rice fields encourages marketers to maintain ownership of and identification with their holdings, however small the harvest. It is only in times of extreme financial need that fields are mortgaged to raise ready cash.

CONCLUSION

In all respects Banaue's female handicraft marketers are local, rural entrepreneurs. They continue to live in or close to their native barangays; they trade with local artisans who produce a local product; and they reinvest any savings back into the local economy through purchases such as rice land, livestock, and means of transportation (see also Rutten 1993). Their only major external investment is the college education of their children, which functions as a source of social capital for the family (see also Seligmann 1989, 705). Their trade is strictly an individual venture. Each marketer develops her own personal trade network and negotiates individually with producers and buyers with very little horizontal cooperation.

At the same time, Banaue's handicraft marketers play a critical role in linking the local economy to wider economic forums. They purchase goods from artisans living in the most distant villages and travel to regional and national capitals to sell their crafts to urban-market buyers. Female marketers, moreover, ground their actions in the values and expectations of their community to maintain ties and of the larger national economy to maximize profits, both of which interact at the local level. While exercising personal agency in response to the varied contexts in which they work, traders' actions, in part, are constrained by past patterns, such as preexisting social and cultural structures and unequal power relations, which "exert determinative pressures and set limits upon future activities" (Roseberry 1988, 171–72). Situated then, at different nodes of economic interaction and constrained by internal and external determinants such as kin and community responsibilities and the opportunities of the market, female traders highlight different aspects of their multifaceted and flexible identities. By building upon the hybrid nature of Banaue's economy, they "combine different types of social relations, deriving from different modes of production and [distribution] and from different institutional contexts . . . [which set them] apart from the stereotype of the capitalist entrepreneur" (Long 1975, 275). The most successful marketers, such as Jane Pinan, are those who are able to maintain the minimum of obligations while still using the traditional suki avenues. They advance gifts in credit relationships to recruit labor and buyers, thus meeting the demands of reciprocity based in commodity transactions.

As highly innovative marketers, female handicraft traders in Banaue draw from their experience in the reproductive sphere to fulfill the requirements of the market. They are thus most effective in "negotiat[ing] the territory between the internal life of the community and the demands of their clients" (Stephen 1996, 388). The fact that women actually control the majority of the local, regional, and national trade means that as crafts have become commercialized inequalities have developed, not along gender lines, but among women along newly formed class lines—between traders and producers and between successful and less successful traders. Differences in the success of marketers' businesses, whether run by men or women, depend upon the extent of traders' control over the means of production and exchange. The former is achieved through their relationship with artisans and their knowledge of production; the latter, through their negotiating skills with urban buyers.

Female marketers have thus crafted "hyphenated identities" (Cook 1995, 35). Through their multistranded associations, they combine the structure and content of traditional sociocultural forms with those rooted in new social and political orders (Stephen 1991, 105). In refashioning their cultural identities in a region experiencing processes of social and economic change, they portray themselves at once as nurturers and shrewd businesswomen. They are producers and cultivators who simultaneously draw from both commodity and gifting transactions. To understand how these female craft marketers identify themselves, one cannot think in terms of monolithic collective identities. Rather, one must be as attentive to their "inner differences, contradictions and inconsistencies as [one is] to their homogeneity" (Hall 1991, 46).

Female herbalist holding forth in an itinerant Moroccan market. Photo credit: Deborah A. Kapchan.

CHAPTER SIX

Gender on the Market in Moroccan Women's Verbal Art: Performative Spheres of Feminine Authority

DEBORAH A. KAPCHAN

ABSTRACT: *The growing presence of women in the Moroccan marketplace has expanded the repertoire for feminine behavior and changed the social imagination with regard to gendered performance in the public sphere. This chapter examines how Moroccan women inhabit public spaces formerly denied them by revoicing discourse genres associated with men and thereby creating new conceptions of gender identity in a specific kind of public sphere. Through an analysis of both men's and women's marketplace discourse, the author demonstrates that neither the rules of genre nor the constraints of context account for the effect of women's performances in the public domain; rather, divining the intentionality of these performances is always an active and emergent process (Bauman 1977), engagement with which enacts a change in the social habitus. The very "irrationality" of these discourses is what gives them their force. Expressing a "counterproject to the hierarchical world of domination" (Habermas 1992, 427), a countersystem of feminine belief and intention (niya), they are reminders of the potential of women's performances to effect changes in the social world.*

I must confess, however, that only after reading Mikhail Bakhtin's great book *Rabelais and His World* have my eyes become really open to the *inner* dynamics of a plebeian culture. This culture of the common people apparently was by no means only a backdrop, that is, a passive echo of the dominant culture; it was also the periodically recurring violent revolt of a counterproject to the hierarchical world of domination, with its official celebrations and everyday disciplines. Only a stereoscopic view of this sort reveals how a mechanism of exclusion that locks out and represses at the same time calls forth countereffects that cannot be neutralized. If we apply the same perspective to the bourgeois public sphere, the exclusion of women from this world dominated by men now looks different than it appeared to me at the time.

— HABERMAS

To indicate that the world is topsy turvy, it is said that "the women are going to the market."

— BOURDIEU

The North African open-air marketplace (*suq*) is one of the most paradigmatic of male institutions. Clifford Geertz (1979) has characterized it as governed by the search for information, a world in flux where prices and identities are perpetually renegotiated (cf. Rosen 1984). Bourdieu makes the marketplace a metonym of the male world, part of a complex of symbols that includes the mosque and all that is outside and "high" (1990). These spatial icons of masculinity in Bourdieu's model are countered by his descriptions of the female world as damp, dark, magical, and (most importantly) squarely inside the walls dividing hearth from field. In other words, the North African suq is symbolic of the public realm, and that realm is indisputably male.

Such patent divisions are ideal constructions, one might even say projections, of a division of labor that upholds the gender status quo. It is easy to find examples of women in Moroccan history who frequented the marketplace not only as buyers but also as sellers of goods—used clothing, foodstuffs, small livestock, and herbs—commodities that were either made or cultivated in the domestic sphere before being marketed to the public. In contemporary Morocco, both the nature of the goods sold as well as an increase in women's participation in selling them have caused a profound transformation in the landscape of the open-air marketplace in the last two decades. Inflation, mass urbanization, and increased privatization have forced women to participate in the capitalist market in new and innovative ways. Whereas men still predominate in market professions related to agriculture and animal husbandry, they must now compete with women in the trades that rely on the arts of persuasion—in particular, herbalism and the sale of goods related to magic. What's more, in some regions, women have cornered the market in the sale of luxury commodities that come from Europe— namely, radios, cut cloth, perfume, and underwear. The presence of women traders in what is recognized (by both Western scholarship and Moroccan oral tradition) as a male domain is significant in studies seeking to analyze the role of women in the informal economy and the expanding service sector in recent Moroccan history. However, my emphasis in this chapter will not be on women's economic roles, but instead on the political implication of women's *voices* in the marketplace. It is my contention that the acceptance of women in new physical and economic landscapes in Morocco is established as much by their verbal artistry as by economic necessity. Tracking this transformation elucidates how incremental changes in performative practices like oratory and bargaining ground women in new relationships to social space and authority. That such openings are occurring at a moment in time when the perpetuation of the marketplace as a semirural institution is being threatened by rapid urbanization and devalued as backwards—an embarrassment to a modernizing nation—is no accident.

This chapter compares women's and men's verbal art in order to ascertain how gender roles take different forms in public discourses. Although a common axiological belief system can be glimpsed in both men's and women's sales spiels, men's discourse veers in a more "modern" direction based on literacy, while women's discourse emphasizes and sometimes essentializes a feminine system, in many ways separate from and parallel to the male model. Moreover, while the carnivalesque ambience of the marketplace allows women to "revoice" extant discourses, infusing them with new and subversive meaning (see Kapchan 1996), my analysis reveals that the import of these voices is tempered, if not largely diffused, by the devaluation of the market-place itself. The changing value of the site permeates the nature of the expression that transpires within it. If women find room to manipulate (in) the public margins, then they are also condemned to inhabit them. Recent celebrations of such festive institutions as the suq in the media and the popularization of (perceived) folk forms like herbalism and marketplace encounters in both the French and Arabic presses in Morocco, however, reveal small pockets where an alternate, or "competing public sphere," becomes visible (Habermas 1992). By linking feminine voices in the marketplace to social transformation, I trace the permutations and ambiguities of this emergent feminine sphere of authority.

THE SPACE OF THE MARKET, THE BAZAAR IMAGINATION

Historically, the itinerant marketplace has rural origins, although the performance traditions found there are also found in performance circles (*halqa*s) in urban centers and at city gates. Often equated with the Middle Eastern urban bazaar (C. Geertz 1979), in actuality the itinerant suq more resembles the open-air events of the European Middle Ages evoked by Bakhtin than the dark, narrow corridors of urban medinas.

> The marketplace of the Middle Ages and the Renaissance was a world in itself, a world which was one; all "performances" in this area, from loud cursing to the organized show, had something in common and were imbued with the same atmosphere of freedom, frankness, and familiarity. Such elements of familiar speech as profanities, oaths, and curses were fully legalized in the marketplace and were easily adopted by all the festive genres, even by church drama. The marketplace was the center of all that is unofficial; it enjoyed a certain extraterritoriality in a world of official order and official ideology, it always remained "with the people." (Bakhtin 1984, 153–54)

The atmosphere of freedom that Bakhtin ascribes to the Rabelaisian literary market is not completely transferable to the ethnographic context of the Moroccan marketplace, where, despite greater freedom of speech than in nonmarket contexts, one is never permitted to defame the monarchy. However, "profanties, oaths, and curses" abound in an atmosphere thick with religious discourse. Not unlike Europe in the Middle Ages, Morocco is a sacred society where the official discourses of Islam provide both counterpoint and drone to the languages of license and commodification that symbolize the marketplace; indeed because "official order and . . . ideology" are perpetually present, the profane and untrustworthy come into relief.

It is unnecessary to defer solely to Bakhtin in delimiting the importance of the marketplace for a plebeian and politicized public sphere. As sensitive registers of the sociopolitical climate, marketplaces are increasingly being recognized as key sites for the redefinition of ethnic and gender identities (Behar 1990; Seligmann 1993). Moroccan writers and theorists themselves found in the marketplace an authenticity upon which to build a Moroccan postcolonial theater in dialect, a "theater of the people" (*misrah an-nas*) as the Moroccan playwright, Taieb Saddiki, called it (Saddiki 1980).[1] For Moroccan intellectuals of the postindependence era, the marketplace—and particularly the halqa, the performance area of the market—expressed a quintessential Moroccan humor, one that was able to withstand, mock, and ultimately disempower the hegemony of colonialism. In this spirit, Abdelkrim Berrechid's 1977 foundational manifesto on "Festive Theater," located "authentic" Moroccan performance in the oral traditions of open-air comedy, poetry, storytelling, and song (Berrechid 1977). Reminiscent of Bakhtin, this document sounded the call for a vital postcolonial Moroccan theater that celebrated the performances of the marketplace as liberating, presenting a challenge to conventionality and rules. Unlike Bakhtin, Berrechid began writing when festive open-air performances were still extant in both rural and metropolitan areas in Morocco. At that time, however—only thirty years ago—the suq was primarily a masculine domain. Indeed, the contemporary marketplace provides a counterexample to modes of patriarchal social relationships built upon genealogy and blood ties that often epitomize North African and Arabo-Islamic segmentary models of social organization and identity (Abu-Lughod 1986; Eickelman 1976; Gellner 1969; D. Hart 1976). Although knowing people (*ma'rifa*) is important to establishing clientelism in the marketplace, the loyalty owed to blood ties does not provide the model of social relations between buyer and seller, making it a space wherein the rules of honor are easily bent, if not ignored altogether.[2]

The suq is the site of popular performance and popularism and has long been equated with plebeian culture and its celebration. At one time this included almost everyone except the urban elite. In contemporary Morocco, however, there is a fast-emerging middle class (along with boutiques and supermarkets catering to them) living in provincial towns that have grown into cosmopolitan cities in the span of a decade. The appearance of a new consumer class means that fewer and fewer educated buyers frequent the market, complaining of its dirt, its smell, its distance from the center of town. The fecund soil of the marketplace is now lower-class dirt in the eyes of many upwardly mobile consumers, who view it as a symbol of backwardness and barbarity. With urbanization, markets are being moved miles outside of town or razed entirely.

Precisely because the suq is the public arena for social license, however—a site where almost anything can be said with impunity—its properties of transgression take on particular political significance. Throughout history, open-air markets have been sites of social upheaval, coming under strict surveillance at times of political and economic instability (Abrahams n.d.; Agnew 1986; N. Davis 1978; Seligmann 1993; Troin 1975). There is a *public* in the marketplace at easy access to anyone interested in rallying sentiment, provoking criticism, and inciting rebellion. What is more, in the marketplace it is possible to disseminate information undercover, as it were, discursive practices working more like gossip than like an official tract. Unhinged from print, opinion rises like a wave, its source untraceable, its author unknown. If, as Clifford Geertz notes, the Moroccan marketplace is first and foremost a "communication network," then it is a highly irregular one characterized not only by the "search for information one lacks and the protection of information one has" (C. Geertz 1979, 125), but also by the active diffusion of information that may enlighten, delude, or mislead.

THE MARKETPLACE: A COMPETING PUBLIC SPHERE?

As a space of carnivalesque subversion—one which represents rural poverty as opposed to urban affluence—the marketplace is an unlikely candidate for the development of rational discourse and consensus in the political realm. No one is taken seriously in the marketplace, especially characters that historically have been marginalized and ignored—fools, clowns, magicians, women, and the poor. There are other, more probable places where a conservative and rational feminine public emerges in Morocco—in feminist publications, national conferences, and political elections and forums, for example (Fernea 1998). However, it is just this nonofficial face of the market that I would like to explore, for in such interstitial and seemingly "irrational" social spaces the work of creating public culture is performed (Lee 1992, 407).

Although quite different than a Habermasian public sphere wherein opinion is discursively negotiated in rational forums of print media, the historically situated marketplace represents an alternate and "competing public sphere," that is class-specific[3] and "takes account of the dynamics of those processes of communication that are excluded from the dominant public sphere" (Habermas 1992, 425).[4] In the Moroccan marketplace, these processes are oral and performative, but they are no less powerful than more literate discursive traditions. Indeed, the oral/performative dimensions of marketplace communication are not survivals that simply *predate* print journalism, but instead are creative strategies that coexist in dialogical relation with a vast array of print and visual media. Marketplace orators watch television, listen to radio, and may read any one of several ideological newspapers. This in addition to their role as verbal performers. The emergence of female orators, then, represents yet another subcultural sphere within the bounded communicative realm of the marketplace. Are women orators contributing to a shift in gendered practice (the gendered habitus) within the larger Moroccan public sphere? If women's revoicing of marketplace oratory constitutes a feminine and "competing public sphere" (which I assert it does), then how are its effects measured? Where is its agency?

Performative Spheres of Authority: Poetic Rules and Unofficial Meanings

Market women make public dimensions of women's experience that have heretofore been private, a process I have referred to as "private publications" (Kapchan 1996). Their discourses about relations between the sexes—in terms that are less than discreet—as well as their playful use of humor and parody, challenge dominant patriarchal notions about the place of women's bodies and voices in Moroccan society. This challenge is embodied, however, via the appropriation of poetic convention and religious formulae in a traditionally male-coded genre—marketplace oratory. By carefully adhering to the "law of genre" (Derrida 1980)—the formal conventions of generic speech (parallelism, rhyme, theme)—as well as to rules for religious speech, market women break the "laws" of appropriate speech for women, bodying forth a female authority that is palpable. They do this through repetition of well-known "primary genres" such as oaths, blessings, and curses, as well as through the use of reported speech and call-and-response techniques that make the audience active coparticipants in the performance of feminine authority (cf. Brenneis 1986; Duranti 1986). Indeed, it is the *performative* force of genres like blessings and curses that carry reverberations of feminine authority into other aspects of daily life, as these genres not only speak about but also are believed to *enact* change in the social world.

Appropriating Genres, Performing Authority

A subaltern feminine and plebeian public sphere in the marketplace is not created by the novelty of women's words, but by their embodiment of performative attitudes usually associated with men. By revoicing extant (male-coded) discourses and infusing them with new meanings, women are enacting their own public authority. Because of the assumed dishonest context of the market, however, the first thing that any orator and salesperson in the suq must establish is credibility. "Believe him or leave him" (*sadq-u au farq-u*)[5] goes a proverb about merchant-client relations. Thus does the herbalist in the following example begin by invoking the name of God, as she holds up the herbal morsels that she is selling:

1

In the name of God.
In the name of God.
Just this bit, how much is mixed in it!
Sit down and you'll see how much.
In the name of God.
In the name of God.
In the name of God.[6]

Trust in the marketplace has frequently been established by the use of oaths, which, for practicing Muslims, should not be said in bad faith (*niya*).

Of course, like oaths in the Judeo-Christian context, they are often said mechanically, without much thought to their meaning. Nonetheless, they pivot between the sacred and the profane and are used strategically to persuade an audience. In the following example, a woman herbalist explicitly calls attention to the importance of establishing trust with her clientele, passing out samples of her herbs and using oaths to vouch for their efficacy:

2

And whoever wants to prepare them by themselves, here they are.
Whoever wants them already ground, I'll gather them up here.
Bring them to your house and pound them and sift them.
Don't call me a liar or the daughter of a bitch.
And whoever of you doesn't know how or doesn't have honey or oil or
    the means to grind them
I'll give them to you prepared.
I gathered them and washed them and pounded them and sifted them
    and cooked the porcupine and sifted all of it.
If they have additions or subtractions, God subtract from my health,
    from here
[she smacks her side].
Whoever wants some from me give me a hundred [riyals].
By the truth of God!
If I've wasted your 100 riyals, tomorrow next to God—here, you are all
    more than twelve witnesses—
if I've wasted your 100 riyals, tomorrow next to God, you'll take a piece
    of my meat, from here.
And whoever wants to taste a little, taste a little, here they are,
mixed with honey and with oil.
If you eat some it's better than ghee or almonds or walnuts.
It's the sweetest thing to eat.
It's good for hemorrhage if it's in your head.
It's good for the person who has grief in his heart.

As the book said,
it's good for stomach problems and pain.

These five herbs, use them for five days in a row as the book states.

If you want to buy these herbs prepared, just have faith [*dir niya*] and
   leave the yoke here on my shoulders.
There's nothing more difficult than responsibility.
Here woman,
even we [my family] eat them in the morning and in the afternoon.
And I have brought up five children on them, by God I swear.

This herbalist invokes Islamic law, which requires twelve witnesses in order for a testimony to become legal fact. She notes that if she is lying she will
suffer in the afterlife when the client will take a piece of her flesh as payment.
If the herbalist does not heal the flesh in this life, then her own flesh will be
(symbolically) diminished in the next. Accountability in kind is promised,
if not assured. There is nothing that is not compensated for, no act that does
not participate in relations of long-term obligation and exchange. This is as
true of verbal acts as of bodily/material ones, as observed in an herbalist's citation and invocation of religious formulae and reported speech:

3
This is protection against *tqaf* [spells that render a person impotent].
And whoever can't gather them,
if you ask me I'll give you some.
Well, compensate me.
           God have mercy on the parents.
I don't hear you at all!
           God have mercy on the parents.
Come, let me ask you:
What did that man say, sir, about these herbs?
These others. What did he say, sir?
           He just spoke well of them.
Were you here sir with that man?
That *shrif* that was here with us?
Come, you woman! That man that was here,
what did he say about these herbs?
           He said they were good.
Right mame? right?
I'll move on from these herbs and I'm going to give you something,

if you pray for the Prophet.
May God pray for you oh Messenger of God.

The testimony that the herbalist draws forth makes the audience responsible for the truth value of her assertions about the benefits of the herbs. Not only does she call forth "objective" testimony, but also she makes other audience members repeat the favorable judgements, thereby becoming active participants in the mutual construction of meaning. The herbalist conducts this verbal symphony, eliciting religious phrases well known to everyone in the audience: "God bless the parents" (*llah y-erhem l-walidin*), and the sentence, "Pray for the Prophet" (*salli 'la nbi*), for which the accompanying obligatory response must always be, "May God pray for you oh Messenger of God" (*salla allah 'l-ih ar-rasul llah*). By performing these reciprocal phrases, the herbalist involves her audience in an exchange of (religious) affect indexing sincerity and good intentions. Her repetition of these formulae grounds her discourse in an ethos of religiosity which references honor, respect for elders, and truth. It is a worldview intimately tied to an ethic of paternalism and male dominance, which the herbalist implicitly challenges by her very performance in public.

The herbalist goes beyond evoking these associations. She causes her auditors to actually embody them, not only by repeating words but also by ingesting samples of her herbs. Such active testing of truth value involves the audience in a mutual exchange: if they are healed, then the herbalist will receive (spiritual) merit, and the audience will then return to the herbalist once again:

4
I'm going to turn to the right and give you all a little,
a little,
a little.
But with a condition . . .
I'm going to give you some of these.
And those.
I'm going to present them to you free again.
Here they are, here.
I want merit.

Today, whoever wants to try them;
and whoever doesn't want to try them can try them at home.
I'm going to give you one little one and you try it and come back
    to me.

The herbalist needs her audience's estimation of "merit" in order to establish her authority in a new public domain. Her strategies are numerous.
Not only does she perform authoritative genres of speech, but also she de-
lineates her genealogy, often through a male line:

5

You see, I'm talking, without you talking about me.
Pray for the Messenger of God.
Even if you just move your lips [in silence]
I know what your business is.
I'm a *majduba* for God.
That's my state and I'm its owner.
I'm not going to tell you that I just got this blessing [*baraka*].
I was a girl of seven and I had this *baraka*.
My father went to God, and we will all return to God;
but I remained in this state.
Oh God, pray for the Messenger of God.
Whoever is experienced, ah little mother, is successful.
and whoever is among the liars, little mother, is lost.

Blessings are also a way of giving something to the potential buyer which
places them in debt to the merchant. Because blessings are performatives—
the act of uttering the blessing is, itself, a bestowal—blessings carry the
power to change belief (*niya*) and, ultimately, practice. Indeed, they elicit re-
action, an exchange—whether verbal (the repeating of "Amen" or of another blessing) or material (the purchase of herbs, for example).

6

My Lord, my Owner, whoever intends to do something,
may God realize it for him.

7

This woman asked me to fix her 100 riyals of herbs.
This 100 wasn't wasted in the wilderness.
Will it come back to her or not?
It will come back double and triple.
God make you find it in paradise.
Say "Amen."
   Amen.
Give me your hand, my sister. God heal you. Say "Amen."
   Amen.

The genre of invocation (*da'wa*) may be negative or positive—a blessing or a curse:

8

Whoever intends to do something, May God realize it for him.
And whoever does harm to his brothers, May God harm him.

9

God kill the woman and the man who do what is forbidden,
whoever commits sins against his brother.
Here's four, here you are (masc.), here you are (fem.), here it is.
I'm beseeching God, if you pray for the Prophet.
   Prayers and Peace be upon Him.

The invocation of religious formulae, blessings, and curses is not unusual for a woman. Women often exchange such formalities in private contexts. What is unusual is the public *performance* of these genres. By voicing the concerns of women in the appropriated "genres of men," market women establish a new relation between gender and the public sphere. Whereas the ambiguous context of the marketplace certainly facilitates this opening, it is neither the "recontextualization" of private themes, nor the playful "frame" of the marketplace (Bauman and Briggs 1990; Goffman 1974, respectively) that accounts for women's resituation in the public domain. In the Moroccan suq, it is impossible to disentangle the serious from the playful. Frames are evanescent and numerous. Through their revoicing and reembodiment of public speech genres, women change the gender relations accepted as natural in the public sphere. Their presence performs their authority.

Given beliefs about the power of women's magic, calling death upon those who "commit ugly crimes" (see #9 above) is not an act that is taken lightly. To the contrary, the herbalist recognizes the power of women, assigning much power to her own clairvoyant abilities:

10

I'm going to say two words.
They bewitched your sons
and they bewitched your daughters.
They bewitched your house.
They bewitched your store.
Consequences [of magic] are following you.
How many children you had!
How much you built!
How much weight you gained!
How powerful you are!
You have lots of newborn sheep.
You had a bountiful harvest.
[But] the eye is following you until your entire house falls.
The eye is following you.
It emptied the castle and filled the grave.
The eye follows you.
It ate the meat and sucked the blood.
Your sins are mine [I'll be responsible for your actions]
Here's your key. Well, compensate me with "God have mercy on the
    parents."
        God have mercy on the parents.

Women orators challenge the circumscribed place of women in Moroccan society in numerous ways. Some challenge the limits of modest speech, speaking about topics considered taboo—especially for women in public (though men herbalists have long voiced these discourses to other men). Others cite Qur'anic verses in classical Arabic, drawing on the symbolic authority of scripturalist Islam and the power of literacy (see discourse #1). What all marketplace women have in common is their appropriation of traditional speech genres to effect new models of female behavior. Conforming to poetic convention and improvising creatively upon it, market women persuade their audience to accept—indeed to help create—a new feminine presence in the public sphere of the marketplace, the bounds of which spill over into the general habitus of society.

INTENTIONALITY AND THE CARNIVALESQUE

> To engage in assigning intentionality means to engage in the economy of power relations in a given community.
>
> — DURANTI

In order to apprise the impact of women's voices in the public sphere—or even to determine if their actions and words can be said to create a competing public sphere—it is necessary to question whether the intentionality of these performers bears upon the force of their performances. Do market women intend their words to resonate in the public consciousness, meaning to create a new zone of permissibility for women in the public domain? What are the effects of this public genre of speech on the social habitus, particularly as it relates to notions of gender? By adopting a socially recognized "male" genre, do women also adopt the misogynist mentality that it has traditionally expressed? How does the carnivalesque context of their discourse influence and determine these issues? In the remainder of this chapter I will go further than poetic analysis, by suggesting that it is neither the code (genre) that governs the meaning of this discourse, nor the context (or frame), but the actual embodiment and coperformance of the genre that has an impact on the public sphere.

Intentionality

As site, the market is a place of assumed license where rules for sincerity in speech are suspended (Grice 1975). People are expected to lie in the marketplace. The market is a social space where lying is acceptable; yet the context does not determine the speech act; rather, it provides an interpretive frame that may be overridden by judging the intentionality of the speaker as truthful. People do tell the truth in the marketplace, although the judgment of truth telling must be earned and is often marked. This is the linguistic premise of the carnivalesque: any clear correspondence between sign and referent is skewed; intentionality in carnivalesque language is always in question, always at play. Because the normal interpretive grounds of truthfulness in linguistic communication are inverted in the marketplace, merchants compete to persuade buyers of the truthfulness of their economic and symbolic exchange. Like information, truth becomes a commodity fiercely bargained for and coveted. Thus does the herbalist in example #2 direct her audience: "Don't call me a liar or the daughter of a bitch." And in example #5 she says, "Whoever is experienced, ah little mother, is successful, and whoever is among the liars, little mother, is lost."

Almost all herbalists assert the truth of their herbs and words, but the salience of the theme of intentionality in women's marketplace discourse distinguishes it from its prototype—male marketplace oratory. Male orators construct their public authority by reference to genealogy, code switching often and drawing on conventional symbols of legitimation and power, such as diplomas and religious literacy. For example,

II

What is written on this diploma?
And what is written on this authorization?
"The Kingdom of Morocco" is written on it:
"Kingdom of Morocco, Ministry of Interior.
"The Ministry of Interior, Province of Fes."
Written here is "the herbalist Mohammed Saadi."
I'll introduce you to natural healing.
They aren't the miracle herbs, or cooking spices or *les epices*.
What kind of diploma is *this*?
It's in *biologie*, the science of herbs.
What's written here?
The kingdom of Morocco, the Ministry of National Education, Higher
     Studies, College of Science, University of Hassan II.
Science of Herbs, *la biologie*,
a B.A. in *la biologie*.
What is written on *this* diploma?
This is from Pakistan.
Here it is.

What is written on it?
This [photo] is my younger brother, not me.
As for me, don't even ask!
Written here: "Diploma of Herbalism." [in English].
That is, it's written in English, *Diplome d'Herboriste.*
Written here is "Republic of Pakistan" [said in English].
"Specialist in Medicinal Herbs.
"The capital of Karachi."
Written here: "Herbalist Mohammed Saadi."
"Born in 1959 in Casablanca.
"Graduate, Herbalist of the State,
"Recognized by the State."
Signed by Doctor Grochola,
the biggest surgeon.
He's the doctor that signed [his name] here.
He's the one that performed an operation on Gorbachov of Russia.
These are the "friends of power" congregated here.
And there are medical doctors, and Ph.D.'s and I am here also.
Not just today.
I've been here for three years every Friday
at the door of the mosque.

12

Be careful not to get angry.
Anger is a part of fire.
There's no one who goes blind,
and his [blood] pressure goes up
and he has asthma attacks,
like the angry one.
The messenger of God said
"Take care, take care not to anger,"
the hadith[7] says,
[for that person] "distances himself from insomnia and nervous-
    ness." [CA][8]

The herbalist in example #11 code switches frequently between Moroccan Arabic, French, and English. He emphasizes the authority of his state-

certified diploma—and that of his brother—in order to distinguish his goods from the "miracle herbs, or cooking spices or *les epices*" [spices] of other herbalists, including women. The herbalist in example #12, by contrast, draws on his years of religious education in classical Arabic to establish a different kind of paternalistic authority—that sanctioned by scripturalist Islam (cf. Schuyler 1993, 1996).

Women orators also use these techniques of authority-construction (Kapchan 1996). Because most are less educated than men, however, women rely more on popular discourses of healing and belief than on diplomas, code switching, and Qur'anic citation. The importance of the client putting their trust in the herbalist, in her herbs, and in God is a primary and recurrent theme. Thus, from the examples cited above:

> yeah!
> Intention [niya] is from you and the impetus is from me
> And completion is from him who created us, our Owner.
> My Lord, my Owner, whoever intends to do something,
> may God realize it for him.
>
> 2
>
> If you want to buy these herbs prepared, just have faith [*dir niya*] and
>   leave the yoke here on my shoulders.
> There's nothing more difficult than responsibility.

The necessity of directed belief is the first ingredient in the herbalist's promised cure. And it is a promise: "If I don't fill you with the blessings of your children, may God make it so my children never see their inheritance," she asserts. And,

> If [after using the herbs] you still have spells, and obstacles, and
>   contention;
> if your children are fighting, your daughters-in-law arguing;
> if they keep arguing, and they don't like you or tolerate you,
> the responsibility will be mine before God.

Women orators profess their intentions as believers in and practitioners of magic, the very force for which their herbs are an antidote. They sell not only potions and cures, but belief in a system that subverts the status quo. In the Moroccan Islamic context, intentionality (referred to as *niya*), is a word that encompasses the English meanings of volition or directed inner state, but carries other meanings as well. Someone who has niya (*'and-u niya*) may be said to have good intentions—that is, to be sincere—but may also be considered naive or "green" (the corresponding color in Moroccan Arabic is blue). In some contexts, niya may mean belief or faith, as in someone who put his faith in herbs (*dar niyt-u f-l-'ashub*) and was consequently healed. A common expression is *dir niya u bat m'a l-haya* ("Just have faith and you can sleep with the viper [and not be hurt]").

Niya is at issue at several levels in the market: (1) the niya (intention) of the merchant is evaluated by the client (Are her goods worthy of purchase? Will they do what she says they will do? Is she telling the *truth*?); (2) the degree of niya (belief, good will) of the client determines whether a sale will take place; and (3) niya, when translated as "belief," will determine whether a remedy will work or not for its purchaser. In this latter case, intentionality not only sells but also heals (see Kapchan 1996; Rosen 1984). A fourth dimension of niya relates to the intention of women marketers and their level of (self-)consciousness in regard to their voice and place in the market economy. Intentionality becomes an important "commodity" in the Moroccan marketplace. People buy according to their belief in the relative sincerity and value of the goods and their marketer. Not only is the evaluation of good intention necessary for a sale to take place, but also the efficacy of the good itself (its power to enact cure) depends on the niya of the client. The system of magical intervention and prophylaxis is thus perpetuated by the oratory that caters to it (see #10 above).

Women herbalists are involved both in economic and ideological competitions. For despite the fact that this genre has traditionally been "in the mouths of men," its inherent ideology (the belief in and practice of magic) is socially marked as feminine. Whereas men have been holding forth in the marketplace with polemical discourses and herbal remedies that counter the powerful effects of feminine magic for decades, women's participation in this performance changes the relations of words and power. Gal has noted, "Resistance to dominant representations occurs in two ways: when devalued linguistic strategies and genres are practiced despite denigration, and when these devalued practices propose or embody alternate models of the social world" (Gal 1989, 349). Both strategies are at work in Moroccan women's public oratory. The devalued genre is marketplace oratory itself; viewed as backward, a remnant of a disappearing peasantry, the genre is at best a folklorized icon of a naive but simple past; at worst, a vulgar and shameful discourse. The "alternate model . . . of the social world" inherent in this genre is the belief in the efficacy and agency of magic, a belief system that many Moroccan intellectuals consider opposed to any possibility of progress or reform (see al-'Arawi 1982). That market women are not denying their competence in magic, but are instead publicly confirming it, has two contradictory effects: on the one hand, women's acknowledgment of the counterhegemonic system of magical agency validates its existence in the social imaginary and underscores the power of women within its bounds; on the other hand, this very affirmation contains the seeds of its own demise, for magic requires secrecy; its subversive power lies in its ability to be covert (Kapchan 1996). Once it is uncovered—admitted, so to speak—it is easier to dismiss as either shameful behavior, or simply as backward foolishness.

Intentionality becomes a theme in these feminized discourses precisely because belief in the power of magic—indeed, the paradigm of magic itself—is under threat. Increasing urbanization, coupled with a massive rise in an upwardly aspiring (as opposed to an upwardly mobile) consuming class and their inundation with televised advertising from all over the world[9] changes notions of power and authority. Marketplaces all over Morocco are being razed and replaced with supermarkets where no bargaining takes place. Not only is oratory being silenced, but also fewer people subscribe to its inherent belief system. It is noteworthy that the discourses by men quoted above are for "scientific" ailments—sexually transmitted disease in the first case, general intestinal malaise in the second. The men are reaching for the authority of Western-informed medicine. They do not need to stress the importance of belief in their cures, because they are based on a system that is in clear ascendance over a more traditional system of sympathetic energies.[10] Women, by contrast, sell antidotes for spells of impotence (*tqaf*), ingestion of potions, and the evil eye—less "modern" ailments. Their emphasis on the intentionality of their audience is thus not gratuitous. Intentionality becomes a sales strategy whose effects reach beyond material exchange to encompass the social habitus of both speakers and auditors.

When interviewed, market women, although conscious that their presence and discourse breaks social convention, do not indicate their intentions to create new roles and models for women in the plebeian public sphere. Their motives are economic; most would prefer to stay home or work a job that is less demanding. Nonetheless their presence changes notions of appropriateness in the public domain. Over the course of the last ten years or so, their presence has become naturalized. The most important effects of women's marketplace oratory then come not from their intended meaning, but from eliciting the intentions of the audience to believe in the herbs and, more importantly, in the words of the herbalist. Such belief requires a performative assent to the authority of women marketers as agents of power and influence. This assent is not only verbal, but is coded in the bodies and environments of the audience—that is, in the very habitus of the marketplace.

AN UNINTENTIONAL COMPETING PUBLIC SPHERE

In a recent publication, Lauren Berlant refers to an "intimate public sphere," a domain whose public nature is constructed via discourses circulating in nonofficial and alternative arenas. Discussing Harriet Jacobs's 1861 publication, *Incidents in the Life of a Slave Girl*, for example, wherein a slave thought that there was a Queen of America who wanted the freedom of slaves and to whom the president was subordinate, Berlant remarks:

> Jacobs shows that a great deal of language and logic circulating through
> the national public sphere is absurd, ignorant, and extremely consequential
> to the ways people understand and act within what they perceive to be the
> possibilities of their lives. She takes seriously this failed communication
> about the nation not only to show how dominated people find ways to sus-
> tain their hopefulness in a cruel world, but also to show how the kinds of
> invention, innovation, and improvisation her illiterate interlocutor prac-
> ticed with only partial knowledge could be used radically, for the reimagi-
> nation of collective political life within the nation. (Berlant 1997, 15)

Similar assertions could be made about the discourse of market women, many of whom are illiterate. Although their discourse is considered "irrational" by some—indexing a premodern world of superstition—or sinful (*haram*) by others, as witchcraft is defined in the Qur'an, it is important to remember that the discourse of magic [11] is one that gains its strength adversarially. Magic is a separatist politics, a counterhegemonic discourse that seeks to wrest power from a patriarchal system in which women are inscribed as powerless (see Kapchan 1996). The discourse of women orators reaffirms the system of magic, in which women have agency and are potentially dangerous, while the discourse of male oratory is turning toward a new paradigm—one based on diplomas and science. Is it accidental that women are finding their voice in the marketplace just as the marketplace itself is being devalued as a cultural institution? Or that women are asserting a feminine discourse at a moment when the public criteria for power are changing?

Spheres of Authority: The Metadiscursive

No public performances are innocent, and few are original. If oratorical performances in the marketplace have been subversive (and still are), they are now self-consciously so. The rapid transformation of the patterns of everyday life in Morocco—primarily because of urbanization, education (Eickelman 1992), unemployment, and transnational mass-media—make all that lends itself to stereotypification an immediate icon of a fast-disappearing traditional and folkloric world. Whereas in postindependence Morocco marketplace performances became the signature of Moroccan theater, expressing an authenticity that Molière and translated Greek tragedy could not, in a postmodern world, Moroccan marketplace performances in situ become tokens of authentic identity tottering on the border between parody and the sincere desire to incorporate old images into new conceptions of self and nation.

The notion of a public and political sphere assumes the existence of a private and inviolable one (the home), a construction as relevant to contemporary Morocco as to eighteenth-century Europe. In both cases, the delineation of the "private" realm (in contract law and other political and religious discourse) constitutes the heterosexual family unit, and especially women and children, as a silent and thus apolitical dimension of life. An unofficial "sexual contract" requiring women's subordination is implicit in the idea of the public sphere, whether documented in the creation of democracy in the Euro-American tradition (Pateman 1990; cf. Habermas 1989) or in the legitimating rituals of the Moroccan monarchy throughout history (Combs-Schilling 1989).

The historical rift between private and public performances in Morocco, and the association of women with the former, has also fostered the existence of a mentality, an oppositional ideology, associated with the feminine world. This ideology is the belief in magic, a system based on covert strategies of feminine control. That women's emergence into the public marketplace takes place in a genre devoted in large part to the remedy of ills incurred through magical intervention is no accident. Women can instantiate themselves as specialists in this field just as long as there is an audience that gives it credence.

CONCLUSION

In this chapter I have inquired into the impact of women inhabiting public spaces formerly denied them and their power to revoice discourse genres associated with men to create new conceptions of gender identity in a very specific kind of public sphere. I have shown that neither the rules of genre nor the constraints of context account for the effect of women's performances in the public domain of the marketplace; rather, divining the intentionality of these performances is always an active and emergent process (Bauman 1977), engagement with which enacts a change in the social habitus. The performative power of these discourses resides in their publicness and in their role in creating the social body. Marketplace women cater not only to a feminine market but also to a feminine ontology: namely, the belief in magic and the power of knowledgeable women to use it effectively to assert their agency. Whether these practices will be subsumed in reactionary projects that define them as either backwards or subversive in order to silence them is impossible to predict. It is clear, however, that the very presence of women in the marketplace in the last decade has expanded the repertoire for feminine behavior and changed the social imaginary with regard to gendered performance in the public sphere. The very "irrationality" of these discourses is what gives them their force. Expressing a "counterproject to the hierarchical world of domination" (Habermas 1992, 427), a countersystem of feminine belief and intention (niya), they are reminders of the potential of women's performances to effect changes in the social world.

Cserépfalu women preparing snowflower bouquets for the Eger market, Hungary.
Photo credit: Éva V. Huseby-Darvas.

CHAPTER SEVEN

Hungarian Village Women in the Marketplace During the Late Socialist Period

ÉVA V. HUSEBY-DARVAS

ABSTRACT: *This chapter argues that for the women of Cserépfalu, a northern Hungarian village, their involvement in national and transnational marketing has had a significant impact upon their gender, class, and local identities. Local responses to centrally directed social change during the late socialist period (1982–1989) resulted in the importance of women in marketing within and beyond the village. Without these marketing ventures neither the socialist economy as a whole nor individual families could have survived. By stressing the value of resourcefulness and a Protestant work ethic, the village women partially conformed to the norms of the local Calvinist community, greatly contributed to the household economy, and enabled conspicuous consumption. Nevertheless, these women were harshly criticized and stigmatized in accordance with the villagers' competing patriarchal ideology. The subsequent emergence of the free market economy ironically led to a decline in women's marketing activities.*

In this chapter, I examine the relationship between village women's marketing activities and their generational, gender, and local identities during and following the socialist period in Cserépfalu, a northern Hungarian rural settlement.[1] For the women of Cserépfalu, a Calvinist village of 1,394 individuals and just under 500 households at the time of this study, marketing and market-related endeavors became critically important during the late socialist period between 1982 and 1989. Women carried on marketing ventures within the scope of the second or third economy as explicated below. These two sectors were considered formally distinct from that of the centralized socialist state economy, yet neither the socialist economy as a whole nor individual families could have survived without women's marketing ventures. Paradoxically, while village women contributed substantially to the household economy and their marketing ventures conformed to local community norms of resourcefulness (*kaparkodás*) (Juhász et al. 1972),[2] they were stigmatized by fellow villagers because their actions challenged the mores of the traditionally patriarchal village.

THREE ECONOMIC SECTORS DURING THE LATE SOCIALIST PERIOD

The conventional manner in which the first, second, and third economic sectors of socialist economies are defined draws clear boundaries between the activities that comprised each sector during the late socialist period. As I show below, these sectors were, in fact, interdependent and overlapped with one another. The first sector involved participation in the state economy, defined as holding a regular wage-earning job that offered social benefits. Nearly all Cserépfalu villagers worked in, or drew pensions from, one of several branches of the state economy.

Regular or occasional work in either the private sector, on the peripheries of the state sector, or employment in irregular, but still more or less lawful,[3] economic activities defined the second sector. Most women's marketing activities were located in the second sector. In all village households, people were involved in some second sector activities, from which they usually earned higher wages than from state sector employment. Second sector economic ventures included working on household or rented plots (*háztáji*); in orchards and vineyards; raising poultry, pigs, and rabbits for sale; engaging in short-term (four to eight weeks per year) seasonal agricultural migrant work; gathering, preparing, and marketing a variety of forest products; and making and selling noodles and other goods (K. Csilléry 1979; Lajos 1959– 1961). In addition to the nearly 100 women who were employed by the state-owned Mezőkövesd Folk-Art Cooperative, at least as many, if not more, women made embroidery for boutique owners and other private entrepreneurs on a piecemeal basis.

In contrast to first or second sector activities the state considered third sector economic pursuits explicitly illegal. Villagers, however, distinguished between those activities in the third sector that they regarded as "natural," "normal," or "part of life" and those that they condemned as illicit. "Everybody does it," people told me with a shrug. Some of them added, "It is fine, but don't get caught by the authorities." Third sector economic pursuits condoned by the villagers included taking alfalfa (or anything else) from cooperative fields, poaching in the woods and gathering medicinal herbs, regularly selling homemade wine or fruit brandy in small quantities; some of the women's marketing activities, such as the selling, buying, and exchanging of goods and other commodities for profit during so-called tourist excursions to Austria, Romania, Czechoslovakia, Yugoslavia, and the Soviet Union; *fusizás*, a kind of moonlighting, in which people made or produced things for individual profit, usually during official working hours, from material that belonged to the state-owned enterprise in which the person was employed; and selling or exchanging first sector labor related services for personal profit, for example, using a state-owned vehicle for the transportation of a neighbor's building materials. Most villagers believed that "it was there for the taking." Third sector activities persisted despite efforts by the local authorities to discourage them via fines and public shaming of offenders.

Economic ventures in the third sector that were condemned by most of the villagers, who described them as "cheating," "theft," "immoral," and "unbefitting of a real, proper and decent *cserépi*," included: exchanges of services within the village in which villagers were directly shortchanged for a single individual's high profit; "horse trading" (*ember kupeckodás*) with other people's labor in such a way that both the state and fellow villagers were cheated; intravillage prostitution; regularly selling wine and fruit brandy in one of the village's clandestine speakeasies (*bögrecsárdas*); stealing from a fellow villager, particularly from kin, fictive-kin, or neighbors; or pursuing activities for one's own benefit that would get a fellow villager into trouble with the authorities.

Almost all villagers regularly participated in first and second sector activities and, occasionally, third sector ones as well. Participation in the first and second economic sectors frequently provided the goods, time, materials, and often the opportunity for villagers to enter into and profit from the third sector. The official boundaries between these sectors were always shifting. For example, any sort of marketing activity for private gain, including selling and buying in local marketplaces, was strictly condemned by the state until the late 1960s, during which time it became tolerated but never really encouraged (Stark 1989; Szelényi et al. 1988; Szelényi 1994). Thus, the socialist state always had some control over the participants, who could seldom be sure in exactly which sector they were participating. Still it is clear that the existence of these sectors, however they may have been variously interpreted and adapted by the Hungarian government and citizens, helped to define the nature of women's marketing and of work and consumer-related identities, attitudes, values, and aspirations in Hungary.

THE HOUSEHOLD DIVISION OF LABOR

The division of labor within Cserépfalu families historically varied according to sex, age, and seasonal work activities (see also Fél and Hofer 1969). The traditional family was a unit of production and consumption, controlled by a male head of the household. In conjunction with a predominant pattern of virilocal postmarital residence, every attempt was made to separate young wives from their natal kin. Even in the early 1960s, strict rules guided a young woman's "visitation rights" to her parents' house. While her father-in-law ruled the household, her mother-in-law tried to have complete control over the young wife's time, work, social behavior, friendships, income, and even her rate of reproduction.[4]

After the late 1940s, with the beginning of state socialism, collectivization, permanent male out-migration, and long-distance commuting, the ideal (and often the actual) postmarital residence pattern became neolocal. This more recent pattern gradually created stronger connections between young and middle-aged married women and their female natal kin. In economic ventures and in all sectors of social life, women began to rely more on their mothers, sisters, aunts, cousins, and *ángy* (ángy is an umbrella term for any female relative by marriage who is older). These connections, similar, for example, to those in rural British communities as reported by Bott (1971) and Strathern (1982, 72–100, 247–77), were continuously validated, reaffirmed, and articulated through the exchange of gifts, visits, labor, and favors. Villagers' verbal expressions and most secular and religious rituals demonstrated the growing strength of ties between women and their female natal kin.

The introduction of the government's New Economic Mechanism (NEM) in January 1968 led to unprecedented material affluence in the Hungarian countryside (Andorka 1979; Balassa 1982; Hanák 1991; Knight 1983; Lampland 1995). The NEM policy made more resources available for the production of consumer goods and took steps to raise the population's standard of living. It placed less priority on the development of industry, stressing instead investment in agriculture and the infrastructure necessary for agricultural development. The new policy also allocated considerable investment capital for the modernization of farming and abandoned the idea that Hungary should aim at economic self-sufficiency (Enyedí 1980, 1982; Hanák 1991, 220; Hann 1980).

This boom had a substantial impact on Cserépfalu. Younger villagers, in particular, placed increasing importance on the accumulation of material goods and on conspicuous consumption. Social pressures intensified in all age groups. Many old and middle-aged villagers became inspired to give more than ever to their children, while many adult villagers found themselves working to the point of physical exhaustion because of these same pressures and desires. Some students of Hungarian rural society (for example, Sozan 1983, 1984) have argued that this phenomenon appears to be self-exploitative, self-destructive, and masochistic. Additionally, growing income differentiation in the wake of the NEM was accompanied by growing socioeconomic stratification. Given these conditions, marketing became an even more significant supplementary activity for village women in Cserépfalu. Women of lower socioeconomic status especially became heavily involved in these activities.

VILLAGE WOMEN IN THE MARKET

The village women of Cserépfalu have become actively involved in local, regional, national, and transnational economic life as a result of their marketing activities. While many villagers have always looked down on marketing activities, it is precisely through marketing strategies that middle-aged women of Cserépfalu have shaped and expressed their own gender, generational, and to some degree, class identities.

Types and Kinds of Marketing

Cserépfalu women's marketing strategies have developed in accordance with whether or not they sell their goods in local, regional, national, or transnational markets, and with the kinds of merchandise they offer for sale. At the time of my study, while there was not a great deal of local marketing activity,[5] what there was went on regularly throughout the year. The most profitable local marketing involved home-brewed spirits and was considered illegal. Four local widows ran three establishments that, in local parlance, were and still are known as bögrecsárda (a wayside inn where drinks are served in mugs rather than in glasses). In these transactions, money almost never changed hands. Rather, the widows received looted produce and other goods for their home-brewed spirits. The poorest villagers—including those whose parents and ancestors, as far back as local memory goes, lived in one of the single- or double-celled cave-dwellings on the periphery of Cserépfalu (cf. Bakó 1977; Kovács 1937; Szabó 1936, 1937)—did not own wine cellars and vineyards. The men from these, and similarly poor, families rarely had the opportunity to participate in pincézés (the village men's institution of drinking and socializing (Huseby-Darvas 1996). Instead, they frequented the bögrecsárda, the village version of underground "speakeasies," where they could obtain spirits at any time of the day or night in exchange for eggs, produce, or practically anything of value. Many villagers, especially the wives whose pantries were pilfered by their thirsty male relatives for drink, cursed and looked down upon the widows who ran these establishments.

The regional sphere of women's marketing geographically was broader. Regular and dynamic marketing took place in a 25-kilometer radius around the village of Cserépfalu. The widows who ran the "speakeasies" often traveled to the regional markets and even to the national markets from time to time to sell the goods they had accumulated in their home-brew businesses. The women also took produce, flowers, and other goods to the weekly markets in Mezőkövesd and Eger. Interestingly, women from neighboring villages did not engage in marketing nearly to the same extent and intensity as the women of Cserépfalu.

Village women did some marketing in Miskolc, the county seat and second most populous city in Hungary; however, the distance and cost of travel prevented them from marketing in Budapest, the country's capital. Nevertheless, women from the village regularly went to markets in Austria, Romania, and Czechoslovakia[6] despite the high cost of travel, investment of time and energy, and risk, because they were able to realize much greater profits there.

Village women were clearly aware of how the global marketplace exploited their labor. They never tired of telling how the blouses, dresses, tablecloths, and other items they embroidered and sold as piecework in the regional center of Mezőkövesd were sold in the boutiques of the United States, Canada, Australia, and Western Europe for a much higher profit.

Sources and Types of Marketed Goods

What kinds of items did village women sell? How did they obtain the goods they took to market? Village women obtained the goods they took to market in four ways. First, they produced goods in their homes, including surplus produce from household plots, home-brewed wine, and occasionally on a household basis, cottage handicrafts made by enterprising fathers, fathers-in-law, husbands, and (very rarely) sons (K. Csilléry 1979; Lajos 1959–1961). These goods they sold primarily at regional markets. Second, groups of village women, most often with the help of their children, gathered wild materials such as mushrooms, snails, flowers, and berries in the forests near the village and sold them in either regional or national markets.[7] Third, the women pilfered goods to which they had gained access. These included some of the produce grown by the local cooperative or on other cooperative or state farm grounds. Villagers would "take" bags of harvested produce, hide them in the baggage compartment of the workers' bus, and bring them home for the women to sell on the various markets.

Fourth, women sold goods they had either purchased, or received as remuneration for their work on state-owned cooperatives. Many women would divide the bags of onions or the boxes of fruit or early vegetables that they received as pay, which they then sold at a considerable profit at the regional or national markets. Another strategy they used was to accumulate birth-control pills and other prophylactics over many months by having doctors prescribe them for themselves and for all their female kin. They had the prescriptions filled in various regional pharmacies[8] and smuggled them, along with much needed butter, coffee, and canned foods, into Romania where birth-control devices were illegal and strictly prohibited.[9] They would then travel by bus to Transylvania and sell the birth-control pills, condoms, and other prophylactics, as well as foods, to ethnic Hungarian[10] women there. After investing some of the profits in Romanian goods they planned to sell elsewhere, the women would return to Hungary and invest the remainder in sweet Soviet champagne and freshly baked Hungarian bread from a bakery said to be the best in the region. They would then travel by bus or train to Austria and sell the champagne and bread there. Finally, the women would buy yards and yards of "Viennese velvet"—a material that in the 1980s was highly valued in the village for making "Sunday suits" and confirmation clothes for teenagers and young men—gold jewelry, yards of other cloth, or what they called "Viennese scarves" and return home.

THE CASE OF SNOWFLOWERING

The most financially rewarding occasional economic marketing activity pursued by Cserépfalu women was the gathering, preparation, and sale of snowflowers (*Galantus nivalis*) in early March and of lilies of the valley (*Convallania maialis*) in May. The flowers have specific symbolic meaning in urban rites celebrating the arrival of spring and summer, respectively. The set of activities associated with each plant is called, in local parlance, *hóvirágozás*, literally "snowflowering," and *gyöngyvirágozás*, "lily of the valleying." In fact, the process of flower marketing consisted of four distinct phases. The first was a long planning period between Christmas and the actual event when open conflict within families and between middle-aged village women (those who were at the time between the ages of thirty and fifty-five years)[11] ensued, a phenomenon which I discuss in greater detail below. In the second phase, small groups of two to five women gathered the flowers in early March or May. Most of the groups formed on the basis of kinship, fictive-kinship, and neighborhood ties. In the third phase, large groups of twelve to eighteen women, usually comprised of a wider network and age range of kin and neighbors, would prepare the bouquets. Even old women were involved in this phase (although their participation was marked by continual complaints). Finally, individual middle-aged village women would sell the flowers in the regional market of Eger, Mezőkövesd, or more rarely in Miskolc or Budapest.

Flower gathering has been a part of Cserépfalu women's economic strategies since long before World War II. In this chapter, I will limit my discussion to snowflowering and how it has shaped the identities of Cserépfalu women. Snowflowering began to involve long-distance travel and complex strategies in the early 1970s when, as I was told, snowflowers "just died out in the nearby woods." As a result, village women began traveling to Budapest to buy large quantities of flowers from Transdanubian vendors at the *Nagy-csarnok* (the Central Market of the capital). They would take the flowers back to Cserépfalu, prepare small bouquets, and then take them to Eger to sell. A forty-two-year-old villager gave this account:

> My husband and my brothers quarreled and yelled at me. Spending all that money, buying all those flowers, they said, was just too big a risk. But my *koma-asszony* (cogodparent) and I did it anyway. We ended up making two to three times the amount we spent in Budapest and on travel. . . . But after a couple of years I said to my koma-asszony, "Let us try to go to Transdanubia and pick our own flowers like my neighbor's neighbor, Rózsi, is doing with her [group]. Why make these Transdanubian *Svábok*[12] rich?" But Rózsi would not tell us where they were going! It was a secret she swore never to reveal. So my koma-asszony and I just had to find our own forests. We always keep it a secret too, like all the other cserépi women do. . . . We lose five day's vacation time or get sick leave from our [state sector] jobs. Plus we lose money on the expensive train and bus tickets and have to pay those Svábok for three to four nights of lodging. . . . They just look down on us as if we were Gypsies, as if we did not have a house or anything of our own. And the city folks on the Budapest metro [en route to another train station] just stare at us and our big *hátyi*[13] baskets as if we

were *négerek* [in Hungarian: African Americans, Blacks] . . . but it is still worth it. In one week I make more money than two-and-a-half to three months of my wages at the [state sector] job. . . . So my husband still yells at me. When I tell him I will go he curses at me; my children are ashamed of me and the foreman gets angry. . . . But if I didn't do it, my children would not have anything, just like I didn't when I was their age.

The small gathering groups began to organize and plan around Christmas. Women listened to weather reports, talked with village men who commuted as woodcutters to Transdanubia, and visited back and forth before they decided on the precise gathering location. Lodging was difficult to get in Transdanubian villages, and a woman never really knew how big the crop of snowflowers would be that year until she had actually arrived in a particular forest. Thus, the chances of finding lodging and enough flowers depended upon the number of people who had found out about a group's destination. Keeping snowflowering destinations secret in a community where everything was known about everybody led to a number of open conflicts year after year.

Conversation, gossip, and family tension related to snowflowering were most intense between Christmas and the second week of March. Within the small gathering groups, women criticized those villagers who "do it as a hobby; like look at my cousin, she gets 18,000 forints into [the family's] budget every month from her husband and children, yet she still goes year after year." After the snowflowering was over, however, these groups would dissolve and might or might not reorganize the same way the following year, as women moved fluidly in and out of different circles. The very same cousin who was openly criticized for participating in snowflowering might soon become a travel and business partner in a selling and buying excursion to one of the neighboring countries, where a portion of the profits from the venture would be "reinvested" in goods not easily available in Hungary.[14]

Once the women returned to Cserépfalu with the flowers from Transdanubia, they began preparing the bouquets immediately, relying on the labor of informal, traditional mutual-help associations (*kaláka*) among the villagers. This was considered a serious obligation, so if a neighbor or relative was sick or could not help for some other reason in the preparation process, she would send someone else, even a child, in her place. During these sessions the women shared details about their journey, lodgings, the gathering process, and the return, but they would never mention the precise location of the forest in front of the helpers "so they will not blab about where we found all these flowers." [15]

With the bouquets packed in baskets, boxes, and suitcases, the women then boarded the bus and traveled to the predominantly Roman Catholic village of Eger. As they said, "the *pápisták* [a pejorative term referring to the Roman Catholics of Eger] are such saintly folk. They always buy flowers, not only to give [on Women's Day], but also to take to their churches and cemeteries." Intravillage competition was keen, not only in the Eger market but also en route to that city on the bus. Yet the women kept a close eye on one another and whenever village women had trouble with Eger authorities or flower vendors, they would form a united group once again, helping their covillager sell her remaining bouquets and cheering her up by cursing at the Eger authorities once the latter were no longer on the scene. Village women purchased the obligatory place-ticket in the market in Eger, theoretically giving them the right to sell, but local flower vendors often called in the authorities, who then tried to send the villagers to other, less favorable locations in the market. Village women also sold bouquets on streets, in front of churches, and at busy intersections away from the market of Eger. If they were caught, they had to pay a fine for illegal vending.

In March of 1983, fifty-three women from Calvinist Cserépfalu sold flowers in Eger. In contrast, only a very few women from the neighboring, primarily Roman Catholic villages of Bogács and Bükkzsérc were engaged in the same activity. While traveling home from Eger, village women joked with one another on the bus, calling the neighboring villagers by pejorative nicknames [16] and comparing not only their individual profits made from selling the flowers but also Cserépfalu's profits versus those of Bogács and Bükkzsérc.

Intrafamily and intravillage conflicts loomed large around this very significant marketing and supplementary income-producing venture because it involved women's long-distance travel. From the moment married women declared their intentions to pick flowers until they returned from selling the bouquets in Eger, their husbands fought against their engagement in these activities. [17] Older village women, who a few years before had picked and sold flowers themselves, now argued with their thirty-, forty-, or fifty-year-old daughters, saying, "Why are you doing this again? You don't sleep for a week;

you don't really need to do this." Even children and teenagers who participated in the preparation and, occasionally, even in the transportation of
bouquets to the markets, refused to help with the actual selling process because, they claimed, their mothers' selling on the market embarrassed them.

Most members of the village elite were also openly critical of the women's
flower-selling ventures. They accosted women vendors at the Eger market
with, "Do you really need to do this? Are you not embarrassed by this when
you don't even need it?" This might appear to be a paradox, but is not, once
it becomes clear that while the village elite valued the accumulation of material goods, they also made distinctions based on who acquired the goods
and how. Certain economic activities were simply not appropriate for those
who desired to achieve or protect their high social status.

The most frequent responses of the women to these negative comments
and queries were: "Yes, we do [need to do this]. We here are the authentic,
resourceful Calvinist women" (igen; mink vagyunk az igazi, kaparkodó Kál-
vinista asszonyok), thus invoking tradition, religion, and ingenuity to defend
their marketing activities.

THE CASE OF MATYÓZÁS

Another important revenue-generating activity the village women pursued
was the making and selling of embroidery on a piecework (matyózás) basis
in groups of three to ten. One group of eight villagers had been embroidering together for twenty-two years. These women jokingly referred to their
group as the "work brigade of the Lower End of the village" (Alvégi Matyózó
Brigád). Within and beyond Cserépfalu, these embroidery groups fulfilled
a quasi-ritual sociocultural function similar to that of the traditional spinning house associations that operated until the mid-1950s. They were the key
centers of intravillage communication and important agents in extravillage
social relationships. During the spring, summer, and early fall when the
groups gathered on the sidewalks, villagers who walked or rode by in their
cars or bicycles stopped and chatted with them, exchanging gossip and information about village affairs, market prices, and events, and what was hap-
pening with the idegen rokonyok (kin who are strangers or who had become
strangers) and the hűtlen hazaárulók (unfaithful traitors, that is, villagers

who had emigrated permanently from the country). Money, marketing, financial obligations, work, and other responsibilities preoccupied participants in these conversations. The women discussed who was behind in their payments of church tithes, known as "the wages of the pastor" (*pap béri*), and where particular villagers obtained the necessary funds to cover essential obligations such as church expenses, wedding presents, baptismal presents, and new clothes and jewelry for godchildren's upcoming confirmations. The behavior of village men was also an important and recurring topic among the Matyózó women. How much, where, and when did men drink? Which bachelor was seen going into the house of the village whore? Who beat his wife? Did she deserve to be beaten on a particular occasion?

Most of the marketing and other commuting women, on their way home, got off the bus and headed directly to the nearest Matyózó group to catch up on all the events of the day and to share news from outside the village with the group.

In addition to serving as key centers of communication within the village, the many members of the embroidery groups, through their marketing strategies, provided a direct link between Cserépfalu and wider regional social and economic networks. Many women traveled by bus to Mezőkövesd where the cooperative's headquarters was located and monthly regional meetings were held for the representatives of the more than 3,000 cooperative employees from the area. The cooperative was the single largest employer in the Mezőkövesd district (Kratochwill 1980, 29). These occasions offered women opportunities to meet women from neighboring villages and make comparisons about the quality of each village's embroidery, prices, and the profits they were making. Within Cserépfalu these comparisons might take place between individuals and between the various embroidering groups, but at the regional meetings the women from the village represented themselves as a united Cserépfalu front.

The embroidery groups also tied the village economy into the global economy. The women knew that the blouses they embroidered were intended for Western export and thus brought Hungary much needed hard currency. The women's favorite topic involved long and argumentative speculations about the Hungarian state's profits in contrast to their individual incomes. Former villagers who lived in and visited from North America informed the Matyózó women that the embroidered blouses retailed for as much as U.S.$80 to $129 in Canada and the United States. For embroidering a child's blouse the women got 46 forints (about U.S.$1 at the time), and for the most elaborately embroidered woman's blouse on which they might work as much as fifteen hours, they earned 115 forints (U.S.$2.50) from the co-op. Young, middle-aged, and some older women believed that "the difference between retail price and piecework wage is pocketed by the state, so they make more money on us per blouse than we earn in almost two months!!" Women involved in Matyózás were aware of their constant exploitation by the socialist state, despite the changes in form it had taken over time.

THE MEANING OF WORK

In Cserépfalu, the attitude of village men and of nonembroidering, and even part-time embroidering, women toward the entire activity of embroidery was uniformly negative. Cserépfalu villagers generally held the attitude that making and selling embroidery was not work; some of the villagers even saw it as a leisure activity. Middle-aged women who worked either for agricultural cooperatives or for one of the local light industries and did embroidery during their lunch hours and their early-morning and late-evening "free times," considered full-time Matyózás a luxury. As one forty-seven-year-old woman, who worked full-time and went to the market regularly, commented:

> These women can afford to waste their time just sitting around and gossiping all day while they embroider. They are all "rich peasants." Their fathers just handed everything over to them: the house, the land, the vineyard. We, who started from nothing, must work for our houses and for our livelihood. Most of these Matyózó women are still *kuláks* [rich peasants]. They did not change even after the land was taken from them; their rank has remained and they don't really have to work. Of course, there are a few poor ones who are weak or sick and that is why they can only embroider. They cannot work regularly, so they just embroider and don't do anything.

Thus, even though women's production and marketing of embroidery subsidized a household's ability to survive in the first economic sector, villagers were reluctant to consider it as work.

REINFORCING LOCAL VALUES AND IDENTITIES

The gathering and marketing of various forest products was a significant supplementary income-producing activity during the late socialist period for village women in Cserépfalu,[18] although it was fraught with generational and familial conflicts. Many middle-aged marketing women were also employed full-time in the local state sector.[19] Villagers from nearby settlements commented to me repeatedly that "these stubborn Calvinists collect a few roots and a couple of berries and down they run to the [Mezőkövesd] market. . . . Even now that the bus fares have doubled, the cserépi women fill the bus on market days."

Even though young people occasionally helped with the gathering, middle-aged women did most of the selling. A sexual as well as generational division of labor was apparent in these marketing activities.[20] Much to the dismay of marketing women, young women were reluctant to participate in the process of selling in the marketplace, even when they accompanied their older kin and helped to carry baskets filled with produce to the market. "They just stand there, as if they were not even cserépi women," a fifty-six-year-old woman commented, adding:

> My grandmother taught me how to talk a lot and how selling on the marketplace must be conducted when I was a little girl. Every market day we were selling in Kövesd and from spring to fall she took me along to the villages south of here. Back when I was a child, we still went house-to-house selling lime. . . . My daughters used to help with everything, but always refused to sell with me in the market. Not that they were pretending to be upper class gentle-folk like so many of these young ones are. It's just that all that schooling ruined them, so selling embarrassed them, and [it] did not come to them naturally like it came to me. My husband did this, it is his fault, even though I told him that all that learning would ruin the girls. But he insisted after he came home from the army. He said, "They should be anything, but not peasants like us. Peasants are treated with such contempt, almost like Gypsies, in this country." We had land before the Coop took it from us. I had hoped that the girls would marry, bring home nice cserépi [local] sons-in-law and we would all work and live here, all together. . . . But we are on pensions now; the girls got all that learning and moved to the city. They have a better life now than the prince[21] had in the old days. Yet my daughters never could earn even a single *Ady* [here: slang

for a 500 forints bill] selling in the marketplace. What kind of cserépi woman is one who cannot sell on the market?

These and other remarks reveal the pejorative status that villagers attributed to those who engaged in marketing and, indirectly, to those women who gained greater autonomy by becoming educated and working outside their homes and the rural village.

Villagers over the age of fifty-five were also highly critical of the increased material demands of younger people and repeatedly made comparisons between traditional and modern consumption patterns. Yet, ironically, they supported the very lifestyles they criticized. As elsewhere in rural regions (cf. Simó 1983), in Cserépfalu older people lived their lives for their children. Their economic actions were shaped primarily by the ever-increasing demands of their children and grandchildren. They deemed it natural, though difficult, that every extra forint from their pensions and supplementary economic activities, would go to their children. Paradoxically, while many young people were embarrassed by their mothers' and other female kin's marketing activities, these endeavors were the very source of cash available to them to spend on luxury items and other goods.

SACRIFICE AND RESOURCEFULNESS

I frequently heard the saying, "A person is crazy without money" (*bolond az ember pénz nélkül*) in Cserépfalu. Offered as an explanation, a cause, and a reason for a person's actions and for intrafamilial tensions, the saying was most common among middle-aged women. To avoid going crazy without money one had to be resourceful. Indeed, the most highly regarded behavior in the ideal male or female villager was to demonstrate resourcefulness. In Cserépfalu, resourcefulness was an essentialized characteristic attributed to and equated with genuine cserépi-ness. When villagers contrasted themselves with people in neighboring settlements, they most frequently mentioned resourcefulness and diligence or the lack thereof. They also considered that these traits defined their own Calvinism which, in turn, constituted a critical component of their ethnic identity and distinguished them from their Roman Catholic neighbors.

Villagers evaluated outsiders as well in the light of their degree of resourcefulness. They openly admired the resourcefulness of the village doctor who, in five years of practice in Cserépfalu and Bükkzsérc, had amassed visible wealth, and the village school principal-cum-Communist Party secretary who, in less than two decades in the village had achieved affluence. Villagers held the local pastor who had moved to Cserépfalu in 1980 with three truckloads of fine furniture and a station wagon in high regard for his perceived resourcefulness and one man described the former director of a nearby agricultural cooperative who had been sent away after being caught for embezzlement as "the best *kaparkodó* [most resourceful] boss we have ever had. Sure, he filled his own pockets first, but took really good care of us too." The new village boss "had empty pockets and a big family; he was too busy being kaparkodó only for himself, without considering us, so we changed jobs." In this last case, while the villagers still considered the new boss's resourcefulness a positive trait, they condemned him for not sharing with the workers as had his predecessor.

The older villagers not only said that they lived for their children; they also continuously gave them everything they were able to give, whether or not their children still actually lived in the village.[22] Both generations insisted that this was a natural part of parental duty and obligation. Middle-aged and older villagers often discussed the size, value, and frequency of cash and other kinds of gifts conveyed to their children, grandchildren, and godchildren. They explicitly competed about who gave more and whose offspring owned more material goods. To give as much as possible was a symbol of high status and a sign of individual worth. With the ever-increasing importance of consumption and accumulation of goods among the young and some of the middle-aged, social pressures to give had intensified tremendously by the 1980s. Giving to one's children was implicitly equated with Calvinist values—working hard, self-exploitation, continuity, and sustained good relations between the generations. During the period of late socialism this type of giving became the raison d'être for the labor of middle-aged and old villagers.

Older villagers still recalled times not long ago—the early 1960s when land collectivization was completed—when their fathers or grandfathers had total control of all the family income, money, and possessions until they died. In contrast to current practices, the younger generation had given all their earnings to the head of the household in which they resided. Most of the old villagers, however, were not bitter about these particular changes, but instead took them as "a matter of course," "the way life is." The younger villagers, and in particular, the middle-aged, including the women most involved in marketing and the men who commuted to their jobs, perceived themselves as sacrificing their lives for their children and families and most frequently uttered the phrase, "I am sacrificing my life." The men pointed to commuting itself and the problems they encountered on the job away from the village as principal evidence of their sacrifice. They explained their problems, conflicts, and life's difficulties in terms of regional and individual differences, rural-urban differentiation, and varying expectations and interests, rather than criticizing the sociocultural contradictions inherent in the society and the economic system in which they participated.

Women between the ages of about forty and fifty years of age explained the reason for their sacrifice by comparing their lives to those of their mothers and grandmothers. As a forty-three-year-old informant maintained:

> My mother always worked, yet she did not have the responsibility on her shoulders like I do and my sister does. You see, it was the father's responsibility that the family had enough food, enough wood. Now women must make do and always have enough. Life was simpler for my mother. Even though we were poor she did not know the meaning of the word "nervous." Now we [her age-group] are all nervous. My husband comes home twice a month [from the city]. He either gives me or the kids the money he did not spend on drinking, or I take it out of his pockets when his [kin] drag him in from the workers' bus.[23] It is on my shoulders that everything goes well; my kids have to have everything like others do. Today we have much more [material goods] than they had in the old days, but we have to sacrifice our lives to keep up.

Conflicts Between Men and Women

One man who commuted worried about the lack of moral constraints on women in the city and viewed their travels as akin to abandoning their domestic responsibilities. He would not let any of his womenfolk go to market, and if they went to the city, he had to accompany them. In his view, [there] are no regular jobs close to the village. Move to the city? Never!! All city women are whores. They confuse the concepts there. Here in Cserép we know what we want in a woman: she must be a quiet lady in company, a peasant when work needs to be done, and a whore in bed. But city women are whores in company, pretend to be great ladies when work should be done, and they are not even peasants, just filthy pigs, in bed. . . . How can they be good mothers? They just fool around, but say that they work overtime, and ignore their kids. . . . You see, here the eyes of the entire village are open all the time. I can be working 200 kilometers from home and even then I know that my woman behaves properly. The foreman said to me, "I want to put your name on the list for a city flat; you could move in two or three years!" I said, "I don't want that dirty decadent underground life for my family." No, I will never move to the city. . . . I just got my nephew a job in the factory. Now the six of us from here will be in the same plant. That is the only way, the best way: if we . . . stick together. The more there are of us the better we can show them in the city. . . . Sure I would like to work fewer hours, spend more time with the kid and the [wife], watch television, and take vacations. But I cannot. I must sacrifice like I do if we are to get ahead. My son has everything. He is happy. He just got a digital watch and an Adidas leisure suit. We paid over 2,000 forints for these. He just completed the first half [of the first year in elementary school] with an outstanding report card. You see that little television set in there? Nobody has this minimodel in the village yet. I just bought it. Now we have three working TVs. . . . I know what I sacrifice my life for and it is the only way.

Incidentally, in this particular family the man was in skilled industrial labor; he commuted three times a week, and earned between 5,500 and 6,500 forints per month. Together, the three women earned about 6,000 forints a month embroidering. In addition, the two older women got state retirement pensions, each receiving 1,650 forints monthly. The family income from supplementary activities was an estimated 4,000 to 8,000 forints a month, depending upon the season and other factors. The women started embroidering at five in the morning and finished at ten or sometimes eleven o'clock at night. Of course, between embroidering, they took care of household and garden chores, vineyard and orchard work, three pigs, many chickens, and one child. Finally, after nine years of what the husband considered "just sit[ting] around," the wife went to work in a village institution as a cook for 2,200 forints per month. In addition to this forty-hour-a-week job she continued to embroider an average of four hours each day, seven days a week. But none of the women from this household were ever allowed to sell or go alone to the marketplace.

While village women emphasized their diligence, thriftiness, and shrewd ability to sell goods on the market, village men extolled their own excellence and good reputation as workers. The maintenance of close-knit social groups during work was equally important to women and men. Since most women worked in the village with covillagers, this was considered a matter of course. Therefore, there tended to be less talk about it among women than among men, although they talked often about how much better they were than any other villager nearby during and after gathering, marketing, and particularly flower vending and embroidering.

Such talk could very likely have been part of women's response to their negative evaluation by the village elite, men, and others. The women maintained a powerful and rather pervasive ideology,[24] which, in effect, underwrote, supported, and justified the reinterpretation of what certainly no longer resembled puritanical, traditional Calvinist values. Acquisition and sacrifice were indeed part of the Protestant ethic Weber (1976) described, but the rampant consumerism I found in Cserépfalu during the late socialist period clearly was not. What opportunities did villagers really have to reinvest their savings in order to expand their own productive enterprises in the Protestant tradition during that particular regime? Thus the new strategy of consumption became a peculiar type of late socialist manifestation of Calvinism, amalgamated to a particular type of socioeconomic idiom[25] that celebrated consumerism. Economic life in the village increasingly centered on obtaining more and more material goods and on the related Calvinist trait— resourcefulness—which these women deemed to be locally specific and central to their ethnic identity. During the late socialist period rural villagers, whether young, old, or middle-aged, appeared to have been "dominated by the making of money, by acquisition as the ultimate purpose of . . . life" (Weber 1976, 53). Thus acquisition appeared as the era's *summum bonum* by which "sacrificing one's life" was explained and justified. The value placed on obtaining, owning, and displaying various goods functioned as—what

Erikson called in a different context—"so many opiates to lull . . . [the vil-
lager] . . . into the new serfdom of hypnotized consumership" (1963, 402).[26]

SUMMARY AND CONCLUSION

Middle-aged women in Cserépfalu during the late period of state socialism
conspicuously demonstrated their capacity to adjust themselves to the system and to ingeniously assert and redefine their identities, taking as much
advantage as possible of the unique opportunities that the peculiar co-
existence of the public and private economic sectors created at that time.
After the New Economic Mechanism was adopted in 1968, these women
revived the tradition of marketing that had been deeply buried or at least
dormant in the early, very difficult periods of state socialism. During the
1980s, marketing began to come back in full force. Discovering the past
led to various traditional and novel extravillage economic ventures by which
cserépi women succeeded in broadening the scope of their economic activity to a transnational scale.

While middle-aged village women were successful in accumulating economic resources in order to increase distributive power and conspicuous
consumption within their households, village men's position within the
household and the village was weakened by their often forced inclusion into
the ranks of socialist urban industry. When most village men began to com-
mute to work, women became the pillars of households and family life.

The long-distance travel and marketing activities women undertook in
the face of economic pressures permitted them to become economically
influential, even as they suffered the criticism of the village men and women
of different age groups. The market women tried to resist and divert these
symbolic and social attacks on them by referring to the much valued, al-
legedly local, and Calvinist trait of resourcefulness.

The often confusing socialist economic system (Berend 1996), which
aimed at fast industrialization and the abolishment of independent private
peasant economic initiatives, shaped the choices of middle-aged women,
who focused on obtaining economic power and control over intrafamily and
intravillage redistribution. Ironically, the intent of ideologues and politicians

was to establish a new kind of socialist society in which individuals would *not* be driven by egotistical and entrepreneurial motives. In this socioeconomic milieu, on the fringes of various sectors of the economy, the women of Cserépfalu forged their niche. At the same time that they represented themselves as resourceful and committed to the family rather than to the satisfaction of individual needs, they succeeded in amassing economic profits. In accord with their intense identification with a Protestant ethic, they turned over the lion's share of the income they accumulated to family members in an act of dutiful generosity that simultaneously enhanced the family's social prestige and moderated the criticism aimed against them. Contrary to the tenets of the Protestant ethos, however, precisely because of the specific nature of the state socialist economy, they were unable to accumulate, save, or reinvest their marketing profits. Instead, these profits were rapidly drained by their children's conspicuous consumption. Paradoxically, the more these village women were embedded in the market, as defined by the socialist economic system, the more their identity rested on Protestant ethics of resourcefulness, diligence, persistence, and sacrifice.

EPILOGUE

Ironically, with the advent of the "real" market economy and the demise of state socialism, the Calvinist women of Cserépfalu have lost their ties to the markets in which they had been so actively involved. Late state socialism, characterized by its multiple economic sectors, has disappeared (Agócs and Agócs 1994). Under these new conditions, marketing women are no longer able to pursue their previous economic strategies. Because of the introduction of the new market economy the state can no longer afford to subsidize mass public transportation. Given the high cost of bus and train fares, women no longer find it profitable to keep "running down to the market with every little root and berry." In addition, Hungary's borders have opened up in all directions. New vendors, attracted by entrepreneurial possibilities, have flooded the country, bringing with them new products. The importance of the embroidery groups has decreased, and embroiderers are sought out to a far lesser extent. With the end of the economic Community of State Socialist Countries (COMECON), transnational commuting and trade have ceased to yield economic profits. Individual socialist entrepreneurs have been replaced by large-scale companies, created and inspired by new capitalist entrepreneurs.

The end of socialist industry has shut down the state-subsidized factories and mines. Workers and miners, forced out of jobs, are unemployed, and many of them have had to return permanently to villages like Cserépfalu. While the economic forces unleashed by the emergence of the real market economy have thus extinguished the types of marketing activities I have discussed in this chapter, they have also encouraged new kinds of marketing undertaken by a different generation of women.

Yet, as I observed during fieldwork in May of 1997 and 1998 in the village, the women of Cserépfalu have responded creatively to many of the formidable challenges that have arisen since 1989. Some of the women who were middle-aged in the 1980s had reached the age of seventy by 1997. Because those over seventy are able to travel free on the buses and trains, it is now the older village women who go to the markets.

The migratory circuits have changed considerably in the years since the demise of communism in the region. As a result of the opening up of borders, a whole array of new vendors—Bosnian, Croatian, Chinese, Russian, Ukrainian, Vietnamese—have flooded the Hungarian markets. Today a different kind of transnational competition for space and customers occurs in the marketplace. The older village women sell flowers and other things side by side with vendors who sell silk and plastic flowers and wreaths. When I visited the village cemeteries, I noticed and commented on the many artificial bouquets and wreaths on the graves. The women of Cserépfalu told me rather sheepishly that they buy these from the competitors because they last longer than fresh flowers do. Besides they, the cserépi women, sell the fresh ones for a good profit anyway.

Bolivian woman selling traditional medicines at the annual Huari fair, Department of Oruro, Bolivia, April 1991. Photo credit: Lynn Sikkink.

CHAPTER EIGHT

Traditional Medicines in the Marketplace: Identity and Ethnicity Among Female Vendors

LYNN SIKKINK

ABSTRACT: *This chapter focuses on the economic practices of women from a rural community on the southern altiplano of Bolivia. It argues that the practices the women use in selling and trading traditional medicines in the marketplace shape their identity and ethnicity. Their marketing practices are defined by their household activities, the products they sell, and by local and national notions of ethnicity and class. Economic and cultural considerations intervene in the construction of market women's identities, based on their entrepreneurial savvy, their membership in rural communities, and their manipulation for business purposes of social perceptions of them as Indians and* cholas *(an "in-between" category).*

On the southern Bolivian altiplano where economic conditions are extremely depressed, some might characterize everyday life and people's beliefs in light of the centuries-old effects of colonialism and exploitation (see, for example, Crandon-Malamud 1991). What is not as obvious is the ability of inhabitants to maneuver within this situation, creating new possibilities and working out a better position—even marginally—for their own family. Although the gains might seem small, the stakes are high for the people involved—perhaps through a mother's efforts her child will get the education necessary for a city job, affecting the future well-being of all the family members. Rural women, as managers of household resources and exchange relations (Sikkink 1994), are particularly attuned to these possibilities. Through careful management of their household's goods, their ability to sell in the marketplace, and the designation of their resources to various ends, they attempt to better their family's situation. Women are the primary vendors in rural, regional, and urban Andean marketplaces. Marketing provides them with economic opportunities at the same time that it may present them with particular societal constraints (Babb 1989; Buechler and Buechler 1971, 1996). What I explore here, drawing from my fieldwork in Bolivia on exchange strategies among rural women from San Pedro de Condo, is how one particular exchange practice of selling (and sometimes bartering) traditional medicines helps to illuminate processes of identity creation and constructions of ethnicity in the Andes, in particular, among women who sell in the market.

THE HOME COMMUNITY OF TRADITIONAL MEDICINE
COLLECTORS AND VENDORS

The village of San Pedro de Condo, Department of Oruro, is situated on the dry and treeless altiplano of southern Bolivia, at 3,800 meters. The colonial village, with its plaza and church, occupies the western edge of its own canton in the Province of Oruro, and its surrounding territory is approximately 65 kilometers across at its widest point. Lake Poopó and its salt-whitened shores are visible from the village and the view of the watery extent on the horizon is a striking contrast to the barren pampas. Rising up on the other side of the village are the hills and high peaks (up to 5,200 meters) where

Condeños live in dispersed herding settlements (*estancias*). Prior to the Inca conquest, Condo was part of the Asanaqi-Killakas federation (Abercrombie 1986; Espinoza Soriano 1981), a history still evident in the social organization of Condo into segments called *ayllus* and in aspects of Aymara ethnicity. Nevertheless, today, fewer and fewer Condeños speak Aymara. Some Condeños say, "We are trilingual!" (in Aymara, Quechua, and Spanish), and it is possible to communicate in Condo by relying on Spanish alone. As a forcibly centralized early colonial resettlement (*reducción*), Condeños have seen hundreds of years of state intervention and involvement with the market economy. The nature of their involvement has certainly changed over time. They have gone from being purveyors of useful goods to mining centers to supplying goods and foodstuffs to other peasants and to urbanites. In Condo, vendors have carved out a unique niche in that they have access to many herbs important to traditional medicine pharmacopoeias. Although residents in other areas have some of these herbs available to them, Condeños have an advantage in that their environment combines a diverse microclimate (from lakeside pampa to the hills and valleys of the Azanaques range), they have marketing know-how (long involvement in markets), and live close to both the Huari and Challapata markets.

In San Pedro de Condo, the women from the community of Kallapa-ayllu are extremely active in selling many goods at the marketplaces in their economic orbit. Known within the region as outwardly oriented merchants (*negociantes*), these women have turned their identities as astute marketers to their advantage. Alongside selling potatoes, freeze-dried potatoes (*chuño*), a native high-altitude grain (*quinoa*), wheat, fava beans, a native Andean tuber (*oca*), and meat in several regional marketplaces, they also collect and sell traditional medicines and household remedies (*medicinas caseras*). Women are the logical purveyors of these goods since they employ medicinal herbs at home to treat their sick family members. The women from Kallapa are ubiquitous at the annual Huari fair, known for its wide array of traditional medicines.

Traditional medicine vending as a specialized market activity is considered unlike any other because of the opportunities it presents. Many scholars have written about markets, marketing, and the activities of marketers (Dilley 1992; C. Geertz 1978; Mintz 1971; Plattner 1989). They have noted that markets are not always characterized by market behavior (Dilley 1992), and that women (Mintz 1971) and nonmonetary exchanges (C. Geertz 1978) are important to marketing transactions in many locales. Traditional medicine vendors, although they all sell similar items, display varying combinations of them in different inventories, procure their inventories in different ways, and have learned to cater to different customers and operate within different vending contexts. Outsiders characterize these women as particularly "traditional" because of the wares they offer. At the same time, the women vendors consider themselves savvy entrepreneurs who help to bring extra income into their households. These two images are at odds with each other and must be negotiated within the setting of the market. Even more important, though, traditional medicine vendors are well aware of how others perceive them and are able to make use of these characterizations in order to further their sales. The same argument might be made about urban purveyors of these medicines, such as the vendors in the "witches' market" (*mercado de brujas*) in La Paz. The latter emphasize their traditional qualities to urbanites and tourists, who are fascinated by the vendors and the mysterious goods they offer. In both of these settings, the vendors' marketing strategies shape characterizations of their own identity and ethnicity as well as others' perceptions of them.

Although female vendors manipulate these perceptions in order to operate successfully in the marketplace, it is not clear to what extent their strategies actually confer power upon them. On the one hand, as Babb points out in the case of the urban Huaraz market women she studied in Peru, there is a "combination of a sense of potential power and a recognition of relative powerlessness" that confronts women vendors even in their roles as permanent marketers (1989, 40). On the other hand, when Condeña women take their marketing to urban centers and identify collectively, as Seligmann has described for Cuzqueña vendors (1989) and Clark for Asante vendors (1994), a potential space opens up for social action and political power. This potential is more limited for Condeña women, mainly because most of them take on marketing as a secondary activity, they continue to reside in Condo, and they tend to restrict their marketing to regional markets, selling only at certain times of the year. Where Condeña vendors are able to exercise greater political power as a result of their marketing activities is primarily at home in their households and home communities, rather than in urban public spaces. By employing their savvy businesswomen roles in their families, they command a stronger voice in decision making and greater authority in general in the home (see also Sikkink 1994).[1]

The economic practices of market women are important to discussions of ethnicity and identity because, even though women are sometimes described as bearers of lore and custom, or as representing in a more "traditional" form their rural / local communities (see, for example, de la Cadena 1991), women are also in situations, particularly in the marketplace, in which they act as mediators (Seligmann 1989) and are involved in crossing and recrossing borders between different contexts of identity and ethnicity (Behar 1993; R. Rosaldo 1993). Harris, citing Seligmann and de la Cadena, argues:

> Increasingly it is women who are the bearers of Indian identity in areas of high migration, and also women—who are the prototypical mestizos. In other words, women's ethnic identity is more clear-cut because of their relatively stable relationships with consumer markets. Peasant men, on the other hand, typically enter and leave markets in a more fluid and mobile way and their ethnic identity is correspondingly less clear-cut. (1995, 372)

Their contradictory possibilities (women as either bearers of Indian identity or as *cholas*[2] who represent prototypical mestizos) means that their identities are more clear-cut while men's identities are less fixed, less anchored to place, and therefore not so concretely categorized. In the case of market women, there is some evidence that they occupy "permanently interstitial" roles (to use Abercrombie's [1991] phrase for a different case), that mark the movement between categorically distinct identities. In these "in-between" roles (Seligmann 1989), these vendors negotiate and shift identities from rural household to marketplace through economic practice. It is inaccurate to see the women involved in these practices or the goods they sell as ultra-traditional, simply because they are women and their wares are those that are commonly used at home in healing. Women, through selling these particular items, are not necessarily resisting change or advocating "alternative" medicine (relative to urban biomedicine). In light of the growing interest in, and demand for, these alternative medicines by the urban sector (and the considerable interest in them that tourists demonstrate), vendors view themselves as entrepreneurs and their marketing practices as aspects of a new or growing business opportunity.

METHODOLOGY

The material for this chapter includes information from interviews with traditional medicine vendors conducted during the period of my initial fieldwork (1990–1992), which centered on women who lived full-time in Condo (see Sikkink 1994, 1995, 1997). I refer to these women as "local vendors" in this chapter. In subsequent fieldwork trips in 1995 and 1996, I interviewed several "urban vendors" who were originally from Condo but lived and worked full-time in Oruro and Cochabamba. I conducted these interviews in the context of participant observation and included only women with whom I had a connection — they were mostly relatives of friends and coparents (*comadres*) in Condo. As such, this work marks the initial phase of my research into these specialized vending practices, which I plan to continue by interviewing both vendors and customers and focusing on the context of healing as well as the business of vending. In characterizing women's identity and ethnicity here, I focus on their comments about themselves as well as the way they dress, their language use, and their ability to operate in various cultural contexts.

MARKET WOMEN AND MULTIPLE IDENTITIES

Questions of Ethnicity

The way in which the identity and ethnicity[3] of a Condeña market woman shifts as she moves back and forth between her home community and the marketplace where she sells her wares is contingent upon her own activities: where and what she sells, how frequently she sells in the market, and the relationship of her marketing to her family and home-community roles. She also confronts and responds to external characterizations that seek to define her variously as campesina, chola, or as *india* (a derogatory characterization). Condeña women themselves tend to identify themselves as "Condeña," rarely self-identifying in terms either of these outside labels or as a larger ethnic category, such as "Aymara" or "indigenous." Drawing on the argument presented in Cook and Joo (1995), rural inhabitants only infrequently identify as an ethnic collectivity (such as Aymara in Bolivia or Peru, or as Zapotec in Mexico), even when there are widespread movements that seek to promote these groups as culturally important to the nation as a whole. Identity among Condeña vendors is context-bound, thus changing and complex. Their ethnicity is not a fixed quality. Therefore, a perspective that views identity and ethnicity as relative and situational is fundamental to the material I present here. As Larson points out, ethnicity is a "social construction that is rooted in concrete historical experiences and struggles at the intersection of material conditions, social practices, and consciousness" (1995, 35). Ethnicity and identity, then, shift through push-and-pull processes in which segments of society and individual actors compete. In the case of Zapotec identity construction, Stephen argues that two dimensions are particularly important: "an ethnic identity for outside consumption," and an "internal version of ethnic identity that allows for contradictions of class differentiation, age, and gender" (1991, 12). I would argue that for Condeña vendors, there is more than one ethnic identity for outside consumption, depending on the degree and kind of vending they undertake, and the extent of their engagement with others who produce and consume their particular ethnic identities.

Although some of these identity-formation processes are confronted by all rural inhabitants, they are especially important in the lives of market women. More than others from their home communities, marketers are actively involved in negotiating their positions relative to various other groups. This puts them in a dynamic position in which they regularly self-identify and are identified by others, often in contradictory ways. Discussing the position of Asante women in the Kumasi Central Market, Ghana, Clark comments that "cross-cutting identities" such as gender, ethnicity, and outside characterizations are important in trading activities and create varying relationships between buyers and their customers (1994, 283). In the Kumasi market, gender is extremely important because not only is the market identified as a site of women traders, but also this identification leads to specific relationships that women have with male customers and officials, in which they are sometimes expected to be "wifely" in market relations with men (Clark 1994, 370).

Work in the Context of the National Economy

Women are in the marketplace not only because they find opportunities there, but also because they are confined to marketing by the national economy and the work options (or lack thereof) that the state provides them. Buying and selling goods in Andean marketplaces has been encouraged by the state and has also provided economic opportunities to Andeans ever since early colonial times. As the contributors to *Ethnicity, Markets, and Migration in the Andes* (Larson, Harris et al. 1995) argue, it is inaccurate to see rural inhabitants' responses to "the" market as either one of accommodation or resistance. Instead, as Platt aptly remarks, participation in the market was an Indian strategy rather than a colonial imposition (1995, 260). One case study of the Tapacarí region indicates that marketing networks have become more regional and horizontal than centralized in recent times. This has not led to an erosion of monetary or monetary exchange transactions, but rather has provided an additional way in which the subsistence economy interacts successfully with market forces (Larson and León 1995, 247).

Rural men and rural women differ in the kinds of restraints they experience in their work lives. A sexual division of labor certainly exists in Condo, marking differences in women's and men's lives. Entering the wage labor sphere, rural men and women experience similar constraints in that they only find certain kinds of jobs available. Occupations open to men tend to be in agriculture, construction, or transport as porters in the marketplace. Even fewer occupational opportunities are open to women, and this is one reason they become vendors—the marketplace is one of the few places where they can earn money and still maintain a rural livelihood and identity.[4] The only other employment opportunity open to women is in domestic labor, mainly in the cities. This pattern has been developing for some time. Gill points out that in 1952 approximately 76 percent of the indigenous female population of workers was concentrated in domestic service and small-scale commerce (1990, 123). In the 1980s and 1990s, the composition of this group changed to one of much younger women who worked temporarily as domestics before marriage and family (1990, 126). The shift in the age of domestics undoubtedly contributed to a heavier reliance on commerce by women workers who sought a cash income. Unlike female domestics, women traders are not constrained by the same expectations on the part of employers of age, status, ethnicity, and childlessness. Gill's study also shows that employers of female domestics actively emphasize their employees' "Indianness" as a way to differentiate themselves from their workers. Because rural vendors are somewhat more autonomous, they are not as compelled to readily accept the ethnic and racial categories of outsiders even though outsiders do not hesitate to attempt to categorize vendors as Indian and rural, whether they are born in the countryside or not. For instance, Sofía Velasquez, whose life history is told by the Buechlers (1996) was an urban market woman, yet treated as rural by officials and customers. While marketing is clearly constrained by national economic opportunities and stereotypes, it may also provide some attractive possibilities to women, not the least of which is a degree of flexibility in terms of work patterns and women's ability to structure their own time and identity around what, when, and where they will sell and to whom.

Time and Space in Identity Formation

Because they are part-time marketers, Condeña women do not share all of the characteristics of urban, chola women in their roles as marketers and traders. Condeña women, rather, are almost always agro-pastoralists first and marketers second. Their work, then, is guided in part by temporal and spatial considerations that do not affect permanent market women. All Condeña vendors sell in accordance with an annual round of subsistence activities (farming and herding) that influences what they sell, how much they can sell (or are forced to sell), and how often they go to the marketplace. For instance, many vendors sell crop products throughout the year which change according to what is available. Since there are no real "cash crops" in Condo, women sell what they have recently harvested or have in storage as dried foods. Traditional medicine vendors also respond to seasonal fluctuations in resource availability, especially during the Huari fair for which they diligently collect large quantities of certain herbs (which are available in flower at this time of year). They are, however, less constrained than crop vendors, because they can collect and dry herbs, trade for other items to augment their wares, and in general, build up a core inventory of goods that can be sold at any time of the year.

Most vendors who sell either at the annual Huari fair (a week-long event) or at the Sunday Challapata fair use a combination of various strategies, from infrequent forays to weekly trips into the marketplace. Vendors may also travel to sell in urban areas such as Cochabamba and Oruro, or to mining centers.[5] Considering these trips alongside their agro-pastoral duties at home points to a larger Andean pattern of trading cycles that correspond to activities and duties in the home community (Collins 1988; Platt 1995), which are important in structuring the overall economic strategies of rural peasants. The temporal and spatial dimensions of rural vendors are thus more widely varying, diverse, and far-flung than those of urban traders.

Condeñas in the Marketplace

Through vending traditional medicines, Condeñas themselves shape their identities and ethnicity. Because vendors are in some sense representatives of their wares, and in turn are considered by others to be represented by their wares, one must consider both processes of self-identification and how their customers and society characterize vendors in general. These processes run up against each other in the marketplace—vendors incorporate some stereotypes of their activities, react against others, and continually negotiate their difference.

One important issue to consider, which illustrates the variation in vendors' self-perceptions and identities, is the extent to which vendors of traditional medicines are also healers. When I asked women this question some women laughed, some pointed to the local diviners/healers (*yatiris*) as the real healers, some indicated that they themselves had a lot of healing knowledge, and some indicated that they indeed were healers (*curanderas*).[6] For instance, one vendor in Cochabamba claimed that she knew many things that doctors did not and was therefore in demand as a healer. In Huari, some vendors assemble a dozen or more ingredients for customers suffering from uterine problems. Condeña women's healing knowledge comes from their roles at home, where, indeed, they are healers for their family. They are not particularly concerned about presenting themselves as traditional curers to their customers, many of whom are women like themselves. Rather, they simply want to successfully sell their home remedies.

Although the vendors of traditional medicines share some obvious similarities and belong to a group that is distinguished by mostly rural women who have chosen this as an activity to accompany their many agro-pastoral tasks at home, there is a basic typology of vendors that varies according to (1) which marketplace(s) they sell in; (2) the frequency of their vending; and (3) their inventories and how they assemble them. Below, I compare and contrast three basic marketing strategies and demonstrate the bearing they have on the formation of traditional medicine vendors' identity and ethnicity. I will discuss the strategies of vendors who sell close to home at the weekly Challapata market; those of vendors who sell at the annual Huari fair (though some vendors do both); and those of vendors who travel to more distant urban marketplaces.

The group of "local vendors" (those that sell in Challapata and/or Huari) is much larger than the group of "urban vendors" (those who sell in Oruro or Cochabamba, or travel to other distant locations). As would be expected, the local vendors maintain closer ties to their home community of Condo, continuing their agro-pastoral livelihoods. Although some Huari vendors sell only at the fair and thus are less closely linked to vending as a permanent identity, some Challapata vendors sell on a weekly basis. Thus Challapata vendors constitute an intermediate category. The majority of Condeña local vendors sell at both the Huari fair and at Challapata and are acknowledged as businesswomen, mostly from the Kallapa ayllu. The range of their inventories varies but most of their wares are locally based, like the women themselves.

The Condeña vendors who sell at the Huari fair have inventories of different sizes. Whereas some of them sell a large array of medicines (sometimes more than eighty different items), others concentrate on only a few varieties (from five to ten). Whatever the size of their inventories, most of the stands at the fair display local specialties, so that women from different locations tend to sell those medicines that come from their territories. Therefore the women from Kallapa sell the herbs *chachacoma*, *lamphaya*, and *pupusa*, along with flamingo feathers, which they get from the shores of Lake Poopó. Intermediaries buy large quantities of these herbs from Kallapa vendors, which has undoubtedly lent to their success.

Although the inventories of these vendors are based around a core of items that they themselves collect from within their ayllus, the vendors also make collecting trips to other areas to obtain distinct medicines. For example, Gabriela, a young vendor from Kallapa, gathers many of her medicines locally. However, she goes outside her ayllu's territory to collect the root called *althiya*, and she mines the yellowish earth called *ajayunki* from a small ranch belonging to a neighboring ayllu. Generally she does not pay for what she collects in these two areas within wider Condo, but instead reciprocates with some coca, perhaps a different medicine, or a gift of a little food. When she travels further afield, for instance to Pampa Aullagas where she mines *jakemasa*, she pays the residents of that area 2 bolivianos per burro-load. From this same place she collects the herb *choquequeña*, paying about 1 boliviano per load for it. Another vendor from Kallapa, Inocencia, puts together a more varied inventory by collecting, buying, bartering, and also by using her relationship to relatives in the Cochabamba area to obtain medicines from that region. She travels to Cochabamba where she stays with relatives and collects and trades for their local medicines, using the medicines she has brought from Condo in exchange.

The vendors who sell at the Huari fair, like Gabriela and Inocencia, also use the fair as an opportunity to broaden their inventories by buying or trading for other medicines there, especially nonlocal varieties. Gabriela is among those vendors whose inventory relies on the plants they collect themselves, and therefore probably seeks little in the way of medicines at Huari. In contrast, Inocencia uses the Huari fair as a place to diversify and amplify her stocks of medicines. In 1991 when I accompanied her at her stand she sold mostly in small quantities to other campesinas. With that money she bought medicines for her inventory—particularly the expensive yellow incense that comes from Peru—so she could sell these items at Challapata and at the mines. Just as Inocencia offers her knowledge to a buyer in dealing with health problems, she also occasionally prepares an offering based on lowland ingredients for a customer who requests it and explains something about the preparation of the offering.

At the Huari fair, the sale of small quantities of certain kinds of local herbs prevails. The typical pattern is for a woman who has collected relatively small amounts of certain herbs to sell or barter them (sometimes for food, sometimes for other herbs) to another woman who is obtaining small quantities for her family's use, or for herself. Hence, the women from Condo who sell at the Huari fair tend to view small-scale vending of traditional medicines in terms of the ongoing maintenance activities of their rural households. That is, they "sell out of necessity"—an infrequent practice that brings in a small amount of cash, which is often quickly converted to household necessities.[7]

In contrast, the second category of vendors, the twenty or so Condeña vendors who sell regularly at Challapata, clearly see what they do in terms of a "business." In describing their business, they emphasize the planning and learning that went into becoming vendors. They organize their stands in such a way as to cater to the varied needs of larger numbers of customers who buy from them. In Challapata, Doña Eustaquia relies on the careful management of her stand to yield a small, regular income. Because she has little land, several children, but no husband, her business is a necessary part of her livelihood. Along with the fifty or more herbs in her inventory she also sells minerals, beans, seeds, and other products that she can knowledgeably combine into particular arrangements for cures. She sells to those with health problems and less frequently assembles offerings customers take home for use in rituals. In this way her knowledge is more clearly for sale along with her products, and her identity is more clearly bound up with her weekly selling in Challapata. In her careful way of dressing and the fastidious arrangement of the items in her inventory, she resembles more the organized and permanent stands of medicine vendors in the cities and their self-conscious identification as vendors who attract customers by filling a specific niche.

There are differences in the self-perceptions of vendors who sell once a year at Huari and those who sell regularly at Challapata. These differences are partly due to the way that their customers perceive them. The occasional Huari vendor extends household practices into the marketplace and has an immediate need for the money she may earn selling there—in this way her identity does not change much and is unlikely to be greatly affected by how outsiders judge her. The vendor in Cochabamba, by contrast, has separated herself from her rural household and must fashion herself first and foremost as a vendor. In these urban marketplaces, women become vendors and cholas at the same time—they reflect this in their more expensive dress, their use of Spanish, and their reliance on monetary transactions (see Seligmann 1989, 1993). These vendors identify with a whole category of chola businesswomen, yet ironically they are differentiated by their wares—they sell "home remedies" considered "traditional" by urban standards, and they hold the promise of healing powers that are exoticized in urban settings.

All of the local vendors differ from the third category of vendors, the urban vendors who have made a more permanent home in the herbal medicine sections of marketplaces in Oruro and Cochabamba. In urban settings, Condeña women have set up more permanent stands in which their much-diversified wares are displayed in bottles and boxes to tempt the buyer, resembling in some ways a pharmacy. Here they sell many of the herbs that come from Condo, but also herbs, incenses, and powders that they have care-fully collected from other places through buying and bartering. Not only do they offer for sale a larger collection of medicines, but also they offer many items beyond the common herbal remedies, including a wide assortment of ingredients for ceremonial ritual offerings called *mesas negras* (black tables). They pride themselves in assembling these ritual offerings properly for customers, and among their wares may be such items as llama and sheep fe-tuses, which constitute parts of more complicated and complete ritual mesas. These vendors, then, offer a wider array of goods than their counterparts in the rural and regional marketplaces.

These women's identities differ from those of their rural sisters—they see themselves clearly as "businesswomen" and emphasize their urban know-how.[8] At their stands in the marketplace they dress in their full skirts (*po-lleras*) and bowler hats. Sometimes, they wear the aprons, jewelry, and shoes that identify them as market women. In Cochabamba, a traditional medi-cine vendor conforms to many of the standards and ideals for urban female vendors and strives to adapt to urban society. However, since she is selling traditional medicines, her customers expect that her identity and knowledge will be rooted in her rural identity. Her authority as a vendor is therefore bound to a contradiction: she must conform to urban ideals by retaining her rural qualities. This is why I argue that urban vendors make more claims for their healing knowledge than do rural women—they must demonstrate the "legitimacy" of their knowledge by harking back to their rural roots.

Whereas some of the vendors in Oruro maintain close ties with their home community of Condo and even continue to farm there, the Condeña vendors in Cochabamba have become full-time residents and vendors in Co-chabamba. Reflecting their more marginalized status within their new envi-ronment, the seven to ten Condeña vendors there sell out on the sidewalk across from the permanent stalls of the central market. Within the walls of the marketplace are traditional medicine stalls similar to those that Con-deñas own in Oruro, but in Cochabamba they are run mainly by urban ven-dors who were raised in Cochabamba. In this marketplace, the Condeña vendors cater to urban customers who are particularly interested in prepar-ing ritual sacrifices, especially at certain times of the year. For them, the ven-dors assemble special ceremonial offerings: mesas negras to cast spells, or to counteract them, and *mesas blancas* [white tables] of various sizes, offerings to be burnt in supplication of good health, luck in business, wealth, or in thanks to Pachamama or the saints). As part of these mesas the vendors use large quantities of *q'uwa*, an aromatic herb from the Chilean border that is sold in the Huari fair but is rarely used in Condo. Acquiring q'uwa therefore becomes important for Cochabamba vendors who may go to Huari solely for this reason. Some claim that customers seek them out because they are Condeñas from the altiplano with superior skills and knowledge. Dressed in their bowler hats and longer polleras, they differentiate themselves from the Cochabamba market women who wear short shiny skirts and straw hats with flowers. The Condeña vendors register their seriousness and lay claim to authority by overtly displaying healing knowledge alongside their wares. One Condeña vendor, Inés, was keenly interested in showing me cures for cancer, diabetes, and prostate problems, ailments that are rarely mentioned by Condeñas living on the altiplano.

Many of the traditional medicine vendors from various marketplaces are linked together through ties of shared work and kinship. For instance, three sisters from one family, all of whom are married and have children, sell traditional medicines in different locations, and name each other as their main source of help in starting out. Margarita lives in Condo year-round and sells every year in Huari and about once a month in Challapata. She occasionally travels to Oruro to sell at her sister Julia's stand. Julia has a permanent stand in Oruro and sells there most days of the year. She and her sister Margarita help each other out by swapping and trading for certain medicines. The third sister, Emiliana, lives full-time in Cochabamba, which is a nine-hour trip from Condo. In Cochabamba, as is true for other vendors, she relies on the selling of mesas and other ritual ingredients like incense that people buy to burn in offerings.

Although not all Condeñas would agree, these three sisters believe that selling in the city is preferable to a rural agro-pastoral livelihood and have adopted some of the characteristics of the other women in the marketplace whom Bolivians characterize as cholas. Emiliana (in Cochabamba) has adopted the dress and look of a chola vendor and has internalized many of the general characterizations of what market women are like, even while she is marginalized from the better locations and higher status of some market women there. From Margarita's rural identity to Julia's and Emiliana's chola-look, they vary because of the depth of their involvement with selling, to whom they sell, and their marketplace locales.

IDENTITY BORDER CROSSINGS

Identity formation and ethnic allegiance is a fluid process that differs from individual to individual and may shift for an individual within her life-time and from activity to activity in a short span of time. Being a market woman is a strong and visible part of a rural woman's identity. I argue that this identity-formation process is for her strongly linked to certain economic practices and the degree to which these practices are either combined with rural livelihood activities or separated from them. Urban vendors of tradi-tional medicines are successful in part because they maintain links to their rural homes and draw on these ties in improving their stands. The women themselves, however, are not the only shapers of identity in these activities. First and foremost they are affected by the expectations their customers have of them—to behave in a certain way, to represent healing traditions linked to the rural areas of Bolivia, and to offer their wares cheaply (which also re-quires skillful management of the economic aspects of these stands). Because of these expectations, women vendors of traditional medicines cannot di-vorce themselves from their rural identities. They offer an ethnicity for con-sumption based on their rural roots. As these vendors control specialized spheres of knowledge linked to indigenous power, the women's rural iden-tities may gain them some measure of power in the eyes of their customers (see Whitten et al. 1997). Yet these women cannot solely play the role of simple rural vendors of traditional medicines who make forays into the city to sell, because they must also meet the expectations of their customers. Their customers demand that they knowledgeably sell certain kinds of wares and that they be capable of interacting with them in conventional ways, such as explaining the proper uses of different herbs and the details of the cures.

Despite the surface similarities of traditional medicine vendors in Huari, Challapata, and Cochabamba, they operate in contexts that require them to behave differently and to assume different identities. Women are not locked into these roles, however, and their identities by the same token are flexible as they move from rural to urban areas. When women "cross borders" from their home villages to rural marketplaces to annual fairs to urban settings, they also cross into new fields of identity formation. A linear scale in which identity and ethnicity correlate with movement from a rural to an urban context does not materialize in the case of market women, precisely because of how market practices operate for these women. Market women are particularly adept at crossing and recrossing borders because, for them, it is not a matter of becoming rural or urban in those respective settings. It is a matter, rather, of mixing their own and other's perceptions of what these identities encompass in order to successfully sell and to make a living in a marginalized world.

PART IV

Research Agendas

Author returned to the marketplace in Huaraz, Peru, in 1997 and found sellers adopting new strategies to increase sales. Sign on cart of oranges reads: "orange juice, vitamin C." Photo credit: Florence E. Babb.

CHAPTER NINE

Market/places as Gendered Spaces:
Market/women's Studies over Two Decades

FLORENCE E. BABB

ABSTRACT: *In this chapter, the author uses her research on Peruvian market women spanning two decades as a backdrop against which to discuss more broadly changing directions in research on market women. She argues that studies are turning from an earlier emphasis on marketers' economic contributions and social position to a more nuanced consideration of their cultural locations and politics. Moreover, she argues, scholars are more attentive to differences of race and ethnicity as well as class among market women and to how these figure in movements for change. Significant negotiations of economic exchange, discourse, and local and national identity are examined in recent work. Finally, she notes that scholars such as those represented in this volume are giving needed attention to social and historical constructions of market women in a number of settings in this period of globalization.*

My research among Peruvian market women began some twenty years ago, and so it may appear a certain conceit to frame this chapter around the last two decades of scholarly work on women marketers. I was hardly the first to research and write on the subject. But when I carried out my doctoral field-work in 1977 there were just a few pioneering studies to guide me (Babb 1981). Ester Boserup's well-known *Woman's Role in Economic Development* had noted that "in no other field do ideas about the proper role of women contrast more vividly than in the case of market trade" (1970, 87). More attention to market women was offered in Judith-Maria Buechler's (1972) dissertation on peasant marketing in Bolivia, Beverly Chiñas's (1973, 1975) books on Mexican women traders, and Niara Sudarkasa's (1973) monograph on Nigerian women marketers. A relatively small number of articles had appeared, including Sidney Mintz's (1971) classic essay on Caribbean women and trade.

The approaches of the 1970s ranged from functionalist to structuralist, but in general they were critical of the historical impact of Western development on women's marketing. Studies of market women in the 1980s and 1990s have built upon the early works, but they have also benefited from the growth of feminist analysis and reflect changing currents in anthropology and related fields. For purposes of discussion, I will consider the emphasis on history and political economy through the eighties and the turn toward cultural analysis in the nineties. I do not wish to suggest any rigid scheme, but rather to trace several currents in recent research. I will conclude by offering some remarks concerning my own changing perspective over twenty years conducting research among market women in the Peruvian Andes.

HISTORY AND POLITICAL ECONOMY

Emerging from earlier critiques of development, a significant body of research has examined market women as economically important yet socially marginalized participants in Third World economies. Some studies have been distinctly historical in orientation, arguing that capitalist development may account for women's involvement but also their exploitation in marketing work. A few authors have emphasized the opportunities afforded women entrepreneurs (Milgram, this volume), but more have identified the inadequate livelihoods and the struggles of market women (Bunster and Chaney 1985; Robertson 1984) and their confrontations with the state (Clark 1988). Several have considered the growth of the urban informal sector and women's trade within it (Hansen 1980; Babb 1985, 1989).

A number of us were drawn to examine women in marketplaces because they were located strategically at the intersection of household work and the wider economy. As feminist analysts of the 1970s and 1980s sought to document the value of housework and the formerly unassessed informal sector, a few of us debated the utility of the Marxist-feminist analysis of production and reproduction to see what it might offer to studies of market women (Babb 1986). Despite the limitations, it enabled us to take into account the full sweep of women's work in and out of the home and to theorize the contribution of women to the national economies of which they formed a part (Babb 1987).

Claire Robertson's (1984) *Sharing the Same Bowl*, a socioeconomic history of women marketers in Ghana, challenged some prevailing models of analysis including modernization theory, "marxist ethnocentrism," and the dualistic usage of formal/informal sectors. Like a number of researchers of the time, she looked to class analysis within a historical framework to account for the changing fortunes of women traders. She united individual life histories with attention to both the local (marriage and family relations) and the national (state-level political economy).

One may see a continuing interest in historical approaches to market women's lives, often with a greater attention to cultural identity, in some recent work. In the anthology *Ethnicity, Markets, and Migration in the Andes*, edited by Brooke Larson and Olivia Harris (1995), historians and anthropologists examine changing relations of Andean peoples to economic exchange from precolonial to twentieth-century times. Critical to their analysis is a challenge to persistent notions of peasant conservatism in the face of growing market exchange, as well as attention to the historical construction of ethnic identities that were often central to the economic and political struggles that were waged. In one essay, Marisol de la Cadena (1995) looks at the recent implications of economic "development" for gender and ethnic identities in one Peruvian community. She argues that women are increasingly perceived and perceive themselves to be "more Indian" than men, since men have greater access to economic opportunities in the wider mestizo society. She acknowledges that women have access to urban culture when they work as marketers or domestic servants, but she judges these to be areas in which women's work is undervalued and hence in which women's indigenous identity goes unchallenged. This view may underestimate women's agency and their success in negotiating identities in both urban and rural marketplaces, although in other respects de la Cadena's analysis has deep resonance for rural Andean women.

In the present volume, Judith Marti draws on historical material from nineteenth-century Mexico as she examines conflicting images and identities of marketers and street vendors. Her work demonstrates that struggles over cultural meanings, social identities, and political spaces for women's marketing are nothing new. Images of market women in newspapers and other popular accounts as well as the legal petitions of vendors themselves, suggest contradictory views of marketers: as respectable businesswomen and as marginal, vulnerable members of society. Marti's reading of the petitions suggests that these women were sometimes clever strategists in their appeals for mercy in avoiding debt payments and other legal problems. She makes rich use of the textual evidence and gives us a look at past negotiations over meanings and identities among market vendors.

CULTURAL IDENTITIES AND CULTURAL POLITICS

Having established the importance of women's market trade and informal commerce in rural and urban areas around the globe, scholars are now turning attention to some other key questions. No doubt influenced by broader currents in anthropological thought, more attention is devoted to less strictly economic and more specifically cultural and political concerns. Just as a growing number of anthropologists are turning from studies of "economic development" to studies of social movements and cultural politics as potential sites of struggle and change, so too this is emerging among those scholars examining market women.

Questions of gender and ethnic identity emerge as central in much of the current research on market women, and the contributors to this volume have been influential in that development. Linda Seligmann's article, "To Be In Between: The Cholas as Market Women," appeared in 1989 in the journal *Comparative Studies in Society and History*. My own book on Peruvian market women, *Between Field and Cooking Pot* (Babb 1989) was published in the same year, and I recall that when I read Seligmann's article I knew she was raising some very important questions that I had barely addressed. In that article, she looks at the way that highland Peruvian marketplaces have been sites of negotiations over Andean and national identity, and the way that chola market women—in transition from Indian or campesino status to mestizo status—claim political power as brokers in the process. A later article (Seligmann 1993) further examines how economic transactions and linguistic exchanges in Peruvian marketplaces bring differences over national identity to the fore.

Ruth Behar's writings based on the life history of a Mexican market woman, Esperanza, have made a valuable contribution to our understanding of the subtle and complex ways in which gender and ethnic identities are framed by one's location in economic and cultural contexts and how these identities and contexts are constantly shifting. Beginning with her 1990 article "Rage and Redemption" in *Feminist Studies* and further developed in her book *Translated Woman* (1993), Esperanza's story is shown to have different meanings when told from Mexico and when read from the United States. In the end, it is less important that the mestiza at the center of this book has traded to gain a living and more important that her life has been made up of a series of experiences, many of them extremely painful, that will be understood in distinct ways on opposite sides of the border.

Another recent work, Deborah Kapchan's (1996) *Gender on the Market*, takes market women as a point of departure for an analysis that is less concerned with economic exchange than with linguistic and cultural exchange. This book offers an ethnographic description of the site of the Moroccan marketplace, principally as a location where women have gained entry in recent years, crossing the divide between private and public spheres. Through their performances of oratory, these women traders have occupied a physical and discursive domain formerly controlled by men. Kapchan presents a rich analysis of the hybrid expressive forms that women bring to the market as they appeal to the public to buy from them. In the present volume, Kapchan's essay reveals that women's verbal artistry in the marketplace has given them increased power, but this may be undermined by urbanization in the modernizing nation. Even so, they have staked out a new social space for women and thereby redefined what is deemed culturally appropriate for women.

Gracia Clark's book, *Onions Are My Husband* (1994), based on a number of years of research in Ghana, devotes more attention to economic aspects of women's marketing, but with an appreciation of cultural questions as well. While there is a detailed account of the economics and politics of women's marketing in Ghana, Clark's book also considers the self-perceptions and multiple identities expressed by women and the way these have been used historically and currently in claims for political space. In Clark's essay in this volume, she shows how traders deploy one of their identities—devoted mothers—to legitimize themselves beyond the market and to protect themselves against the national government, which would hold them responsible for rising inflation.

It is notable that in the work discussed in this section there is a reflexive turn that is enriching the scholarship. Just as researchers are becoming more conscious of the mediating of identities found among market women in the places studied, they are also beginning to recognize and discuss publicly the way that their own insertion in different cultures follows from shifting identities and intellectual preoccupations. This is especially apparent in the writings of Behar and Clark.

Lynn Sikkink's essay in this volume on women vendors of traditional medicines in Bolivia shows that gender and ethnic identity construction is contingent upon a number of factors. She argues that the particular economic practices of vending influence the way that sellers present themselves, whether they emphasize their rural connection to traditional medicine or their urban know-how, and that these self-presentations are played against consumers' expectations. Vendors mediate cultural differences over time, offering their rural ethnic identity for public consumption, to command better sales. This conscious construction of cultural identity to further economic ends has parallels in other areas, for example among handicraft sellers in the Philippines (Milgram, this volume) and among rural Ecuadorian women in the tourist trade (Crain 1996).

The shifting and rather ambiguous identities of market women in the Ecuadorian setting are taken up by Mary Weismantel (1995). In that context, cholas present a cultural mix, or bricolage, of elements, rural and urban, Indian and mestizo, female and male, which, as she says, disrupt regional expectations and nationalist dreams. As other authors have noted, cholas are both raced and gendered, but Weismantel calls attention to the ways that both feminine and masculine elements are often present in the cholas' dress and in their practices. Indeed, she likens them to cross-dressers in other cultural contexts, who may pass for something they are not. As she suggests, there may be some problems in making this comparison, but there is value in drawing gender and sexuality into our analyses of market women.

Perhaps it was the earlier fascination, particularly among some male writers, with the perceived sexuality of West African market traders, or the image of matriarchal Zapotec traders, that made some turn away from examining sexuality in the marketplace. But at this point researchers know more about the force of sexuality in history, culture, and politics. Some contributors to this volume, including Gracia Clark and Johanna Lessinger, have looked at the way that sexuality figures in the work and lives of market women in Africa and South Asia. The sexuality, or perceived sexuality, of Andean market women was described much earlier in the writing of the novelist and ethnologist José María Arguedas, author of *Deep Rivers* (1978), and it is time for us to bring a feminist perspective to this question.

This discussion of the changing approaches to studies of women marketers suggests how wide-ranging the questions are that circulate around market women. This is a point made by Seligmann in her introduction to this volume, and by others (Babb 1989, 43; Kapchan 1996, 17). While the pendulum has recently swung in the direction of cultural analysis, there has been somewhat less attention to the work relations and economic practices of market women, so that one hears less regarding social and economic differentiation among traders. While researchers provide a more complex reading of the ambiguous position of cholas, for example, they may also have an underlying notion that all sellers' identities in a particular marketplace are similarly contingent. However, studies have revealed the heterogeneity of sellers, not only in terms of rural and urban background and ethnic identity, but also in terms of their relative independence or dependence on other economic interests, their participation as wholesalers or retailers, and their domestic responsibilities.

Market women remain one of the major occupational groups in many societies, and their place within wider economies will clearly influence the way they participate in political struggles and social change. In this volume,

Lessinger writes of the impact of global restructuring on market women in India, and Clark considers the effect of structural adjustment on market women in Ghana. Éva Huseby-Darvas addresses the economic importance of marketing for middle-aged village women in late socialist Hungary, and concludes by noting that the new market economy following the collapse of socialism has meant the loss of this employment. That scholars are now taking seriously some neglected cultural aspects of marketers is heartening. That they are drawing together perspectives that are at once culturally, politically, and economically informed as they continue to discuss market women is also encouraging.

ANDEAN MARKET WOMEN TWENTY YEARS LATER

My primary field research on Peruvian market women was in the Andean city of Huaraz in 1977 and was followed by revisits in 1982, 1984, and 1987, a decade that framed my book, which was published two years later. With the prospect of a forthcoming revised edition of my book, I returned to the site of my fieldwork in summer 1997 in order to observe some of the changes of the last decade and to renew relationships begun twenty years before. The trip also gave me the opportunity to return to Peru with a different outlook than before and to raise questions I had not thought of addressing during earlier visits. The world had changed over this period of time and so had Peru; my own interest had shifted from a narrower focus on gender and political economy to include cultural questions as well.

My earlier work had emphasized the work of women as marketers in the production process, arguing that these women contributed to the value of the goods they sold and played a key role in the context of the underdeveloped Peruvian economy. I suggested that the national campaign to scapegoat small-scale marketers for the country's economic problems was unjustified given the hidden work these women performed and their self-employment, which relieved the state of the need to provide for them. I was also interested in the link between women's household work and their marketing, theorizing that both were critical to the society. I remain satisfied by and large with my earlier analysis, but I believe that there are a number of areas that I may have overlooked.

While I was concerned during earlier visits to examine the Huaraz marketers' strategies for claiming space in the streets and marketplaces, I returned to Peru with a greater interest in struggles over urban space. Just after my trip to Peru in 1987, the major city market was torn down and a large number of marketers were sent to sell in the streets, with the vague assurance of a new model market to be constructed. It was not until 1994, however, that the new market opened, and in 1997 I found that only the most economically privileged sellers were able to sell there. Unlike the former market where stalls were rented, the new market stalls had to be purchased and few people could afford that expense. At the same time, city officials were cracking down on street sellers, making the situation most difficult for many marketers. Zones designated for selling were often marginal to the downtown area and many complained that sales were lower than ever.

A growing number of children as well as women had entered marginal areas to sell, some of them wandering the streets to avoid city officials. Interviews revealed how impoverished their conditions were and how they strategized to survive under adverse circumstances. Because the Andean city where I worked was a tourist center, some had fashioned themselves and their trade to appeal to travelers' interests. From innumerable shoeshine boys who capitalized on the dusty shoes of visitors to the area, to small children begging to have their photo taken alongside a baby alpaca for a "tip," to fruit drink vendors with signs proclaiming the value of "vitamin C," many had adapted to a changing cultural climate. My attention was thus drawn to the ways that sellers sought to make themselves more marketable when the economy itself appeared intransigent. As elsewhere in Latin America, Peru in the 1990s was experiencing the harsh effects of neoliberalism, with its structural adjustment measures, privatization, and reduction of social services.

Most marketers feel fairly powerless to improve their own and their families' situation when economic and political conditions conspire against them. When marketplaces, like other institutions, are undergoing privatization, only a minority will benefit from the management's effort to build "community" among them. And when a member of the city council advises that the townspeople suffer from low self-esteem and need to work on "self-identity," many find their situation worsening daily, with little to feel good about. Yet there are still ways that marketers are forging cultural identities rooted in traditions that are resistant to the onslaught of neoliberalism. Not wholly dependent on economic success in the manner of late-twentieth-century capitalism, Andean market women continue to find ways of enduring and also of imagining another future.

My interest in Peruvian women marketers continues to gravitate to the conditions of economic hardship they are experiencing and how they manage to get along under current circumstances. But more than before, I turn my attention to the ways that market women and others come to terms with persistent poverty in the face of an apparently modernizing urban space. Newly paved roads, impressive plazas, thriving tourism, all contribute to the appearance of a town making progress. Yet, how do low-income marketers assess the abundance of high-priced restaurants lining city streets? How do shoeshine boys compare their experiences of low-paid work with the evident leisure time of middle-class school children who share the same space with them in video arcades? How do street vendors and marketers interpret the efforts of city officials to "clean up" the streets and restrict their activity to fairs? What new cultural identities will emerge in these neoliberal times? Will some market women who are carving out a space in the free market economy move beyond individual success and press for systemic change? These are questions that I now ask.

When I showed copies of my book to marketers and their families in Huaraz, I discovered how painfully close they were still to the events of a decade ago. My *comadre* and her daughter, my goddaughter, remembered the tearing down of the old central market as though it were yesterday. When I read aloud from the preface the words of my goddaughter, who had written the details of that time in a letter to me, their eyes welled up with tears. "The market was demolished, as though there had been another earthquake," I read, translating back into Spanish for them. Now, in the revised edition, I provide further details about the new privatized market and how urban commercial space is more tightly controlled in the interest of the local middle class and the tourist industry. I also give more attention to the various discourses of development that are invoked to make authority claims at the local and national levels. Finally, informed by current studies of market women, I consider the ways that Andean sellers are negotiating far more than their economic survival in the marketplace: they are negotiating the terms of their very lives and cultural identities.

The current scholarship on market women, including that of authors in this volume, has taken research and writing in directions I would not have imagined when I began my work in Peru two decades ago. When I returned to my field site recently, I had the advantage of a far broader perspective informed by these authors and others, enabling me to reconsider market women in the context of cultural politics and globalization at century's end. I look forward to seeing what promising new approaches to studies of market women will be taken in the years ahead, building upon and perhaps challenging the impressive scholarship to date.

An informal vendor of condiments along San Pedro Street, Cuzco, Peru, 1998.
Photo credit: Linda J. Seligmann

Conclusion: Future Research Directions

The chapters in this volume lead one to reflect on where anthropological research on market women might go in the next century and how future scenarios might reshape the world of women's work and lives. There are inherent difficulties in generalizing about market women, even within one nation (and still greater difficulties in determining whether market women's experiences are relevant to those of other women). As exchange patterns proliferate transnationally, this becomes an even greater challenge. The chapters in this volume have established that the ways market women are perceived by others and the ways they fashion their own identities become very much a part of their economic practices. Yet the question of market women's identities is complex, precisely because they straddle households and workplaces, rural and urban environments, and ethnic cleavages and operate in spaces where local, national, and global divides exist but are also blurred by the circulation of people and commodities.

Because of the straddling nature of market traders' activities, it is critical that scholars engage in multisited field research. In an essay entitled "Imagining the Whole," George Marcus argues that "the place-focus of the ethnography should be preserved, but the ethnographic text, and the project behind it, has to do more than it has." The market as a subject of anthropological focus requires "studying complexly interconnected local or micro worlds, all at once." Marcus elaborates, "The idea is that any cultural identity or activity is constructed by multiple agents in varying contexts or places, and that ethnography must be strategically conceived to represent this sort of multiplicity, and to specify both intended and unintended consequences in the network of complex connections within a system of places" (Marcus 1998, 51, 52). Akhil Gupta also addresses the question of how to understand identity when it is not fixed. Observing that "processes of migration, displacement, and de-territorialization are increasingly sundering the fixed association between identity, culture and place," he argues that "to understand these phenomena, we need to pay bifocalized attention to two processes . . . structures of feeling that bind space, time, and memory in the production of location [and] those processes that redivide, reterritorialize, and reinscribe space in the global political economy" (1997, 196–97). The contributors to this volume have recognized the methodological usefulness of engaging in multisited fieldwork that requires research, not only in markets but also in households, religious institutions, and a range of political and economic domains, including NGOs and trading blocs and associations, in order to understand women traders' activities and identities.

Judith Marti's chapter suggests one productive avenue for future anthropological research on market traders that has been woefully underutilized, that of ethnohistorical research. While her contribution raises more questions than it answers, it clearly suggests that women traders do not have monolithic identities. The influences on how they present and represent themselves appear in somewhat muffled and nuanced but very important ways in the ethnohistorical record. Not only will historical depth provide a clearer grasp of men's and women's participation in informal marketing; it will also give us a sense of changing perceptions of their participation and of how marketing itself has undergone transformations over time. Finally, ethnohistorical research is one of the most useful means available to create a picture of the many institutions and agents which, in one way or another, have been involved in structuring and manipulating marketing activities.

The comparative framework of this volume has allowed the contributors to address seriously the general proposition that cultural practices and values shape women's economic participation in the marketplace. Authors have also specified the kinds of economic forces and institutional conditions that lead to particular employment trajectories and, in a dialectical fashion, they trace the cultural considerations that undergird and shape the economies in which market women participate. The chapters have examined the ways that household dynamics, gender ideologies (operating within the family as well as within nations and development agencies), interethnic relations, generational differences, the sexual division of labor, genres of discourse, and religious beliefs encourage or discourage women's marketing operations and shape the manner in which they conduct their marketing.

The authors also discuss the nature of market women's political lives, the issues they face, their capacity for resistance and mobilization, and the manner in which distinct classes, policymakers, governments, and international organizations view the activities of market women. All of these themes can be usefully pursued by scholars examining markets in other societies. Political mobilization, in particular, is an ever-evolving topic as traditional markets come under pressure from modernizing capitalism as well as late capitalism, and gender itself becomes a battleground between modernizers and traditionalists.

This kind of comparative framework illuminates that macroeconomic and political forces and ideologies create particular conditions that set the stage for the participation of men and women in informal sector employment and may cause, in a general fashion, adjustments to their behavior. However, it is impossible to ignore how existing local cultural ideas, morals, ideologies, and religious faith channel these general forces, often in unexpected directions. Ideologies that work against empowering women traders, economically and politically, prevail across many societies. Yet it would be naive to think that women and men do not manipulate these ideologies instrumentally to their advantage for purposes of encouraging consumption, as Sikkink, Lessinger, and Kapchan have demonstrated, and for ensuring their own welfare, as Babb, Clark, and Milgram find. Furthermore, the ways that they manipulate these ideologies in order to make a living—for example, by selecting particular kinds of commodities to sell, by using discourse that refers to a magical and traditionalist world, or by presenting themselves as helpless—reveals their willingness to seize onto images, ideals, and desires that are conveyed by various kinds of media images, tourists who visit from afar, or by very local notions of appropriate behavior. Andrew Sayer describes the relationship between economy and culture most aptly in a thoughtful article, "The Dialectic of Culture and Economy," arguing:

> Economy and culture do not impose upon each other as wholly external forces but are always intimately associated. Nevertheless, they have different logics, the one dialogical and including certain intrinsic or non-instrumen-

tal values, the other having instrumental values related to external goals of reproduction. Their interactions are complex. . . . Culture can be instrumentalized to serve economic ends, but this can be accepted precisely because of the value of those cultural elements. Commodification can degrade cultural values, by subjecting them to an economic calculus, but it can also enrich cultures. (1997, 25)

Multisited ethnography ruptures the artificial and dualistic divide between political economy and cultural strategies and is wonderfully rich in its potential; it is also more confused. In work to come, one would hope that systematic research of this kind will allow scholars to follow the dizzying and complex paths that underlie the production, distribution, and consumption of commodities, knowledge, and ideologies so that they can better comprehend how they interact and become integrated, even in a contradictory fashion.

Scholars who take account of both political economy and cultural analysis in studying women traders find it useful to discern cultural and social practices at work as they are embedded and informed by more generalizable market forces. Yet, even in this latter instance, particular ideas and ideological assumptions underlie the design of market forces. The notion that informal sector workers constitute a nascent, extremely entrepreneurial, middle class leads many NGOs and government aid projects to believe that if the proper conditions can be established by their organizations and through their policies, informal sector workers will help themselves and solve some of the country's economic problems. They ignore critical linkages between economic work, on the one hand, and the daily relentless cultural work of religiosity, gender ideologies, household dynamics, or of scheduling complex and diversified agricultural and nonagricultural regimes, on the other hand, as the articles by Clark, Lessinger, and Sikkink so clearly show. Perhaps because they are perceived as more malleable and in more need, women traders are often the target of such policies. In a very different case, the Alexanders have carefully traced how colonial gender ideologies, in part, led to far greater attention being paid to men's, rather than women's, presence in Indonesia's markets at the same time that local gender ideologies hardly considered it exceptional that women asserted themselves in the marketplace. The Alexanders also have found, however, that women are not granted political or social standing equivalent to that of men and that as shops and modern department stores proliferate, women's economic power is diminishing in the informal pasars of Indonesia.

A rich area for future research is the way reciprocity and social networks shape market women's exchange practices, their use of space, their identities and politics. Exactly what kinds of values and meanings are carried and conveyed by the exchange of goods in the marketplace?[1] How do exchanges outside the marketplace impinge on market transactions? How are market women's networks and the knowledge that constitutes them transmitted from one generation to the next? Does female networking permit market women to organize politically within repressive regimes because it is less visible and more flexible? How do men's and women's social networks differ and in what ways are they deployed for economic and political purposes? This volume has overwhelmingly addressed these questions in the light of women traders' identities and activities. Important research remains to be done that takes into account the ideologies and cultural values surrounding men's employment trajectories.

The anthropological lens has shifted, allowing researchers to recognize more readily the permeability of constructed boundaries. This moving back and forth across borders also requires that one not simply accept the definitive existence of these spaces and their borders but rather that one uncover how the borders themselves arise, the models and maps upon which they may be based, and what causes them to shift. In order to move in that direction, I would propose that three metaphorical concepts guide research: bridges/mediation, contradictions, and blockades. These concepts have served as a scaffolding for the chapters in this volume. By concentrating on these dimensions of social life, scholars will better be able to move out of spaces, categories, and assumptions that have sometimes distorted and often limited their understanding of sexuality, gender relations, and economic and political dynamics.

For example, marketplaces and the women and men who work in them may act as bridges that mediate value from one domain or institution into another, transforming use value into commodities and providing services and products that people need but cannot obtain easily. This is particularly salient in regions where physical space matters, rural and urban spheres are not readily accessible to all inhabitants, and racial ideologies may predominate. Many women, as traders, link these spheres and facilitate flows that, in turn, appear to hold the nation together.

These same women may nevertheless experience enormous contradictions within their households where at one and the same time they are responsible for subsidizing the economic reproduction of the household through their marketing activities and are roundly criticized for rupturing ideal notions of how women and men should behave. Men confront these contradictions as well, particularly when they are unable to support the household and find their pride at stake and their frustration high. Hence, both men and women may experience heightened tensions that are eventually felt socially, particularly when they become widespread in the context of gender ideologies and generational norms that are challenged by neoliberal measures, economic restructuring, or postsocialist regimes. How these contradictions are dealt with is an open question as the Alexanders, Babb, Clark, Huseby-Darvas, and Lessinger demonstrate in this volume.

It is not enough to describe these domains and their dialectical interactions. Scholars must not be blindsided by placing too much emphasis on women alone as mediators of contradictions; they must systematically document how men's and children's lives and work intersect and interact with those of women in the marketplace. The marketplace itself, as so many of the volume's authors have noted, is a place where the IMF of global economic policies and the "nursing mother" of the household meet each other.

It seems to make less sense to conceptualize private and public spheres as separate domains which interact or influence each other than to regard these spheres as complex interpenetrations of ideologies and practices, some of which may originate in the household but be extended into other domains and vice versa. A good example of this is Clark's discussion of social acceptance on the part of Akan men and women of the dribble of income on the part of Kumasi women traders yet rejection of women's capital accumulation, at the same time that women are expected to uncomplainingly service their husbands who can no longer provide them with appropriate allowances because of increasing male employment. Or, to take another instance of how the interpenetration of what is considered private and public entails contradictions, Clark contrasts women traders' tolerance of new traders entering the ranks to provide for their children with the government's refusal to respond to women's demands, for exactly the same reasons, for additional child care or school support services.

As Gupta and Ferguson (1997) observe in their edited volume, precisely because policies of an economic and political nature have become global in impact, institutions, such as households, families, age grades, or other kin structures, cultural practices, and the knowledge of specific geographical loci become increasingly important to the innovative ways that people apprehend change and the tactics they fashion to deal with unpredictable consequences. In the course of confronting these changes, the institutions, practices, and familiar spatial relations upon which people rely also become transformed. Tracing these dynamics, as they unfold in the lives of market women, provides us with an interesting window onto the ways that market women and their families construct their identities, whether their efforts succeed in being legitimated and by whom, and if and why they change over time.

It is easier to discern bridges/mediation and contradictions, to trace their workings in different settings, and to meditate on their consequences than it is to identify barricades. Barricades tend to appear as consequences or as naturalized bounded entities and obstacles without history when, in reality, they are processes or ideologies rather than structures. For example, household structure might constitute a barricade separating women as well as men from particular kinds of work or channeling them into certain kinds of economic activities rather than others. Yet the structure of the household is itself the consequence of kinship and inheritance patterns, generational dynamics, the imposition of colonial regulations, state policies, and the nature of nationalism. Gupta, in a discussion of nationalism, notes:

> The recognition that different ethnic groups, different locales, and different communities and religions have each their own role to play in the national project underlines their difference at the same time that it homogenizes and incorporates them. . . . Women are generally recognized only in their role as the producer of citizens and are thus precariously positioned as subjects of the nation. (1997, 191–92)

Even more dramatically, one can see in the late twentieth century how transnational cultural flows, while they mask growing economic inequalities that create barricades to the equitable distribution of wealth and encourage

the concentration of a small but powerful elite both nationally and transnationally, may simultaneously and unexpectedly encourage new kinds of
consumption patterns, such as the desire for exotic medicinal herbs sold by
"Indian" women. They may also give the impression, through media images
and narratives, that globalization is a positive, unifying process, available and
accessible to all. John Durham Peters, in an eloquent critique of the tendency to romanticize the fluidity of identities, cautions anthropologists to
recognize that

> the world beyond the local exists as a visible totality only in discourse and
> images, though its fragmentary and scattered effects are all too evident in
> the lives of flesh-and-blood people. Ethnography . . . may seem old-fash-
> ioned in a time when locality no longer guarantees the link between sym-
> bol and soul as it once seemed to. But there is the danger of . . . over-
> celebrat(ing) the contingent bricolage of cultural and personal identity
> in a delirious dance with "Mr. In-Between." . . . The improvisation of iden-
> tity is wonderful if you have the cultural and finance capital to cushion
> you against the traumas of postmodernity, but most of the human species
> still lives out its days in localized spaces, dependent in various ways on
> people they have known for years. The means for making one's identity a
> poetic work are inequitably distributed. Distance from the local is often
> a luxury . . . and in-betweenness can be a profoundly painful—not just
> playful—condition. (1997, 91)

As many of the contributors to this volume have pointed out, despite some
exceptions, the consequences of globalization for women traders' identities,
political power, and economic clout are far less likely to be positive than ambiguous and are often destructive. Florence Babb (this volume) argues that
future researchers must keep their eye on how the people they work with
perceive and respond to contrasts—between urban planners' designs of urban space and how urban space is actually used and contested, in the juxta-
position of radically different consumption patterns and styles, between the
towering concrete edifices that dwarf the ever-diminishing sites of imper-
manent open-air markets, and between the remarkable economic flexibility
of ever-increasing numbers and generations of traders and service providers
and the "intransigence" of state policies and economic forces at work.

A qualitatively different kind of barricade to these flows is apparent as well that takes the form of political mobilization or, more moderately, opposition in the form of manipulation, strategic representation, and subtle reluctance among women traders. Not infrequently, even as they grease the wheels of the economy as bridges or mediators, these women come to constitute a threat to a national sense of identity because they reveal economic fissures and insecurities and, in their own place and behavior, question widely accepted social and cultural etiquette, points that Huseby-Darvas and Kapchan make. Because of the subdued nature and near invisibility of some of these behaviors and practices, scholars tend not to give them much attention. Yet they may be of great significance in understanding moments of social uprising, explicit rejection of the status quo, or eventual transformations in economic practices and cultural values. Because of the particular sites that women traders occupy, they are at once more vulnerable to negative social sanctions, more sensitive to changing market forces, and more able to catalyze opposition to existing political and economic policies, interrupting flows of commodities and people, and challenging social mores. And, as Marcus points out astutely, the locus of such opposition, in the case of women traders, for example, may not be in the market, but rather in neighborhoods, schools, churches or mosques, or movie theaters.

Finally, scholars must move toward asking some hard questions, questions that Babb raises in her chapter: Do some of these relationships and processes carry more weight than others and, if so, why? In what ways does scale matter? What kinds of changes might give women greater control over their own lives and work and can activist scholars contribute to facilitating any of those changes? Certainly the research findings of the contributors to this volume could be of potential benefit to many nongovernmental organizations, microcredit lending facilities, banks, and development planners. In reconsidering their assumptions about women's options and constraints as traders and, in general, as entrepreneurs engaged in casual labor, such institutional personnel may have to devise more complex models and courses of implementation that take account of both economic conditions and cultural values. They may have to reconsider why they are so intent on facilitating particular kinds of development; and their reassessment may lead them to abandon entirely wrongheaded projects until they learn to read the complex maps that constitute the logic of women's lives as traders in informal markets.

The explosion of wildly different kinds of commodities for sale in the informal marketplace is an indicator of the current state of globalization, but bazaars have always been carnivalesque, creating the context for the appearance of the familiar yet unexpected. The authors in this volume bring us closer to understanding the experiential worlds of women who work in markets, the conditions they encounter in their daily lives, and the patterns that emerge from their activities as gateways, mediators, and, occasionally, stalwart blockades, among a multitude of diverse exchanges and identities.

Reference Matter

Notes

Introduction

1. Behar 1990; Buechler and Buechler 1996; Buechler 1997; Seligmann forth-coming; and Valderrama et al. 1996 have collaborated on translating market wom-en's life histories. Babb 1989 and Buechler and Buechler 1992 have written pioneer-ing studies of market women's economic and political lives in Peru and Bolivia, respectively. Seligmann 1989 and Tinker 1987 offer useful overviews of diverse re-search on market women. Gill 1994; Kapchan 1996; Seligmann 1989, 1993; Tice 1995; Weismantel 1995; and E. F. White 1987 explore the ways in which the dy-namics of sartorial display, language exchanges, and interethnic relations contrib-ute to the construction of market women's identities. Larson and Harris's 1995 edited volume, while it does not focus specifically on market women, offers a much-needed history of the interaction between ethnicity, markets, and migration in the Andes.

2. Alexander 1992; Babb 1989; Clark 1994; Mintz 1964, 1971; and Einhorn and Yeo's 1995 edited volume pay close attention to market women's economic prac-tices and class relations. Miles and Buechler's (1997) edited volume includes sev-eral examples of market women's experiences of economic exchange in the Andes. Sheldon's 1996 edited volume on urban women in Africa includes a section on women in markets. Among the many scholars who have discussed market women's participation in informal economies and the changes wrought by neoliberal eco-nomic policies are Babb 1998, 1985; Breman's 1996 edited volume on India's infor-mal economy workforce; Bromley and Gerry's 1979 edited volume; Bunster and Chaney 1989; Clark 1988; de Oliveira and Roberts 1994; House-Midamba 1995; Hoyman 1987; Ingram 1991; Kalpagam 1994; Moser 1994; Murray 1991; Robert-son 1993; Seligmann 1998; Shaw 1995; Portes 1981, 1983, 1989, 1994; Stephen 1996; Tinker 1987; Tripp 1989; Uzzell 1994; and Wilson and Marti forthcoming.

3. Dilley's 1992 edited volume, *Contesting Markets: Analyses of Ideology, Discourse and Practice*, is the best work to date on how culture shapes economic model making and theory building as well as economic practices themselves. Of particular interest is Gudeman's 1992 discussion of "local" and "universal" models of knowledge in that volume.

4. Babb 1996; Benería 1992; Clark 1994; Gill 1994; Horn 1994; House-Midamba 1995; Lessinger 1986; Osirim 1995; Rowbotham 1995; Tripp 1989; Ver-Eecke 1995; Seligmann 1989; and Wilson 1993 discuss the relationships between household and market activities for women.

5. E. F. White (1987, 19), citing Sidney Mintz and Richard Price, argues that at least in West Africa, women's activities as traders stemmed directly from a cultural "habitus" in which women's position in households was "naturally" considered to be an economically autonomous one. It was not so much that a woman had female ancestors who had traded in Africa, but rather that in the postslavery era, Afro-Jamaican women in Sierra Leone took up trading because of the "cultural predilection of West African women to be economically autonomous from men. . . . They had maintained a culturally based notion of how women should behave economically within the family."

6. In reviewing the literature on markets, a pattern emerges whereby if women and men both engage in farming, crops tend to be divided between "male" and "female" crops. Women may help with the actual agricultural labor required for the cultivation of "male" crops, but they have total control over what they do with their designated crops, including trading or selling them. When changes in economic and political systems take place, generated, for example, by colonial efforts to seize native agricultural lands, or by global economic cycles that favor particular export crops rather than others, they have repercussions for the agricultural division of labor, the gender relations between men and women, their respective economic activities, and their ability to make a livelihood. In some instances, women are able to enter into income-generating activities that previously they were proscribed from pursuing.

7. For a discussion of how the social construction of "private" and "public" spheres of activity correlate with unequal gender relations and for debate about the validity of this argument, see Rosaldo 1974, 1980; Reiter 1975; Collier and Yanagisako 1987; MacCormack and Strathern 1980; Molyneux 1985; Stephen 1997; and Westwood and Radcliffe 1993.

8. See also Milgram, this volume, on female traders of tourist handicrafts and wood carvings in the upland Philippines; Stephen 1991; Tice 1995.

9. See Falola 1995, 32.

10. Weismantel (1997) offers a telling example of how daily and seasonal temporal rhythms are bound up with the appropriate cultural etiquette of when, where, and what to eat in a Quichua highland village of Ecuador, Zumbagua. These rhythms are disrupted by the introduction of formal schooling, wage labor, and new kinds of food, all of which impose a different "economy of time." Residents, in turn, consider affirmations of their "cultural identity (as well as expressions of an intention to renounce specific aspects of it)" to be "articulated through the language of material life" and some of them make concerted efforts to reassert their control over the structuring of time and its pace (33).

11. Buechler and Buechler (1977, personal communication, 1996) have observed that male leadership is primarily concentrated at the national level in Bolivia and that at the local level, more women occupy high-ranking positions. In Peru, this did not appear to be the case, although it does appear to be changing. Generally, women held leadership positions for offices concerned with secretarial skills or social welfare. Recently, I encountered a woman who was the secretary general of the Central Market Union in Cuzco, so it may be that more openings now exist for women to attain high leadership positions. If women are able to make their needs and voices heard within unions, then this can serve as a powerful tool of organizing.

12. See also Horn 1994, 51.

13. Smith offers an excellent discussion of the history of construction of race/class/gender ideologies, particularly as Western colonial powers asserted themselves and "created the political and cultural conditions by which new nations would interpret race, class, and gender in distinctive ways" (1996, 56). She discusses at length Stolcke's (1981) contributions to understanding how Spanish notions of kinship and marriage influenced those of indigenous societies in Latin America. See also Stoler (1995) for a similar discussion.

14. Stephen (1997, 9) offers a useful summary of the problems with the formal/informal divide, given the complexity of the way people work in reality. For discussion of the concept of formal/informal economies, see ILO 1972; Moser 1994; Rakowski 1994; Portes 1981, 1983.

15. See Stephen 1997.

Chapter 1

1. Archival research for this chapter was conducted in 1992 under a California State University, Northridge Research Competition for New Faculty grant. I want to thank Linda J. Seligmann and John Clendenning for their excellent sug-

gestions; Florence Babb, Theodore Bestor, and the anonymous readers for their valuable comments; my research assistants Celina G. Bacerra, Alejandro Solis, Marcy Adamik, Clementine Reyes, Ana Elena Magis, and Alethea Marti for their immeasurable help; and Mr. Adam Jenkins for informing me that the Spanish *cilindro harmónico* is the pipe organ. As always, I am grateful to Eric van Young for introducing me to Mexican archives. Any errors are, of course, entirely my own.

Chapter 2

1. Acknowledgments: Fieldwork was supported by a grant from the Australian Research Council. Most of the chapter was written in 1995–1996 when the authors were enjoying the hospitality of the Program in Agrarian Studies, Yale University.

Chapter 3

1. Research for this paper was carried out originally in 1971–1972, and updated in 1986. The earliest fieldwork was done under an NSF predoctoral fellowship. Interviewing and observation were carried out in eleven retail marketplaces in Madras (now Chennai), containing a total of 955 vendors, and in the central wholesale market, then located in Kottuwal Chavadi in the old city center, which had 380 male commission agent/wholesale merchants. During a period of eighteen months, interviews were conducted with 249 male and female retail traders and 85 wholesalers (Lessinger 1976).

2. *Purdah* is a North Indian term for a complex of behaviors that exist in that part of India involving the strict seclusion of women within the household or immediate neighborhood and some form of veiling in public spaces and even in the household before some categories of male relatives. The result is to curtail much male/female interaction. In Tamilnadu, by contrast, gender segregation is both more subtle and more flexible, although it still exists. The presence of unveiled women in public places, so startling to the North Indian eye, masks the slight physical separation of the genders in both household and public space, the averted gaze, the silences and absences of interaction.

3. The emphasis in this chapter is on the parameters of gender segmentation in one portion of the informal sector labor market—petty trading.

4. I would argue that to many Tamils, the fact that a household is very poor lessens the family's innate honor in the eyes of others. Since such families have less honor to lose by sending women out to work, it is pointless to criticize them. By

contrast, even within poor families suspicions about female chastity, fueled by neighborhood gossip, remain and are a frequent source of conflict between husbands and wives, or even between parents and children, with fathers beating wives and daughters or adult sons threatening to abandon their working mothers.

5. The increase in family standing brought to the middle and upper classes by female employment takes several forms: prestige if the job itself is a high-status one, increased access to consumption items if the job is well-paid, or, most often, wider choices in the marriage market. Increasingly, middle-class families want to marry their sons to employed brides for purely economic reasons. Many middle- and lower-middle-class girls work in order to accumulate a dowry, which they hope will give them a wider choice of grooms, even though the cultural ideal insists a girl should leave the social and financial issues of marriage entirely to her elders. Yet most girls know that all over urban India, dowry levels are increasing astronomically, with employed men able to command enormous sums from anxious parents of young women. By the 1990s, the spread of garment factory work meant that some girls began to see that their earning power gave them leverage in marriage negotiations.

6. In contrast to the general trend, a few occupations in Madras do remain defined by caste membership, largely because they deal with the sacred or the polluted, at the two ends of the caste spectrum. Priests who serve households or large traditional temples are Brahmins (although priests in smaller, non-Sanskritic shrines are often not). Nevertheless most Madras Brahmins have today abandoned priestly occupations for the professions or business. Some of the city's oldest temples are still surrounded by Brahmin residential enclaves, historical relics of a period when a house in the Brahmin street near the temple was a priestly perquisite (see Mines 1994). At the other end of the social scale, latrine cleaning, sewer cleaning, municipal garbage removal, and jobs such as hospital orderly remain largely in the hands of former Untouchables. Some of the scavenging specialties are dying out and large numbers of former Untouchables have today found other, less degrading and caste-bound work. Single-caste Untouchable residential areas are also rarer than they once were.

7. Since the mid-1980s, India has been in the process of an economic "liberalization" designed to make it more competitive within the global economy. The country has been opened to foreign investment; state industries are in the process of privatization; and government controls on industry, trade, imports, banking, and currency have been loosened. This abandonment of India's historic stance of nonalignment and anticolonialism has had the effect of fueling inflation, so that the cost of basic commodities has risen steeply. At the same time, this policy has not provided new sources of employment for the poor, whether urban or rural.

"Structural adjustment" refers to the economic changes imposed by international lending agencies as India seeks to repay the foreign debt that it has, for the first time, incurred on a large scale. India has cut back sharply on the level of state funding for public services and public employment.

8. Working-class women assert that prolonged joblessness or low-wage employment encourages heavy male drinking. Drinking in turn leads to fights and wife beating as women demand a share of male wages for food and men assert their right to keep their earnings for drink. Women become verbally abusive, withhold sex, or refuse to cook; men retaliate by thrashing the women. Women who begin to earn money because they can get none from their husbands may still find an alcoholic taking the money away from them by force. A man's frequent accusation during domestic fights is that a working woman has become "arrogant," or that she has been unfaithful, and so on.

9. Both these innovations were justified on the grounds of gender separation. Female police constables would preserve the modesty of female complainants and detainees (and reduce the number of rape charges leveled against the police). Female passengers, it was argued, would feel more comfortable traveling with female rickshaw drivers. In nineteenth-century India, the same kinds of arguments were used to promote the training and employment of female doctors and teachers.

10. Such besieged illegal markets may remain the sites of ongoing police-vendor conflict, or they may eventually legitimate their status through political connections and gradually become official city markets. In the 1980s and 1990s these settlements had become more frequent in Madras, and the level of police harassment had decreased as both the city administration and the police force itself became more professionalized. When this study was first done in the 1970s, however, conflicts with the police were a major problem for virtually all retail markets in the city.

11. In the 1980s Madras City authorities, overwhelmed by the sanitation, traffic, and public order challenges of the Kottuwal Chavadi area, began efforts to relocate the wholesale market to a newly constructed area at the outskirts of the city. By the mid-1990s this relocation, bitterly resisted by wholesale merchants, was finally complete. Whether women retailers' access to wholesale merchants will be eased by the new setting is presently unclear. The new location is in the tidy new middle-class suburb of Anna Nagar, not in a red-light district dotted with cheap hotels. Of course, there is always the possibility that prostitution may eventually relocate too.

12. In certain cases, of course, male and female vendors may actually be related to each other. The privilege of introducing relatives into a marketplace is one of the benefits of stall "ownership" that marketers assert for themselves. In many in-

stances, however, the use of kinship terminology is a familiar Tamil mechanism for bridging social distance between the sexes in a manner that maintains propriety. Male and female neighbors and family friends use the same technique.

13. Unlike parts of North India, where women are often wholly absent from streets or shops, Tamil women can traverse streets, squares, and temple grounds or enter shops during daylight hours (and after dark when accompanied). However, women should move briskly and purposefully, not linger. A woman who is seen stopping to window shop or to idle in a coffee shop is probably not respectable. In other words, Tamil women can use public space, but they cannot inhabit it as fully or in as leisurely a manner as men.

Some public space in Chennai is demarcated by gender. City buses, for instance, have "ladies' seats" and the percentage of bus seats given over to women had increased since the 1970s, reflecting the growing numbers of female passengers. Train ticket offices, ration shops, and polling stations have "ladies' queues." Many suburban and long-distance trains have ladies' compartments. Traditional religious events, such as prayer meetings, classical music concerts, or weddings once offered separate male and female seating areas, which is now increasingly rare. Middle-class people prefer seating that allows mixed-sex family groups to sit together. Nevertheless, at such events unrelated men and women will not sit next to each other, instead leaving an empty seat between.

14. Crucial to this strategy is a traditional cultural attitude, still strong in Tamilnadu and Kerala, of courtesy and protectiveness toward women. Thus a man who touches or makes obscene remarks to a woman in a public place may find himself the subject of a shaming public tongue-lashing and general disapproval from the crowd. Older women frequently instigate such tirades, acting as the voice of the moral community. Nevertheless, poor women such as market vendors are likely to be treated less respectfully than middle-class women and to be harassed by higher status men who think they are unobserved. Such behavior is seen as part of class privilege. As working-class women grow older, most develop the ability to defend themselves verbally, but they are inhibited when the man is in a position of power over them, as wholesale traders are in relation to female retailers.

15. Household managers by tradition, women are no strangers to arithmetic, weights and measures, and money management. The purely financial aspect of retailing holds no terrors for most of them. A few elderly men and women traders seemed unable or unwilling to use a scale, perhaps because their mental powers had waned along with their physical strength. Some suggested they were still entangled in the nondecimal coinage and the highly localized, nondecimal systems of weight and volume measures that were current in their youth.

16. Wholesalers' appraisal of women traders as poor credit risks is realistic. In addition to the barriers to large earnings discussed in this chapter, Noponen (1991) suggests that women traders are more likely than men to allow their daily earnings to be engulfed by domestic crises because of their sense of maternal and familial responsibility. Amid the pressure to buy food, repay family loans, and keep a husband supplied with snacks, cigarettes, or alcohol, women are indeed unlikely to repay their wholesalers promptly.

17. These kinds of difficulties in traveling and entering into commercial negotiations with strange men also serve to keep women from becoming institutional suppliers—a form of business expansion some male retailers adopt. As one woman said, to supply vegetables in quantity to small restaurants, school kitchens, or workplace canteens, she would have to "wander here and there all over the city" to visit customers and enforce contracts. It is a set of delocalized commercial relationships in which public chaperonage would be useless.

Likewise women cannot undertake the kinds of visiting, chatting, and ingratiating of oneself that allow a man to move from a declining market to establish a foothold in a better, busier one. Unless women have prior kinship ties, they cannot relocate since their inability to travel or to initiate autonomous social interaction prevents them from creating new social ties on an individual basis.

Chapter 4

1. The life history materials cited in this chapter were recorded in Kumasi, Ghana, from August 1994 to July 1995. Funding for this research from a Fulbright Senior Fellowship for Regional Research and a Social Science Research Council Advanced Area Studies grant is gratefully acknowledged. I have been working with some of these traders in Kumasi Central Market since 1978, so some of their statements date from earlier research visits. Quotations are dated here when this seems relevant, but personal context is minimized to allow identities to remain confidential. See Clark 1994, for a fuller account of research methodology.

2. Quotations from individual life histories are not attributed here by name, so that when the complete edited narratives are eventually published the narrators' identities can remain confidential at their option.

3. Hill (1963) details these use claims and inheritance patterns for cocoa land in the 1920s and 1930s, confirmed more recently by Okali (1983). For more examples of gender discrimination in inheritance of rural cocoa farms, an important form of Asante lineage wealth, see Mikell 1989. The traders interviewed in Kumasi more often contested urban assets, mainly housing, market stalls, and trading capital.

4. A substantial proportion of stalls in Kumasi Central Market was held by Yoruba women, according to a study by Sudarkasa in the 1960s (Sudarkasa 1973). Yoruba women also traded in many, if not most, smaller markets throughout the region. Yoruba men were also very active in commerce throughout Ghana, though more often as hawkers or store owners (Eades 1979). Foreign nationals trading in Ghana were expelled in large numbers in 1969 by the Busia regime, to create more opportunities for Ghanaians in commerce. A number of the Ghanaian market traders interviewed in Kumasi for this study acquired market stalls, equipment, and other assets cheaply at that time from those leaving the country.

5. Market women were particularly noted as fundraisers and organizers. Various authors report in passing that they were giving speeches in support of the cocoa boycott of 1938, collecting donations for the independence movement of the 1950s, and providing food and information to striking railway workers in the 1960s. (Nkrumah 1957; Drake and Lacy 1966; Chazan 1983).

Chapter 5

1. Field research for this chapter was conducted from November 1994 to September 1995 and from January to July 1998. I acknowledge the financial support for this research provided by the Social Sciences and Humanities Research Council of Canada (SSHRC) doctoral and postdoctoral fellowships, and by the Canada/ASEAN (Association for Southeast Asian Nations) Centre, Academic Support Programme. In the Philippines, I am affiliated with the Cordillera Studies Center (CSC), University of the Philippines College Baguio, Baguio City. I thank the faculty at CSC for their generous support of my research. I also thank Linda Seligmann for her editorial advice and thoughtful comments. To the residents of Banaue, I owe a debt of gratitude. All personal names of individuals identified herein are pseudonyms.

2. Recent scholarship (Atkinson and Errington 1990; see especially Errington 1990; Brenner 1998, especially Chap. 4) argues that in upland Southeast Asia where women are noted for their control of household finances and where there is a high degree of gender autonomy, men still largely control the prestigious political and religious spheres, as spiritual potency (men's domain) is more highly regarded than economic control (women's domain). Although this pattern is also common in Banaue, I suggest that the potential for women to assume more public responsibilities is increasing. In the 1995 election, two women were elected as Banaue municipal councilors from a possible eight positions. In the six barangays in which I worked, women also maintained a strong presence in the local position of barangay official. Two barangays elected women as their council directors or cap-

tains and of the seven executive council positions available, three to four spaces were held by women.

3. The figures indicating the number of craft traders and craft shops are drawn from research conducted in 1995. In 1998 these figures remained relatively the same. As some businesses have failed, others have taken their place, and women have maintained their prominent positions in craft trade.

4. This contrasts with Lynn Sikkink's (1995) study of marketing in the Bolivian Andes, in which men's and women's marketing is product specific and linked to their household application—men sell musical instruments, while women sell herbal medicines.

5. Parallels can be drawn with the general rise of new merchant elites in the knitting and weaving industries in neighboring Sagada, Mt. Province. Villia Jefremovas (1985) has demonstrated how at the village level, a small group of female entrepreneurs who have established workshops producing high-quality knitwear and functional woven products have been able to accumulate capital and identify themselves as belonging to a new local elite class.

6. Florence Babb (1989, 62) quoting Andean researchers Carmen Deere and Magdalena León de Leal, points out that while women's work in the productive sphere may resemble domestic work, one cannot regard women's paid work as a mere extension or reflection of their domestic roles, but instead must consider the diversity of women's productive activity.

7. Rita Mataag, a wood-carving trader in barangay Tam-an, has tried to foster cooperative enterprises in order to maximize her small business, but she has encountered problems. On two occasions, Rita has been embroiled in confrontations with other traders. In early 1995, she decided to help other female traders by allowing them to accompany her on selling trips to Manila. She introduced these traders to her buyers, only to later discover that they had returned to these buyers offering the same items at a lower price. Rita lost her business with one of the Manila buyers and now works only on her own. When this occurred with Ida, a close village friend of Rita's, the two women were able to settle their differences and work out a subsequent arrangement. When they travel to Manila together, they split the cost of the hired truck or watch each other's baggage at the Manila bus station, but they do not sell to the same outlets. Indeed, they often split up once they reach Manila.

In 1994, the Central Cordillera Agricultural Programme (CECAP), a joint EU/Philippine government-funded organization with their head office in Banaue, established the Banaue Handicraft Sellers Association to regulate the marketing of Banaue's crafts. A number of marketers in Banaue lobbied for an avenue through which to control the quality of the products being produced and the method of pricing to eliminate the fierce price undercutting and product copying that were taking place. However, when the building site designated to house the Handicraft Sellers' offices proved physically unsuitable, and with the subsequent evaluation of CECAP projects in mid-1995 and the change in project directors, this initiative lost momentum. When I left Banaue in September 1995, the new CECAP administration had not identified the sellers' association as a priority and individual marketers had been unable to come together to form a cohesive group on their own.

8. As the demand for weavings in Oaxaca, Mexico, grows larger and more dependable, Scott Cook (1986, 63–64) notes that younger male weavers are beginning to divorce themselves from their agricultural responsibilities as a consequence of capitalist development. This suggests that in Oaxaca, unlike Banaue, producers do not weigh the cultural value of their farms; they simply equate the economic value of the income from weaving with that from farming.

Chapter 6

1. During the colonial period and before, theater in Morocco was largely in the French language or, less frequently, in classical Arabic, targeted toward an elite audience of literati.

2. Although family members often work together, their clients are usually not related to them.

3. In the Moroccan case, it takes the form of what Habermas would call a "plebeian public sphere" (Habermas (1992, 426).

4. Habermas goes on to say, "The exclusion of the culturally and politically mobilized strata entails a pluralization of the public sphere in the very process of its emergence. Next to, and interlocked with, the hegemonic public sphere, a plebeian one assumes shape" (1992, 426). Whether a public sphere in the strict Habermasian sense can exist in an ideal monarchy is a question I will reserve for another discussion. As a parliamentary monarchy, however, with several political parties and opposition newspapers, it is quite possible to speak of several rational competing and print-mediated public spheres in Morocco.

5. Westermarck 1980, 171, #806.

6. Original Arabic versions of the following chants are available from the author.

7. The hadith contains the sayings of the Prophet.

8. The original is in classical scriptural Arabic.

9. Satellite dishes are the newest commodity in Morocco, bringing in images from all over the globe to local living rooms.

10. Many male herbalists still subscribe to an ideology of traditional "humoral" medicine—based on the temperaments and typologies of human beings (Nasr 1964). Some herbalists—male and female—code the Western system as evil and insufficient, treating only part of the individual instead of the whole (see Kapchan 1996). There is enough of a trend toward more "Western" and scientific epistemologies, however, to chart a change in women's and men's oratory.

11. Despite its roots in medieval Islamic geomancy and esotericism, magic as practiced in contemporary Morocco is associated with the domain of women. This, despite the fact that many of the recognized magical specialists are men. In practice, most magic is consumed by/performed for women.

Chapter 7

1. I lived in Cserépfalu for a little over a year in 1982–1983 and have visited it regularly for varying lengths of time since then. This chapter is based on participant observation, life histories, and formal and informal interviews, supplemented by archival, statistical, and other documented data.

I thank the people of Cserépfalu, particularly Ibolya and the other women, for their kindness, warmth, hospitality, and patience. For careful reading of earlier drafts of the present chapter and for helpful suggestions, I am most appreciative of György Csepeli, Norma Diamond, Linda Seligmann, and Katherine Verdery. Without generous grants from the American Council of Learned Societies, Fulbright-Hays, the Hungarian Academy of Sciences, and the International Research and Exchanges Board, my research over the years would not have been possible.

2. Many of the Hungarian terms cited here are either local-specific or region-specific.

3. The interactions between legality and illegality, formal and informal economies, or first, second, and third sectors were much more shady and complex than I have the space to discuss here. For example, for the several weeks of seasonal agrarian labor, or for preparing for and selling on the markets, village women often obtained partially paid sick leave from their first sector jobs for a month or more each time by bribing regional doctors for a written certificate.

4. Older and middle-aged village women often recalled that when they themselves were young, mothers-in-law held total control over their sons' wives. In turn, the mother-in-law was responsible to her husband, the head of the household, for the young woman's behavior. In particular, mothers-in-law kept careful watch over the fertility of young couples in order to protect the already small family property from fragmentation. "When the bed was creaking in the middle of the night, my mother-in-law yelled out, 'Stop that! Why are you at it again!?!'"

(See Morvay 1981). The most affluent family, with 25 *hold* of land, lost a daughter-in-law when she became pregnant with a third child and her mother-in-law forced her, I was told, to permit the midwife to induce abortion with a sharp instrument. Within ten days the twenty-four-year-old woman died of peritonitis. This was far from a singular episode in the village (cf. Tóth 1939); having one, two, or at most three children with subsequent pregnancies forcibly aborted seems to have been the reproductive strategy of villagers who held substantial land. In contrast, the landless poor often had from four to eight children per couple.

5. Shortly after the end of the Second World War, the twice-weekly local market closed for good.

6. My initial research took place between 1982 and 1989, when there still was a Czechoslovakia.

7. Snails, in particular, were gathered expressly for sale abroad. The women sold them to the regional state-employed collector who delivered the snails in wet sand to a central state distributor who, in turn, sold them to France. Only one large family, considered the very poorest in the village, actually ate *snail-paprikás* for which the children received much ribbing from other villagers.

8. During the socialist period, medicines were heavily subsidized by the state so that "investment" in these ventures was minimal, mere *fillérs* (the Hungarian equivalent of pennies).

9. During much of Romania's Ceausescu regime (between 1965 and 1989) pronatalist policies prevailed and birth control was not allowed. It was illegal for a Romanian citizen to buy, own, have or use birth-control devices, so this particular marketing activity was a rather dangerous one (Verdery 1994; Kligman 1998). Regardless, women from Cserépfalu were more than willing to take the risk because it was a highly profitable venture to fill an obvious need.

10. The two million ethnic Hungarians in Transylvania represented a ready market for the village women, who felt more comfortable conducting illegal business with customers who shared their ethnicity and spoke their language.

11. Those fifty years old and older would be considered not middle-aged, but old in Cserépfalu. Here I use my own definition of middle age, based on the demographic profile of Cserépfalu's female population in the 1980s. Elsewhere I discuss in detail how age is perceived and expressed in Cserépfalu (Huseby-Darvas 1987).

12. Many of the approximately 200,000 German-speaking Hungarian citizens who are often referred to as Swabian, or in Hungarian *Sváb* (singular) and *Svábok* (plural), indeed live in Transdanubia. However, the Cserépfalu women refer to everyone in that region of Hungary, German-speaking or not, as Swabian.

13. *Hátyi* is a region-specific woven basket carried like a backpack.

14. The village women spent part of their profits on church dues, clothes for children, and gifts for baptisms, confirmations, and weddings.

15. I asked my landlady to read the proofs of a paper I wrote on snowflowering. She commented that it was fine, but got upset because "any Swabian who reads this will realize how profitable snowflowering really is and will go to *our* forests in Transdanubia and *our* market in Eger." She calmed down when I deleted the names of the forests from the paper and assured her that the villagers in Transdanubia were not likely to read that particular paper anyway.

16. The population of each village in the area has a nickname by which neighboring villagers know them. Depending on the context and tone, nicknames might be used and perceived as either camaraderie, jokes, or insults. If no competition is intended, for example, when an individual meets a villager from a neighboring settlement at a regional medical clinic, they might use nicknames to express closeness and camaraderie. Use of a nickname when going to the market to sell flowers might express hostility in a joking manner; after the flowers are sold, nicknames might be used jokingly and as a form of boasting at the same time; during or after soccer games between teams from neighboring villages, nicknames often serve as insults, resulting in serious fights especially when alcohol is involved (Huseby-Darvas 1984, 1988).

17. Even those husbands who worked in Transdanubia and readily gave their wives Transdanubian weather reports fought against these ventures, and cursed their wives for wanting to gather and market the flowers. The men claimed that these activities were "too risky, too embarrassing, and too *cigányos* [Gypsylike]."

18. It is interesting to note that poachers and women who gathered medicinal herbs conducted their activities in the forests alone, while women who were gathering fruits, berries, mushrooms, and flowers always worked in groups (cf. Bakó 1977, 148).

19. Occasionally, women loaded down with forest and domestic products would fill the first buses of the day headed to the Mezőkövesd market. They sold either to individual buyers or to a single city buyer who had a stall at the market, thus earning three to five times their daily first sector wages by seven o'clock in the morning. Then they returned to Cserépfalu to put in their eight hours of labor in the state sector for the 100 to 120 forints per day rate. Usually there was a specific reason for the market trip: money was needed for confirmation or wedding gifts, children's new clothes, for "greasing the palm" of an official, or to "smooth" a permit, or for a doctor, so that he or she would treat a sick relative "better" or would prescribe birth-control pills to be sold in Romania in an upcoming marketing trip.

20. As one nineteen-year-old commuting village man said to me, "[I would not be caught dead selling anything with the women folk on the market]; I still help my mother and grandmother with picking snails and gathering flowers and berries for the market. There is always lots of work to be done here. Of course, there is good money too and my mother always saves my share [for when I will get married]."

21. She is referring here to Prince Coburg, who according to local residents, is the last descendant of the Coburg family. He owned landed estates in and around the region and large parts of the village until 1945.

22. For example, former villagers living in the cities and working as professionals or skilled industrial workers estimated that, in addition to eggs, meat, fruits, and various produce, they received between 30,000 and 100,000 forints in cash annually from their parents and grandparents who were residing in Cserépfalu.

23. As I already mentioned in passing, heavy drinking is widespread in Cserépfalu, as the former village physician, Dr. Ferenc Kaucsek, has described in great detail (See Kaucsek 1981). As elsewhere in Hungary—where alcoholism is officially recognized as a major social problem with an estimated 1,500,000 people afflicted by the disease out of a total population of slightly more than 10,000,000 (estimated by the National Council of Anti-Alcoholism, Alkoholizmus Elleni Országos Bizottság, cited in Kaucsek 1981, 306–8)—alcoholism and all it entails is a serious, growing, and apparently fairly recent phenomenon in Cserépfalu. At least according to village elders and the nonnative former elite, the villagers in this grape-growing settlement

> always liked to drink and our lives were in part centered around the vineyards and the wine cellars. Yet having and serving *ó-bor* [old wine, last year's wine] at each harvest was the sign of *a jó gazda, a jó cserépi* [a good master of the land, a good villager]. We were always moderate in drinking too. A man was not a man if he got drunk. We condemned drunkenness in the old days. Now most cellars are empty by March [grape harvest is in October] and all these young ones drink in excess.

Commuting, living in worker's hostels, and waiting for trains and buses seem to invite more drinking. This is substantiated by present and former commuters and by their families. At the same time, some of the old village sayings and rules, both unwritten as well as recorded in the local church archives, indicate that at least some villagers did drink in excess in the old days as well. For example, it was recorded in the local church archives that "going through the cemetery while drunk [was] punishable. . . ." There are also written and unwritten laws about men's proper behavior in wine cellars and vineyards (cf. Bakó 1977; Gönczi 1910; Szendrey Ákos 1938, 124−37; Ujváry 1975, 123−28). This is not intended, however, to cast doubt on the fact that widespread and heavy drinking is more a current and growing social phenomenon in Cserépfalu than a traditional one. According to most villagers, drinking in excess is explicitly due to various stresses involved in commuting to urban-industrial jobs and implicitly connected with radical changes in lifestyles, demands, and values.

24. It is worth noting the contradiction between both the official socialist ideology and the Calvinist notions of simplicity and frugality vis-à-vis the village socioeconomic ideology and strategy I describe in this chapter. According to socialist ideology, the ideal combined measure of human value is "talent, culture, social usefulness, and the degree of participation in important decisions" (Szántó 1977, 377). By contrast, in capitalist systems the basis for rank and social status are money, success, and career, along with a petty bourgeois mentality that centers on conspicuous consumption for its own sake. Increasingly, since the 1960s, the villagers' ideology, which guided their socioeconomic behavior, has come to fit the pattern of the capitalist model as defined by Szántó, rather than either the Calvinist model or the socialist model.

25. Here I mean "idiom" in the same sense as Anthony Cohen (1982, 319) defines it: "Entire behavior . . . including the total ideological and cultural apparatus which supports it." There was a growing abyss between official and local ideology insofar as explaining, justifying, and guiding socioeconomic strategies and lifestyles in the village.

26. It seems to me that these were harbingers of the values and conspicuous consumption patterns that appeared in full force after 1989—that is, the end of socialism—reinforced by advertisements and officially accepted and encouraged practices (see also Róna-Tas 1995, 1997; Vörös 1996).

Chapter 8

1. For an important early discussion of women's roles in exchange relations and the power they confer, see Weiner 1976.

2. Defined by Larson as "part Indian, part mestizo," cholas are in a privileged position in that they are associated with "mercantile savvy." Their nonchola rural counterparts are less fortunate (1995, 37).

3. I use identity and ethnicity here to refer to similar processes, but identity signals a focus on the individual woman: how she perceives herself and how her activities together define her position and image relative to other individuals in her social world. Ethnicity in part makes up this identity, but ethnicity signals

group membership: both how she identifies herself as part of a racialized collectivity and how others position her in a "racial" (social) category.

4. Of course many urban women make permanent livings as marketers in city markets—these women are often recent migrants and/or maintain close ties to their rural communities.

5. In the past, one possibility was to sell one's crops or medicines at the mining centers where they could be sold for a higher price than at regional fairs like Challapata. This option has been lost with the closing or reduction of operations at many mines around Bolivia due to the fall in mineral prices. Another possibility is to sell in cities like Potosí, Oruro, Cochabamba, and La Paz. Selling in cities differs from selling in a marketplace like Cochabamba, and I differentiate these practices in what follows.

6. Some vendors are very specific about their roles as healers. Said one participant of the Huari fair: "Those that sell medicine, all are healers; they know what they're selling; we are healers." [Los que venden medicina, todos son curanderos; saben qué están vendiendo, somos *jampiris*] (cited by Alba 1989, 181). Alba and Tarifa (1993) have written about a group of healers/medicine vendors from the Cochabamba region.

7. Interestingly, in the case of the Huari fair, women often use the money they earn to buy school supplies for their children before the beginning of the school year. Classes in Condo, which officially should begin before the Huari fair, are often postponed until after the fair because so many parents use the opportunity to sell goods in order to purchase new school supplies for their student children.

8. Their stands, however, often depend on their rural livelihoods and identities too because they are provisioned in part by herbs from Condo, and the business itself is based on a household strategy of continuing agro-pastoral livelihood.

Conclusion

1. Anthropologists have been interested in understanding the multivalent nature of exchange as well as the manner in which circuits of exchange are distinguished from, and interact with, each other. (See, among others, Appadurai 1986; Bloch and Parry 1989; Gudeman 1992; Harris 1995; Larson and León 1995; Mauss 1954; Platt 1995; Sahlins 1972; and Weiner 1976.) Far more can be done on the operation of networks, reciprocal exchange, and the social side of money among market vendors in informal markets.

References

Archives

AHCM Archivo Histórico de Municipal del Ayuntamiento de la Ciudad de
México (Mexico City, Mexico)
AHJ   Archivo Histórico de Jalisco (Guadalajara, Mexico)
AHMG Archivo Histórico de Municipal de Guadalajara (Guadalajara, Mexico)
BPE   Biblioteca Pública del Estado de Jalisco (Guadalajara, Mexico)
CA   Coleccíon del Sr. Juan Victor Arauz (Guadalajara, Mexico, private collection)

Secondary Sources

Abercrombie, Thomas. 1986. The Politics of Sacrifice: an Aymara Cosmology in
Action. Unpublished Ph.D. dissertation, Department of Anthropology, University of Chicago.
———. 1991. To Be Indian, To Be Bolivian: "Ethnic" and "National" Discourses
of Identity. In Gregory Urban and Joel Sherzer, eds., *Nation States and Indians
in Latin America*, 95–130. Austin: University of Texas Press.
Abrahams, Roger D. n.d. Folklore at the Marketplace.
Abu-Lughod, Lila. 1986. *Veiled Sentiments: Honor and Poetry in a Bedouin Society*.
Berkeley and Los Angeles: University of California Press.
Agnew, Jean-Christophe. 1986. *Worlds Apart: The Market and the Theater in Anglo-
American Thought, 1550–1750*. Cambridge and New York: Cambridge University Press.
Agócs, Péter, and Sándor Agócs. 1994. "The Change Was but an Unfulfilled Promise": Agriculture and the Rural Population in Post-Communist Hungary. *East
European Politics and Societies* 8, no. 1: 32–57.
Aguilar, Filomeno V., and Virginia A. Miralao. 1984. *Handicrafts, Development and*

Dilemmas over Definition (The Philippines as a Case in Point). Handicraft Project Paper Series No. 1. Manila: Ramon Magasaysay Award Foundation.

al-'Arawi, Abdellah. 1982. *L'idéologie Arabe contemporaine*. Paris: Maspero.

Alba, Juan José. 1989. El ocaso de una feria colonial: vigencias y transfiguraciones sociales. Unpublished manuscript.

Alba, Juan José, and Lila Tarifa. 1993. *Los jampiris de Raqaypampa*. Cochabamba: Centro de Comunicación y Desarollo Andino.

Alexander, Jennifer. 1986. Information and Price Setting in a Rural Javanese Market. *Bulletin of Indonesian Economic Studies* 22: 88–112.

———. 1987. *Trade, Traders and Trading in Rural Java*. Singapore: Oxford University Press.

Alexander, Jennifer, and Paul Alexander. 1991a. Protecting Peasants from Capitalism: The Subordination of Javanese Traders by the Colonial State. *Comparative Studies in Society and History* 33, no. 2: 370–94.

———. 1991b. What's a Fair Price? Price-setting and Trading Partnerships in Javanese Markets. *Man* 26, no. 3: 493–512.

———. 1991c. Trade and Petty Commodity Production in Early Twentieth Century Kebumen. In P. Alexander, P. Boomgaard, and B. White, eds., *In the Shadow of Agriculture*, 70–91. Amsterdam: Royal Tropical Institute.

Alexander, Paul. 1992. What's in a Price: Trading Practices in Peasant (and other) Markets. In Roy Dilley, ed., *Contesting Markets: Analyses of Ideology, Discourse and Practice*, 79–96. Edinburgh: Edinburgh University Press.

Altamirano, Ignacio Manuel. [1871] 1961. *Christmas in the Mountains* (La navidad en las montañas). Translated by Harvey L. Johnson. Gainesville: University of Florida Press.

Anderson, James N. 1969. Buy-and-Sell and Economic Personalism: Foundations for Philippine Entrepreneurship. *Asian Survey* 9: 641–68.

Andorka, Rudolf. 1979. *A Magyar községek társadalmának átalakulása* (The Transformation of Hungarian Village Society). Budapest: Magvető.

Appadurai, Arjun, ed. 1986. *The Social Life of Things: Commodities in Cultural Perspective*. Cambridge: Cambridge University Press.

Arguedas, José María. 1978. *Deep Rivers*. Translated by Francis Barraclough. Austin: University of Texas Press.

Atkinson, Jane Monnig, and Shelly Errington, eds. 1990. *Power and Difference: Gender in Island Southeast Asia*. Stanford, Calif.: Stanford University Press.

Azad, Nandini. 1981. *Working Women's Forums: A Case Study of a Self-Help Movement Accelerating Social Transformation Among Slum Women of Madras*. Madras: Working Women's Forum.

Babb, Florence E. 1981. Women and Marketing in Huaraz, Peru: The Political

Economy of Petty Commerce. Unpublished Ph.D. dissertation, Department of Anthropology, State University of New York at Buffalo.

————. 1985. Middlemen and "Marginal" Women: Marketers and Dependency in Peru's Informal Sector. In Stuart Plattner, ed., *Markets and Marketing*, 287–308. Monographs in Economic Anthropology, No. 4. Lanham, Md.: University Press of America.

————. 1986. Producers and Reproducers: Andean Market Women in the Economy. In June Nash and Helen I. Safa, eds., *Women and Change in Latin America*, 53–64. South Hadley, Mass.: Bergin and Garvey Publishers.

————. 1987. Marketers as Producers: The Labor Process and Proletarianization of Peruvian Market women. In David Hakken and Hanna Lessinger, eds., *Perspectives in U.S. Marxist Anthropology*, 166–83. Boulder, Col.: Westview Press.

————. [1989] 1998. *Between Field and Cooking Pot: The Political Economy of Market Women in Peru*. Austin: University of Texas Press.

————. 1996. After the Revolution: Neoliberal Policy and Gender in Nicaragua. *Latin American Perspectives* 23, no. 1: 27–48.

————. 1997. Women, Informal Economies, and the State in Peru and Nicaragua. In Ann Miles and Hans Buechler, eds., *Women and Economic Change: Andean Perspectives*, 89–100. Washington, D.C.: American Anthropological Association.

————. 1998. From Cooperatives to Microenterprises: The Neoliberal Turn in Postrevolutionary Nicaragua. In Lynne Phillips, ed., *The Third Wave of Modernization in Latin America: Cultural Perspectives on Neoliberalism*, 109–22. Wilmington, Del.: Scholarly Resources.

Bacdayan, Albert. 1977. Mechanistic Co-operation and Sexual Equality Among the Western Bontoc. In Alice Schlegel, ed., *Sexual Stratification: A Cross-Cultural View*, 270–91. New York: Columbia University Press.

Bakhtin, M. M. 1984. *Rabelais and His World*. Translated by Helene Iswolsky. Bloomington: Indiana University Press.

Bakó, Ferenc. 1977. Bükki barlanglakások (Cavedwellings of the Bükk). *Borsodi Kismonográfiák*, No. 3. Miskolc: Hermann Ottó Múzeum.

Balassa, Béla. 1982. Reforming the New Economic Mechanism in Hungary. *World Bank Staff Papers*, No. 534. Washington, D.C.: The World Bank.

Barnes, Sandra. 1986. *Patrons and Power: Creating a Political Community in Metropolitan Lagos*. Bloomington: Indiana University Press.

Barton, Roy F. 1919. Ifugao Economics. *University of California Publications in American Archaeology and Ethnology* 15, no. 1: 1–186.

————. [1938] 1963. *Philippine Pagans: The Autobiographies of Three Ifugaos*. London: George Routledge and Sons.

Bauman, Richard. 1977. *Verbal Art as Performance*. Prospect Heights, Ill.: Waveland Press.

Bauman, Richard, and Charles L. Briggs. 1990. Poetics and Performance as Critical Perspectives on Language and Social Life. *Annual Review of Anthropology* 19: 59–88.

Behar, Ruth. 1990. Rage and Redemption: Reading the Life Story of a Mexican Marketing Woman. *Feminist Studies* 16, no. 2: 223–58.

———. 1993. *Translated Woman: Crossing the Border with Esperanza's Story*. Boston: Beacon Press.

Benería, Lourdes. 1992. Accounting for Women's Work: The Progress of Two Decades. *World Development* 20, no. 11: 1547–60.

Berend, Iván T. 1996. *Central and Eastern Europe, 1944–1993: Detour from the Periphery to the Periphery*. Cambridge: Cambridge University Press.

Berlant, Lauren. 1997. *The Queen of America Goes to Washington City: Essays on Sex and Citizenship*. Durham, N.C., and London: Duke University Press.

Berrechid, Abdelkrim. 1977. "Alif Ba: Al-waqu'iyya al-ihtifalliyya." *at-taqafa al-jadida* 7 (Spring): 156.

Bhatt, Ela. 1979. Organizing Self-Employed Women Workers. In Rounaq Jahan and Hanna Papanek, eds., *Women and Development, Perspectives from South and Southeast Asia*, 425–33. Dacca: Institute of Law and International Affairs.

Bloch, Maurice, and Jonathan Parry, eds. 1989. *Money and the Morality of Exchange*. Cambridge: Cambridge University Press.

Boomgaard, Peter. 1989. *Children of the Colonial State: Population Growth and Economic Development in Java, 1795–1880*. CASA Monographs, No. 1. Amsterdam: Free University Press.

Booth, Anne, and R. M. Sundrum. 1988. *Employment Trends and Policy Issues for Repelita V*. Jakarta: UNDP/ILO.

Boserup, Ester. 1970. *Woman's Role in Economic Development*. New York: St. Martin's Press.

Bott, Elizabeth. [1957] 1971. *Family and Social Network*. London: Tavistock.

Bourdieu, Pierre. 1966. The Sentiment of Honour in Kabyle Society. *Honour and Shame: The Values of Mediterranean Society*. London: Weidenfeld and Nicolson.

———. 1990. *The Logic of Practice*. Translated by Richard Nice. Stanford, Calif.: Stanford University Press.

Breman, Jan. [1976] 1989. Particularism and Scarcity: Urban Labour Markets and Social Classes. In Hamza Alavi and John Harriss, eds., *Sociology of "Developing Societies," South Asia*, 268–75. New York: Monthly Review Press.

———. 1996. *Footloose Labour: Working in India's Informal Economy*. Cambridge: Cambridge University Press.

Brenneis, Don. 1986. Shared Territory: Audience, Indirection and Meaning. *Text* 6, no. 3: 339–47.

Brenner, Suzanne April. 1991. Competing Hierarchies: Javanese Merchants and the Priyayi Elite in Solo. *Indonesia* 52: 55–84.

———. 1998. *The Domestication of Desire: Women, Wealth and Modernity in Java.* Princeton, N.J.: Princeton University Press.

Brocklehurst, Thomas Unett. 1883. *Mexico To-Day: A Country with a Great Future, and a Glance at the Prehistoric Remains and Antiquities of the Montezumas.* London: John Murray.

Bromley, Ray, and Chris Gerry, eds. 1979. *Casual Work and Poverty in Third World Cities.* Chichester, Eng.: John Wiley and Sons.

Brown, Judith K. 1970. A Note on the Division of Labor by Sex. *American Anthropologist* 72: 1073.

Buechler, Hans, and Judith-Marie Buechler. 1971. *The Bolivian Aymara.* New York: Holt, Rinehart, and Winston.

———. 1977. Conduct and Code: An Analysis of Market Syndicates and Social Revolution in La Paz, Bolivia. In June Nash, Juan Corradi, and Hobart Spaulding, eds., *Ideology and Social Change in Latin America,* 174–84. New York: Gordon and Breach Science Publishers, Inc.

———. 1992. *Manufacturing Against the Odds.* Boulder, Col.: Westview Press.

———. 1996. *The World of Sofía Velasquez: The Autobiography of a Bolivian Market Vendor.* New York: Columbia University Press.

Buechler, Judith-Marie. 1972. Peasant Marketing and Social Revolution in the Province of La Paz, Bolivia. Unpublished Ph.D. dissertation, Department of Anthropology, McGill University.

———. 1997. The Visible and Vocal Politics of Female Traders and Small-Scale Producers in La Paz, Bolivia. In Ann Miles and Hans Buechler, eds., *Women and Economic Change: Andean Perspectives,* 65–87. Society for Latin American Anthropology, vol. 14. Washington, D.C.: American Anthropological Association.

Bunolna, Jacinto N. 1995. Interview with J. Bunolna, Provincial Director, Ifugao Provincial Operations, Philippine Department of Trade and Industry, Lagawe, Ifugao, March 1995.

Bunster, Ximena, and Elsa M. Chaney. 1989. *Sellers and Servants: Working Women in Lima, Peru.* Granby, Mass.: Bergin and Garvey.

Caplan, Patricia. 1985. *Class and Gender in India: Women and Their Organizations in a South Indian City.* London: Tavistock Publications.

Carey, Peter. 1986. Waiting for the "Just King": The Agrarian World of South-Central Java from Giyanti (1755) to the Java War (1825–30). *Modern Asian Studies* 20: 59–137.

Castells, Manuel, and Alejandro Portes. 1989. World Underneath: The Origins, Dynamics, and Effects of the Informal Economy. In Alejandro Portes, Manuel Castells, and Lauren Benton, eds., *The Informal Economy: Studies in Advanced and Less Developed Countries*, 11–40. Baltimore, Md.: Johns Hopkins University Press.

Causey, C. Andrew. 1997. Stealing a Good Idea: Innovation and Competition Among Toba Batak Woodcarvers. Paper presented at the Association for Asian Studies meetings, Chicago, Ill., Mar. 13–16, 1997.

Chamlee, Emily. 1994. Indigenous Credit, Mutual Assistance Societies, and Economic Development: Prospects and Impediments. Unpublished manuscript.

Chazan, Naomi. 1983. *An Anatomy of Ghanaian Politics: Managing Political Recession 1969–1982*. Boulder, Col.: Westview Press.

Cherneff, Jill. 1982. Gender Roles, Economic Relations and Cultural Change Among the Bontoc Igorot of Northern Luzon, Philippines. Unpublished Ph.D. dissertation, Graduate Faculty of Political and Social Science, New School for Social Research.

Chiñas, Beverly L. 1973. *The Isthmus Zapotecs: Women's Roles in Cultural Context*. New York: Holt, Rinehart and Winston.

———. 1975. *Mujeres de San Juan: La mujer Zapoteca del istmo en la economía*. Mexico City: Sep/Setentas.

Clark, Gracia. 1988. Money, Sex and Cooking: Manipulation of the Paid/Unpaid Boundary by Asante Market Women. In Benjamin Orlove and Henry Rutz, eds., *The Social Economy of Consumption*, 323–45. Monographs in Economic Anthropology, No. 6. Lanham, Md.: Society for Economic Anthropology and University Press of America.

———. 1991. Colleagues and Customers in Unstable Market Conditions in Kumasi, Ghana. *Ethnology* 25: 31–47.

———. 1994. *Onions Are My Husband: Survival and Accumulation by West African Market Women*. Chicago: University of Chicago Press.

———. Forthcoming. Historical Transitions in Gender and Ethnic Identification with Specific Trading Roles in Asante, 1900–1985. In Tamar Diana Wilson and Judith E. Marti, eds., *Women in the Informal Sector: Case Studies and Theoretical Approaches*. Albany: State University of New York Press.

Clark, Gracia, ed. 1988. *Traders vs. the State: Anthropological Approaches to Unofficial Economies*. Boulder, Col.: Westview Press.

Clark, Gracia, and Takyiwaa Manuh. 1991. Women Traders in Ghana and the Structural Adjustment Programme. In Christina Gladwin, ed., *Structural Adjustment and African Women Farmers*. Gainesville: University of Florida Press.

Coatsworth, John Henry. 1981. *Growth Against Development: The Economic Impact of Railroads in Porfirian Mexico*. Dekalb: Northern Illinois University Press.

Cohen, Anthony, ed. 1982. *Belonging, Identity and Social Organization in British Rural Cultures*. Manchester, Eng.: Manchester University Press.

Collier, Jane, and Sylvia Yanagisako, eds. 1987. *Gender and Kinship: Essays Toward a Unified Analysis*. Stanford, Calif.: Stanford University Press.

Collins, Jane. 1988. *Unseasonal Migrations: The Effects of Rural Land Scarcity in Peru*. Princeton, N.J.: Princeton University Press.

Combs-Schilling, M. E. 1989. *Sacred Performances: Islam, Sexuality, and Sacrifice*. New York: Columbia University Press.

Comitas, Lambros. 1973. Occupational Multiplicity in Rural Jamaica. In L. Comitas and D. Lowenthal, eds., *Work and Family Life: West Indian Perspectives*, 157–73. Garden City, N.Y.: Anchor Books.

Cook, Scott. 1984. Peasant Economy, Rural Industry and Capitalist Development in the Oaxaca Valley, Mexico. *Journal of Peasant Studies* 12: 3–40.

———. 1986. The "Managerial" vs. the "Labor" Function: Capital Accumulation and the Dynamics of Simple Commodity Production in Rural Oaxaca, Mexico. In S. M. Greenfield, A. Strickon, and R. T. Aubey, eds., *Entrepreneurship and Social Change*. Monographs in Economic Anthropology, No. 2, 54–95. New York: University Press of America.

Cook, Scott, and Leigh Binford. 1990. *Obliging Need: Rural Petty Industry in Mexican Capitalism*. Austin: University of Texas Press.

Cook, Scott, and Jong-Taick Joo. 1995. Ethnicity and Economy in Rural Mexico: A Critique of the Indigenista Approach. *Latin American Research Review*. 30, no. 2: 33–59.

Crain, Mary M. 1996. The Gendering of Ethnicity in the Ecuadorian Andes: Native Women's Self-Fashioning in the Urban Marketplace. In Marit Melhuus and Kristi Anne Stolen, eds., *Machos, Mistresses, Madonnas: Contesting the Power of Latin American Gender Imagery*. London: Verso.

Crandon-Malamud, Libbet. 1991. *From the Fat of Our Souls: Social Change, Political Process, and Medical Pluralism in Bolivia*. Berkeley and Los Angeles: University of California Press.

Crane, Stephen. 1973. *Tales, Sketches, and Reports*. Edited by Fredson Bowers. Charlottesville: University Press of Virginia.

———. 1967. *The Complete Novels of Stephen Crane*. Edited by Thomas A. Gullason. Garden City, N.Y.: Doubleday.

Dannhaeuser, Norbett. 1983. *Contemporary Trade Strategies in the Philippines: A Study in Marketing Anthropology*. New Brunswick, N.J.: Rutgers University Press.

Danquah, J. B., Hon. Dr. 1947. Irregularities in Import Control. Motion 26/3/47. Ghana National Archives, Accra, No. 0028 SF8.

Davis, Natalie Zemon. 1978. Women on Top: Symbolic Sexual Inversion and Political Disorder in Early Modern Europe. In Barbara A. Babcock, ed., *The Reversible World: Symbolic Inversion in Art and Society,* 147–90. Ithaca, N.Y.: Cornell University Press.

Davis, William G. 1973. *Social Relations in a Philippine Market: Self-Interest and Subjectivity.* Berkeley and Los Angeles: University of California Press.

De la Cadena, Marisol. 1991. Las mujeres son más indias: etnicidad y género en una comunidad del Cusco. *Revista Andina* 9, no. 1: 7–29.

———. 1995. "Women Are More Indian": Ethnicity and Gender in a Community near Cuzco. In Brooke Larson and Olivia Harris, eds., *Ethnicity, Markets, and Migration in the Andes: At the Crossroads of History and Anthropology,* 329–48. Durham, N.C.: Duke University Press.

De Oliveira, Orlandina, and Bryan Roberts. 1994. The Many Roles of the Informal Sector in Development: Evidence from Urban Labor Market Research, 1940–1989. In Cathy A. Rakowski, ed., *Contrapunto: The Informal Sector Debate in Latin America,* 51–71. Albany: State University of New York Press.

Derrida, Jacques. 1980. The Law of Genre. In *Glyph,* 202–32. Baltimore, Md.: Johns Hopkins University Press.

Deventer, C. Th. van. 1904. *Overzicht van den economischen toestand der inlandsche bevolking van Java en Madoera.* The Hague: Nijhoff.

Dewey, Alice G. 1962. *Peasant Marketing in Java.* Glencoe, Ill.: The Free Press.

Dilley, Roy, ed. 1992. *Contesting Markets: Analyses of Ideology, Discourse and Practice.* Edinburgh: Edinburgh University Press.

Diskin, Martin. 1995. Review essay, "Anthropological Fieldwork in Mesoamerica: Focus on the Field." *Latin American Research Review* 30, no. 1: 163–75.

Drake, St. Clair, and Leslie Lacy. 1966. Government Versus the Unions: The Sekondi-Takoradi Strike, 1961. In G. Carter, ed., *Politics in Africa: 7 Cases.* New York: Harcourt, Brace and World.

Duranti, Alessandro. 1986. The Audience as Co-Author: An Introduction. *Text* 6: 239–47.

Eades, Jeremy. 1979. Kinship and Entrepreneurship Among Yoruba in Northern Ghana. In William Shack and Eliott Skinner, eds., *Strangers in African Societies,* 169–82. Berkeley and Los Angeles: University of California Press.

Egnore, [Trawick] Margaret. 1980. On the Meaning of Sakti to Women in Tamil Nadu. In Susan Wadley, ed., *The Powers of Tamil Women,* 1–34. Syracuse, N.Y.: Foreign and Comparative Studies, South Asian Series, No. 6.

Ehlers, Tracy. 1990. *Silent Looms*. Boulder, Col.: Westview Press.

Eickelman, Dale F. 1976. *Moroccan Islam: Tradition and Society in a Pilgrimage Center*. Austin: University of Texas Press.

————. 1992. Mass Higher Education and the Religious Imagination in Contemporary Arab Societies. *American Ethnologist* 19, no. 4: 643–55.

Einhorn, Barbara. 1995. Introduction. In Barbara Einhorn and Eileen Janes Yeo, eds., *Women and Market Societies: Crisis and Opportunity*, 1–10. Aldershot, Eng.: Edward Elgar.

Einhorn, Barbara, and Jane Yeo, eds. 1995. *Women and Market Societies: Crisis and Opportunity*. Aldershot, Eng.: Edward Elgar.

Ellis, George R. 1981. Arts and Peoples of the Northern Philippines. In G. Ellis, ed., *The People and Art of the Philippines*, 183–264. Los Angeles: Museum of Cultural History, University of California.

Enyedi, György. 1980. *Falvaink sorsa* (The Fate of Our Villages). Budapest: Magvető.

————. 1982. Part-time Farming in Hungary. *GeoJournal* 6, no. 4: 323–26.

Erikson, Erik. [1950] 1963. *Childhood and Society*. New York: W. W. Norton and Co.

Errington, Shelly. 1990. Recasting Sex, Gender and Power: A Theoretical and Regional Overview. In J. M. Atkinson and S. Errington, eds., *Power and Difference: Gender in Island Southeast Asia*, 1–58. Stanford, Calif.: Stanford University Press.

Espinoza Soriano, Waldemar. 1981. El reino Aymara de Quillaca-Asanaques, siglos XV y XVI. *Revista del Museo Nacional* (Lima) 45: 175–274.

Etienne, Mona. 1980. Women and Men, Cloth and Colonization: The Transformation of Production-Distribution Relations Among the Baule (Ivory Coast). In M. Etienne and E. Leacock, eds., *Women and Colonization*, 214–38. New York: J. F. Bergin.

Everett, Jana, and Mira Savara. 1991. Institutional Credit as a Strategy Towards Self-Reliance for Petty Commodity Producers in India: A Critical Evaluation. In Haleh Afshar, ed., *Women, Development and Survival in the Third World*, 239–59. London: Longman.

Falola, Toyin. 1995. Gender, Business, and Space Control: Yoruba Market Women and Power. In Bessie House-Midamba and Felix K. Ekechi, eds., *African Market Women and Economic Power: The Role of Women in African Economic Development*, 22–40. Westport, Conn.: Greenwood Press.

Fél, Edit, and Tamás Hofer. 1969. *Proper Peasants*. Chicago: Aldine.

Fernando, M. R., and David Bulbeck. 1992. *Chinese Economic Activities in Nether-*

lands India: Selected Translations from the Dutch. Singapore: Institute of Southeast Asian Studies.

Fernea, Elizabeth Warnock. 1998. *In Search of Islamic Feminism.* New York: Doubleday.

Finney, B. R. 1973. *Big Men and Business: Entrepreneurship and Economic Growth in the New Guinea Highlands.* Honolulu: University Press of Hawaii.

Flandrau, Charles Macomb. [1908] 1964. *Viva Mexico!* Edited by C. Harvey Gardiner. Urbana: University of Illinois Press.

Forshee, Jill. 1996. Powerful Connections: Sumbanese Textiles and Global Exchange. Paper presented at the annual meetings of the American Anthropological Association, San Francisco, Calif., Nov. 20–24, 1996.

Fraser, Nancy. 1992. Rethinking the Public Sphere: A Contribution to the Critique of Actually Existing Democracy. In Craig Calhoun, ed., *Habermas and the Public Sphere*, 109–42. Cambridge, Mass., and London: MIT Press.

Fry, Howard T. 1983. *A History of the Mountain Province.* Quezon City, Philippines: New Day.

Gal, Susan. 1989. Language and Political Economy. *Annual Review of Anthropology* 18: 345–67.

Gallo Pérez, Celina Guadalupe. 1986. *Una visión de la Guadalajara de fines del siglo XIX y principios del actual.* Colección Temática Jalisciense 14. Guadalajara, Jal.: Gobierno del Estado de Jalisco, Secretaría General de Gobierno, Unidad Editorial.

García Cubas, Antonio. 1876. *The Republic of Mexico in 1876: A Political and Ethnographical Division of the Population, Character, Habits, Costumes and Vocations of its Inhabitants.* Translated by George F. Henderson. Mexico: "La Enseñanza" Printing Office.

Gardiner, C. Harvey. 1964. Introduction. In Charles Macomb Flandrau, *Viva Mexico!*, xi–xxv. Urbana: University of Illinois Press.

Geertz, Clifford. 1960. *The Religion of Java.* New York: Free Press.

———. 1978. The Bazaar Economy: Information and Search in Peasant Marketing. *American Economic Review* 68, no. 2: 28–32.

———. 1979. Suq: The Bazaar Economy in Sefrou. In C. Geertz, H. Geertz, and L. Rosen, eds., *Meaning and Order in Moroccan Society: Three Essays in Cultural Analysis*, 123–310. Cambridge, London, and New York: Cambridge University Press.

———. 1991. Between Speech and Silence: The Problematics of Research on Language and Gender. In Micaela Di Leonardo, ed., *Gender at the Crossroads of Knowledge: Feminist Anthropology in the Postmodern Era*, 175–203. Berkeley and Los Angeles: University of California Press.

Geertz, Hildred. 1961. *The Javanese Family: A Study of Kinship and Socialization*. Glencoe, Ill.: Free Press.

Gellner, Ernest. 1969. *Saints of the Atlas*. Chicago: University of Chicago Press.

Gill, Lesley. 1990. Painted Faces: Conflict and Ambiguity in Domestic Servant-Employer Relations in La Paz, 1930–1988. *Latin American Research Review* 25, no. 1: 119–36.

————. 1994. *Precarious Dependencies: Gender, Class, and Domestic Service in Bolivia*. New York: Columbia University Press.

Ginkel, H. Fievez de Malines van. 1926. *Verslag van den economischen toestand der inlandsche bevolking van 1924*. 2 vols. Weltevreden, the Netherlands: Kolff.

Goffman, Erving. 1974. *Frame Analysis: An Essay on the Organization of Experience*. New York: Harper and Row.

Gönczi, Ferenc. 1910. *Szőlőhegyi mulatozások Zalában* (Frolicking in the Zala Vineyards). Budapest: Uránia.

Gonggrijp, G. 1925. Het arbeidsvraagstuk in Nederlandsh-Indie. *Koloniaal Tijjdschrift* 14: 485–522, 618–48.

Gouda, Frances. 1993. The Gendered Rhetoric of Colonialism and Anti-Colonialism in Twentieth-Century Indonesia. *Indonesia* 55: 1–22.

Grice, Paul. 1975. Logic and Conversation. In P. Cole and J. Morgan, eds., *Syntax and Semantics*. New York: Academic Press.

Gudeman, Stephen. 1992. Markets, Models and Morality: The Power of Practices. In Roy Dilley, ed., *Contesting Markets: Analyses of Ideology, Discourse and Practice*, 279–94. Edinburgh: Edinburgh University Press.

Gupta, Akhil. 1997. The Song of the Nonaligned World: Transnational Identities and the Reinscription of Space in Late Capitalism." In Akhil Gupta and James Ferguson, eds., *Culture, Power, Place: Explorations in Critical Anthropology*, 179–99. Durham, N.C.: Duke University Press.

Gupta, Akhil, and James Ferguson, eds. 1997. *Culture, Power, Place: Explorations in Critical Anthropology*. Durham, N.C.: Duke University Press.

Guttman, Matthew C. 1996. *The Meanings of Macho: Being a Man in Mexico City*. Berkeley and Los Angeles: University of California Press.

Haber, Stephen H. 1989. *Industry and Underdevelopment: The Industrialization of Mexico, 1890–1940*. Stanford, Calif.: Stanford University Press.

Habermas, Jurgen. 1989. *The Structural Transformation of the Public Sphere: An Inquiry into a Category of Bourgeois Society*. Translated by Thomas Burger, with the assistance of Frederick Lawrence. Cambridge, Mass.: MIT Press.

————. 1992. Further Reflections on the Public Sphere. In Craig Calhoun, ed., *Habermas and the Public Sphere*, 421–61. Cambridge, Mass. and London: MIT Press.

Hall, Stuart. 1991. Old and New Identities, Old and New Ethnicities. In A. King, ed., *Culture, Globalization and World Systems*, 41–68. Binghamton: State University of New York.

Hanák, Péter, ed. 1991. *The Corvina History of Hungary*. Budapest: Corvina.

Hann, Chris M. 1980. *Tázlár: A Village in Hungary*. Cambridge: Cambridge University Press.

Hansen, Karen Tranberg. 1980. The Urban Informal Sector as a Development Issue: Poor Women and Work in Lusaka, Zambia. *Urban Anthropology* 9, no. 2: 199–225.

Hardgrave, Robert. 1965. *The Dravidian Movement*. Bombay: Popular Press.

Harris, Olivia. 1995. The Sources and Meanings of Money: Beyond the Market Paradigm in an *Ayllu* of Northern Potosí. In Brooke Larson and Olivia Harris, with Enrique Tandeter, eds., *Ethnicity, Markets, and Migration in the Andes: At the Crossroads of History and Anthropology*, 297–328. Durham, N.C., and London: Duke University Press.

Harrison, Faye V. 1991. Women in Jamaica's Urban Informal Economy: Insights from a Kingston Slum. In Chandra Talpade Mohanta, Ann Russo, and Lourdes Torres, eds., *Third World Women and the Politics of Feminism*, 173–96. Bloomington: Indiana University Press.

Hart, David M. 1976. *The Aith Waryaghar of the Moroccan Rif: An Ethnography and History*. Tucson: University of Arizona Press.

Hart, Keith. 1992. Market and State After the Cold War: The Informal Economy Reconsidered. In Roy Dilley, ed., *Contesting Markets: Analyses of Ideology, Discourse and Practice*, 214–27. Edinburgh: Edinburgh University Press.

Hasselman, C. J. 1914. *Algemeen overzicht van de uitkomsten van het Welvaart-Onderzoek gehouden op Java en Madoera in 1904–1905*. The Hague: Martinus Nijhoff.

Hatley, Babara. 1990. Theatrical Imagery and Gender Ideology in Java. In J. M. Atkinson and S. Errington, eds., *Power and Difference: Gender in Island Southeast Asia*, 177–207. Stanford, Calif.: Stanford University Press.

Hefner, Robert. 1985. *Hindu Javanese: Tengger Tradition and Islam*. Princeton, N.J.: Princeton University Press.

Hill, Polly. 1963. *Migrant Cocoa Farmers of Southern Ghana*. Cambridge: Cambridge University Press.

Horn, Nancy E. 1994. *Cultivating Customers: Market Women in Harare, Zimbabwe*. Boulder, Col., and London: Lynne Rienner Publishers.

House-Midamba, Bessie. 1995. Kikuyu Market Women Traders and the Struggle for Economic Empowerment in Kenya. In Bessie House-Midamba and Felix K. Ekechi, eds., *African Market Women and Economic Power: The Role of*

Women in African Economic Development, 81–97. Westport, Conn.: Greenwood Press.

Hoyman, Michele. 1987. Female Participation in the Informal Economy: A Neglected Issue. *Annals, AAPSS* 493: 3–21.

Huseby, Éva Veronika. 1982. Hóvirágozás (Snow-drop Ventures: Supplementary Economic Activities of Cserépfalu Village Women). *Múzeumi Kurír* (edited by Imre Dankó) XXXX: 95–105. Debrecen: Déry Múzeum.

———. 1984. Community Cohesion and Identity Maintenance in Rural Hungary: Adaptations to Directed Social Change. Unpublished Ph.D. dissertation, Department of Anthropology, Ann Arbor, University of Michigan.

Huseby-Darvas, Éva Veronika. 1987. Elderly Women in a Hungarian Village: Childlessness, Generativity, and Social Control. *Journal of Cross-Cultural Gerontology* 1: 87–114.

———. 1988. Migrating Inward and Out: Validating Life Course Transitions Through Oral Autobiography. In Tamás Hofer and Péter Niedermüller, eds., *Life History as Cultural Construction/Performance*, 379–408. Budapest: Hungarian Academy of Sciences.

———. 1990. Introduction; and Migration and Gender: Perspectives from Rural Hungary. Gender Contradictions/Gender Transformations: Cases from Eastern Europe. *East European Quarterly*, Special Issue XXIII, no. 4 (Jan. 1990): 385–88, 487–98.

———. 1996. Pincézés. Paper presented in Tampere, Finland, July 2, 1996.

ILO (International Labor Office). 1972. *Employment, Incomes and Equality: A Strategy for Increasing Productive Employment in Kenya*. Geneva: ILO.

INEGI (Instituto Nacional de Estadística, Geografía e Informática Estadísticas Históricas de México). 1985. Vol. I. Mexico City: INEGI, SEP, INAH.

Ingram, Judith. 1991. Hungary's Gypsy Women: Scapegoats in a New Democracy. *Ms.* (Oct.): 17.

Irschick, Eugene. 1969. *Politics and Social Conflict in South India: The Non-Brahman Movement and Tamil Separatism, 1916–1929*. Berkeley and Los Angeles: University of California Press.

Jefremovas, Villia. 1985. Exploitation and Resistance: Kinship and Community Ties in Northern Luzon. In A. B. Chen, ed., *Contemporary and Historical Perspectives in Southeast Asia*, 273–90. Ottawa: University of Ottawa Press.

———. 1992. Gender, the Household and Cash Cropping in Sagada, the Philippines. In Penny and John Van Esterik, eds., *Gender and Development in Southeast Asia*, 51–58. Montreal: Canadian Asian Studies Association.

Jenista, Frank Lawrence. 1987. *The White Apos: American Governors on the Cordillera Central*. Quezon City, Philippines: New Day.

Jhabvala, Renana. 1992. Women's Struggles in the Informal Sector: Two Case Studies from SEWA. In Sujata Gothoskar, ed., *Struggles of Women at Work*, 63–91. New Delhi: Vikas Publishing House.

Johns, Michael. 1997. *The City of Mexico in the Age of Diaz*. Austin: University of Texas Press.

Johnson, Harvey L. 1961. Introduction. In Ignacio Manuel Altamirano, *Christmas in the Mountains* (La navidad en las montañas), ix–xix. Translated by Harvey L. Johnson. Gainesville: University of Florida Press.

Johnson-Odim, Cheryl, and Nina Mba. 1997. *For Women and the Nation*. Urbana: University of Illinois Press.

Juhász, József et al., eds. 1972. *Magyar értelmező kéziszótár* (Hungarian Dictionary of Definitions). Budapest: Akadémiai Kiadó.

K. Csilléry, Klára. 1979. Hór völgyi fafaragások (Wood Carvings of the Hór Valley). In *Magyar néprajzi lexikon* (Hungarian Ethnographic Encyclopedia), vol. II: 534.

Kalpagam, U. 1994. *Labour and Gender: Survival in Urban India*. New Delhi: Sage Publications.

Kapchan, Deborah. 1996. *Gender on the Market: Moroccan Women and the Revoicing of Tradition*. Philadelphia: University of Pennsylvania Press.

Karim, Wazir Jahan. 1995. Introduction: Genderising Anthropology in Southeast Asia. In Wazir Jahan Karim, ed., *'Male' and 'Female' in Developing Southeast Asia*, 11–34. Oxford, Eng., and Washington, D.C.: Berg.

Katz, Friedrich. 1981. Labor Conditions on Haciendas in Porfirian Mexico: Some Trends and Tendencies. *Hispanic American Historical Review* 54: 1–47.

Katz, Joseph, ed. 1970. *Stephen Crane in the West and Mexico*. Kent, Ohio: Kent State University Press.

Kaucsek, Ferenc. 1981. *A lakosság egészségkulturáltság hiányosságainak okai és káros következményei* (Causes and Detrimental Results of the Population's Inadequate Healthcare and Hygiene). *Egészségügyi Munka* XXVIII: 306–8.

Keeler, Ward. 1987. *Javanese Shadow Plays, Javanese Selves*. Princeton, N.J.: Princeton University Press.

Kligman, Gail. 1998. *The Politics of Duplicity: Controlling Reproduction in Ceausescu's Romania*. Berkeley and Los Angeles: University of California Press.

Knight, Alan. 1998. The United States and the Mexican Peasantry, circa 1880–1940. In *Rural Revolt in Mexico: U.S. Intervention and the Domain of Subaltern Politics*. Expanded ed. Durham, N.C., and London: Duke University Press.

Knight, G. R. 1982. Capitalism and Commodity Production in Java. In H. Alavi, ed., *Capitalism and Colonial Production*, 119–59. London: Croom Helm.

Knight, Peter. 1983. Economic Reform in Socialist Countries: The Experiences of China, Hungary, Romania, and Yugoslavia. *World Bank Staff Papers*, No. 579. Washington, D.C.: The World Bank.

Kovács, Imre. 1937. *Néma forradalom* (Silent Revolution). Budapest: Cserépfalvi Könyvkiadó.

Kratochwill, Tivadar, ed. 1980. *Dél borsod* (South Borsod County). Budapest: Révai.

Lajos, Árpád. 1959–1961. Diszes fafaragás a Hór Völgyén (Ornamental Wood Carving in the Hór Valley). *Miskolci Hermann Ottó Múzeum Évkönyve* (1959–1961): 103–35.

Lamphere, Louise. 1992. Introduction. In Louise Lamphere, ed., *Structuring Diversity: Ethnographic Perspectives on the New Immigration*, 1–34. Chicago: University of Chicago Press, 1992.

Lampland, Martha. 1995. *The Object of Labor: Commodification in Socialist Hungary*. Chicago and London: University of Chicago Press.

Larson, Brooke. 1995. Andean Communities, Political Cultures, and Markets: The Changing Contours of a Field. In Brooke Larson and Olivia Harris, with Enrique Tandeter, eds., *Ethnicity, Markets, and Migration in the Andes: At the Crossroads of History and Anthropology*, 5–53. Durham, N.C.: Duke University Press.

Larson, Brooke, and Olivia Harris, with Enrique Tandeter, eds. 1995. *Ethnicity, Markets, and Migration in the Andes: At the Crossroads of History and Anthropology*. Durham, N.C., and London: Duke University Press.

Larson, Brooke, and Rosario León. 1995. Markets, Power, and the Politics of Exchange in Tapacarí, c. 1780 and 1980. In Brooke Larson and Olivia Harris, with Enrique Tandeter, eds., *Ethnicity, Markets, and Migration in the Andes: At the Crossroads of History and Anthropology*, 224–56. Durham, N.C., and London: Duke University Press.

Lee, Benjamin. 1992. Textuality, Mediation, and Public Discourse. In Craig Calhoun, ed., *Habermas and the Public Sphere*, 402–18. Cambridge, Mass., and London: MIT Press.

Lepowsky, Maria. 1993. *Fruit of the Motherland: Gender in an Egalitarian Society*. New York: Columbia University Press.

Lessinger, Johanna. 1976 Produce Marketing in Madras City. Unpublished Ph.D. dissertation, Department of Anthropology, Brandeis University.

———. 1985. "Nobody Here to Yell at Me": Political Activism Among Petty Retail Traders in an Indian City. In Stuart Plattner, ed., *Markets and Marketing*, 309–31. Lanham, Md.: University Press of America.

―――. 1986. Women, Work and Modesty: The Dilemma of Women Market Traders in South India. *Feminist Studies* 12, no. 3: 581–600.

―――. 1988. Trader vs. Developer: The Market Relocation Issue in an Indian City. In Gracia Clark, ed., *Trader Versus the State: Anthropological Approaches to Unofficial Economies,* 139–64. Boulder, Col.: Westview Press.

―――. 1989. Petty Trading and the Ideology of Gender Segregation in Urban India. In Haleh Afshar and Bina Agarwal, eds., *Women, Poverty and Ideology in Asia: Contradictory Pressures, Uneasy Resolutions,* 99–127. Houndmills, Basingstoke, Eng.: Macmillan Press, Ltd.

Lindholm, James. 1980. A Note on the Nobility of Women in Popular Tamil Fiction. In Susan Wadley, ed., *The Powers of Tamil Women,* 137–51. Syracuse, N.Y.: Foreign and Comparative Studies, South Asian Series, No. 6.

Lomnitz, Larissa. 1988. Informal Exchange Networks in Formal Systems: A Theoretical Model. *American Anthropologist* 90: 42–55.

Long, Norman. 1975. Structural Dependency, Modes of Production and Economic Brokerage in Rural Peru. In F. Oxala, T. Barnett, and D. Booth, eds., *Beyond the Sociology of Development,* 253–82. London: Routledge & Kegan Paul.

―――. 1977. *An Introduction to the Sociology of Rural Development.* London: Tavistock.

MacCormack, Carol, and Marilyn Strathern, eds. 1980. *Nature, Culture and Gender.* Cambridge: Cambridge University Press.

MacEwen Scott, Alison. 1991. Informal Sector or Female Sector? Gender Bias in the Urban Labour Market Model. In Diane Elson, ed., *Male Bias in the Development Process,* 104–31. Manchester, Eng.: Manchester University Press.

―――. 1994. Gender Segregation and the SCELI Research. In Alison MacEwen Scott, ed., *Gender Segregation and Social Change: Men and Women in Changing Labour Markets,* 1–38. Oxford: Oxford University Press.

Mahler, Sarah. 1995. *American Dreaming: Immigrant Life on the Margins.* Princeton, N.J.: Princeton University Press.

Manderson, Lenore, ed. 1983. *Women's Work and Women's Roles: Economics and Everyday Life in Indonesia, Malaysia and Singapore.* Canberra: University of Australia Press.

Marcus, George. 1998. Imagining the Whole: Ethnography's Contemporary Efforts to Situate Itself. In *Ethnography Through Thick and Thin,* 33–56. Princeton, N.J.: Princeton University Press.

Mariani, Giorgio. 1992. *Spectacular Narratives: Representations of Class and War in Stephen Crane and the American 1890's.* American University Studies. New York: Peter Lang.

Marti, Judith. 1990. *Subsistence and the State: Municipal Government Policies and Urban Markets in Developing Nations: The Case of Mexico City and Guadalajara, 1877–1910*. Unpublished Ph.D. dissertation, Department of Anthropology, University of California, Los Angeles.

———. 1993. Breadwinners and Decision-Makers: Nineteenth Century Mexican Women Vendors. In Mari Womack and Judith Marti, eds., *The Other Fifty Percent: Multicultural Perspectives on Gender Relations*, 218–24. Prospect Heights, Ill.: Waveland Press.

———. 1994a. Subsistence and the State: The Case of Porfirian Mexico. In Elizabeth Brumfiel, ed., *The Economic Anthropology of the State*, 315–24. Lanham, Md.: University Press of America/Society for Economic Anthropology.

———. 1994b. Vendors and the Government: Towards Case Studies in Institutional Economics. In James E. Acheson, ed., *Anthropology and Institutional Economics*, 195–211. Lanham, Md.: University Press of America/Society for Economic Anthropology.

Mather, Celia. 1983. Industrialisation in the Tangerang Regency of West Java: Women Workers and the Islamic Patriarchy. *Bulletin of Concerned Asian Scholars* 15, no. 2: 2–17.

Mauss, Marcel. 1954. *The Gift: Forms and Functions of Exchange in Archaic Societies*. Translated by I. Cunnison. London: Cohen and West.

Mayoux, Linda. 1995. *From Vicious to Virtuous Circles? Gender and Micro-Enterprise Development*. Geneva: United Nations Research Institute for Social Development.

Mba, Nina. 1982. *Nigerian Women Mobilized: Women's Political Activity in Southern Nigeria, 1900–1965*. Berkeley and Los Angeles: University of California Press.

Meyer, Michael C., William L. Sherman, and Susan M. Deeds. 1998. *The Course of Mexican History*. Oxford and New York: Oxford University Press.

Mies, Maria. 1982. *The Lace Makers of Narsapur*. London: Zed Books.

Mies, Maria, K. Lalitha, and Krishna Kumari. 1986. *Indian Women in Subsistence and Agricultural Labour*. ILO Women, Work and Development Series 12. Geneva: International Labour Organization.

Mikell, Gwendolyn. 1989. *Cocoa and Chaos in Ghana*. New York: Paragon House.

Miles, Ann, and Hans Buechler, eds. 1997. *Women and Economic Change: Andean Perspectives*. Society for Latin American Anthropology, vol. 14. Washington, D.C.: American Anthropological Association.

Milgram, Lynne. 1997. Crossover, Continuity and Change: Women's Production and Marketing of Crafts in the Upland Philippines. Unpublished Ph.D. dissertation, Department of Social Anthropology, York University, Toronto.

————. 1998. Making and Marketing Contemporary Baskets in Ifugao, Upland Philippines. In Roy W. Hamilton, ed., *Basketry of the Luzon, Cordillera, Philippines*, 52–68. Los Angeles: UCLA Fowler Museum of Cultural History.

————. 1999a. Crafts, Cultivation, and Household Economies: Women's Work and Positions in Ifugao Northern Philippines. In Barry L. Isaac, ed., *Research in Economic Anthropology* 20: 221–61. Greeenwich, Conn. and London: JAI Press.

————. 1999b. Locating "Tradition" in the Striped Textiles of Banaue, Ifugao. *Museum Anthropology* 23, no. 1: 3–20.

Mines, Mattison. 1994. *Public Faces, Private Voices: Community and Individuality in South India*. Berkeley and Los Angeles: University of California Press.

Mintz, Sidney. 1964. The Employment of Capital by Market Women in Haiti. In Raymond Firth and S. B. Yamey, eds., *Capital, Saving and Credit in Peasant Societies*, 256–86. London: George Allen and Unwin Ltd.

————. 1971. Men, Women and Trade. *Comparative Studies in Society and History* 13, no. 3: 247–69.

Molyneux, Maxine. 1985. Mobilization Without Emancipation?: Women's Interests, the State and Revolution in Nicaragua. In David Slater, ed., *New Social Movements and the State in Latin America*, 233–60. CEDLA Amsterdam: Latin American Studies: 29

Morvay, Judit. [1956] 1981. *Asszonyok a nagycsaládban* (Women in the Extended Family). Budapest: Akadémiai Kiadó.

Moser, Caroline. 1994. The Informal Sector Debate, Part 1: 1970–1983. In Cathy A. Rakowski, ed., *Contrapunto: The Informal Sector Debate in Latin America*, 11–29. Albany: State University of New York Press.

Murray, Alison J. 1991. *No Money, No Honey: A Study of Street Traders and Prostitutes in Jakarta*. Singapore and Oxford: Oxford University Press.

Muriá, José María, ed. 1981. *Historia de Jalisco: De la primera república centralista a la consolidación del Porfiriato*. Vol. III. Guadalajara: Gobierno del Estado de Jalisco, Secretaría General de Gobierno, Unidad Editorial.

————. 1982. *Historia de Jalisco: Desde la consolidación del Porfiriato hasta mediados del siglo XX*. Vol. IV. Guadalajara: Gobierno del Estado de Jalisco, Secretaría General de Gobierno, Unidad Editorial.

Muriá Rouret, José Ma. 1983. *A Thumbnail History of Guadalajara*. Translated by Michael Matnes. Guadalajara, Mexico: Editorial Colomos.

Musisi, Nakanyike. 1995. Baganda Women's Night Market Activities. In Bessie House-Midamba and Felix K. Ekechi, eds., *African Market Women and Economic Power: The Role of Women in African Economic Development*, 121–39. Westport, Conn.: Greenwood Press.

Nasr, Seyyed Hosein. 1964. *An Introduction to Islamic Cosmological Doctrines: Con-*

ceptions of Nature and Methods Used for Its Study by the Ikhwan Al-Safa, Al-Biruni, and Ibn Sina. Cambridge: Harvard University Press.

Nkrumah, Kwame. 1957. *The Autobiography of Kwame Nkrumah.* New York: Thomas Nelson.

Noponen, Helzi. 1987. Organizing Self-Employed Women Traders and Home-based Producers. In A. M. Singh and A. Kelles-Viitanen, eds., *Invisible Hands: Women in Home-based Production,* 229–49. Delhi: Sage Publications.

———. 1991. The Dynamics of Work and Survival for the Urban Poor: A Gender Analysis of Panel Data from Madras. *Development and Change* 22: 233–60.

———. 1992. Loans to the Working Poor: A Longitudinal Study of Credit, Gender and the Household Economy. *International Journal of Urban and Regional Research* 16, no. 2: 234–51.

Núñez, Lorena. 1993. Women on the Streets, Vending and Public Space in Chile. *Economic and Political Weekly* (Oct. 30 1993): WS67–82.

Okali, Christine. 1983. *Cocoa and Kinship in Southern Ghana: The Matrilineal Akan of Ghana.* London: Kegan Paul International.

Omvedt, Gail. 1993. *Reinventing Revolution, New Social Movements and the Socialist Tradition in India.* London: M. E. Sharpe.

Ong, Aihwa. 1989. Center, Periphery and Hierarchy: Gender in Southeast Asia. In Sandra Morgan, ed., *Gender and Anthropology,* 294–312. Washington, D.C.: American Anthropological Association.

Osirim, Mary Johnson. 1995. Trade, Economy, and the Family in Urban Zimbabwe. In Bessie House-Midamba and Felix K. Ekechi, eds., *African Market Women and Economic Power: The Role of Women in African Economic Development,* 157–75. Westport, Conn.: Greenwood Press.

Pateman, Carole. 1990. *The Sexual Contract.* Stanford, Calif.: Stanford University Press.

Pescatello, Ann M. 1976. *Power and Pawn: The Female in Iberian Families, Societies, and Cultures.* Westport, Conn.: Greenwood Press.

Peters, John Durham. 1997. Seeing Bifocally: Media, Place, Culture. In Akhil Gupta and James Ferguson, eds., *Culture, Power, Place: Explorations in Critical Anthropology,* 75–92. Durham, N.C.: Duke University Press.

Phillips, Lynne. 1996. Toward Postcolonial Methodologies. In Parvin Ghorayshi and Claire Bélanger, eds., *Women, Work, and Gender Relations in Developing Countries: A Global Perspective,* 15–30. Westport, Conn.: Greenwood Press.

Pineda, R. Vergara. 1995. Domestic Outwork for Export-Oriented Industries. In Amaryllis T. Torres, ed., *The Filipino Woman in Focus,* 153–67. Quezon City, Philippines: University of Philippines Press.

Platt, Tristan. 1992. Divine Protection and Liberal Damnation: Exchanging Metaphors in Ninteenth-century Potosí (Bolivia). In Roy Dilley, ed., *Contesting Markets*, 131–58. Edinburgh: Edinburgh University Press.

———. 1995. Ethnic Calendars and Market Interventions Among the Ayllus of Lipes During the Nineteenth Century. In Brooke Larson and Olivia Harris, with Enrique Tandeter, eds., *Ethnicity, Markets, and Migration in the Andes: At the Crossroads of History and Anthropology*, 259–96. Durham, N.C.: Duke University Press.

Plattner, Stuart. 1985. Equilibriating Market Relationships. In S. Plattner, ed., *Markets and Marketing*, 132–52. Lanham, Md.: University Press of America.

———. 1989. Markets and Marketplaces. In S. Plattner, ed., *Economic Anthropology*, 171–208. Stanford, Calif.: Stanford University Press.

Portes, Alejandro. 1981. Unequal Exchange and the Urban Informal Sector. In Alejandro Portes and John Walton, eds., *Labor, Class and the International System*, 67–106. New York: Academic Press.

———. 1983. The Informal Sector: Definition, Controversy, and Relation to National Development. *Review* 7, no. 1: 151–74.

———. 1989. Latin American Urbanization in the Years of the Crisis. *Latin American Research Review* 3, no. 24: 7–44.

———. 1994. When More Can Be Less: Labor Standards, Development, and the Informal Economy. In Cathy A. Rakowski, ed., *Contrapunto: The Informal Sector Debate in Latin America*, 113–29. Albany: State University of New York Press.

Raffles, T. S. 1817. *The History of Java*. 2 vols. London: John Murray.

Raillon, Francois. 1991. How to Become a National Entrepreneur: The Rise of Indonesian Capitalists. *Archipel* 41: 81–119.

Rakowski, Cathy A. 1994. The Informal Sector Debate, Part 2: 1984–1993. In Cathy A. Rakowski, ed., *Contrapunto: The Informal Sector Debate in Latin America*, 31–50. Albany: State University of New York Press.

Rattray, Robert S. 1927. *Religion and Art in Ashanti*. Oxford: Clarendon Press.

Reiter, Rayna R. 1975. The Search for Origins: Unraveling the Threads of Gender Hierarchy. *Critical Anthropology* 3, nos. 9–10: 5–24.

Reynolds, Holly. 1980. The Auspicious Married Woman. In Susan Wadley, ed., *The Powers of Tamil Women*, 35–60. Syracuse, N.Y.: Foreign and Comparative Studies, South Asian Series, No. 6.

Robertson, Claire. 1983. The Death of Makola and Other Tragedies: Male Strategies Against a Female-Dominated System. *Canadian Journal of African Studies* 17, no. 3: 469–95.

———. 1984. *Sharing the Same Bowl: A Socioeconomic History of Women and Class in Accra, Ghana*. Bloomington: Indiana University Press.

————. 1993. Traders and Urban Struggle: Ideology and the Creation of a Militant Female Underclass in Nairobi, 1960–1990. *Journal of Women's History* 4, no. 3: 9–42.

Róna-Tas, Ákos. 1995. The Second Economy as a Subversive Force: Erosion of Party Power in Hungary. In Andrew G. Walder, ed., *The Waning of the Communist state: Economic Origins of Political Decline in China and Hungary*, 61–84. Berkeley and Los Angeles: University of California.

————. 1997. *The Great Surprise of the Small Transformation: The Demise of Communism and the Rise of the Private Sector in Hungary*. Ann Arbor: University of Michigan Press.

Rosaldo, Michelle. 1974. Woman, Culture, and Society: A Theoretical Overview. In Michell Rosaldo and Louise Lamphere, eds., *Woman, Culture and Society*, 17–42. Stanford, Calif.: Stanford University Press.

————. 1980. The Use and Abuse of Anthropology: Reflections on Feminism and Cross-Cultural Understandings. *Signs* 5, no. 3: 389–417.

Rosaldo, Renato. 1993. *Culture and Truth: The Remaking of Social Analysis*. Boston: Beacon Press.

Rose, Kalima. 1992. *Where Women Are Leaders: The SEWA Movement in India*. London: Zed Books.

Roseberry, William. 1988. Political Economy. *Annual Review in Anthropology* 17: 161–85.

Rosen, Lawrence. 1984. *Bargaining for Reality: The Construction of Social Relations in a Muslim Community*. Chicago and London: University of Chicago Press.

————. 1995. "Have the Arabs Changed Their Mind?": Intentionality and the Discernment of Cultural Change. In Lawrence Rosen, ed., *Other Intentions: Cultural Contexts and the Attribution of Inner States*, 177–202. Sante Fe, N.M.: School of American Research Press.

Rowbotham, Sheila. 1995. Consumer Power: Women's Contribution to Alternatives and Resistance to the Market in the United States, 1880–1940. In Barbara Einhorn and Eileen Janes Yeo, eds., *Women and Market Societies: Crisis and Opportunity*, 11–29. Aldershot, Eng.: Edward Elgar.

Russell, Susan D. 1983. Entrepreneurs, Ethnic Rhetorics and Economic Integration in Benguet Province, Highland Luzon, Philippines. Unpublished Ph.D. dissertation, Department of Anthropology, University of Illinois at Urbana-Champaign.

————. 1987. Middlemen and Moneylending: Relations of Exchange in a Highland Philippine Economy. *Journal of Anthropological Research* 43, no. 2: 139–61.

Rutten, Rosanne. 1993. *Artisans and Entrepreneurs in the Rural Philippines: Making a Living and Gaining Wealth in Two Commercialized Crafts.* Quezon City, Philippines: New Day.

Sacks, Karen Brodkin. 1989. What's a Life Story Got to Do With It? In Joy Barbre, Amy Farrell, Shirley Garner et al., eds., *Interpreting Women's Lives: Feminist Theory and Personal Narratives,* 85–95. Bloomington: Indiana University Press.

Saddiki, Taieb. 1979. *Al-mawqif al-adabi.* Special Issue, IVième Festival du Théâtre Arabe. Damascus.

————. 1980. Interview in *Al-Maghrib* 8: 17–18. Rabat.

Safa, Helen. 1995. *The Myth of the Male Breadwinner: Women and Industrialization in the Caribbean.* Boulder, Col.: Westview Press.

Sahlins, Marshall. 1972. *Stone Age Economics.* Chicago: Aldine.

Saptari, Ratna. 1991. The Differentiation of a Rural Industrial Labour Force. In P. Alexander, P. Boomgaard, and B. White, eds., *In the Shadow of Agriculture,* 113–26. Amsterdam: Royal Tropical Institute.

————. 1995. Rural Women to the Factories: Continuity and Change in East Java's Cigarette Industry. Unpublished Ph.D. dissertation, Center for Southeast Asian Studies, University of Amsterdam.

Sassen, Saskia. 1988. *The Morality of Labor and Capital.* Cambridge: Cambridge University Press.

————. 1991. *The Global City: New York, London, Tokyo.* Princeton, N.J.: Princeton University Press.

Sayer, Andrew. 1997. The Dialectic of Culture and Economy. In Roger Lee and Jane Wills, eds., *Geographies of Economies,* 16–26. London and New York: Arnold.

Scaglion, Richard. 1996. Chiefly Models in Papua New Guinea. *Contemporary Pacific* 8, no. 1: 1–31.

Schuyler, Phillip. 1993. Entertainment in the Marketplace. In Donna Lee Bowen and Evelyn A. Early, eds., *Everyday Life in the Muslim Middle East,* 276–80. Bloomington: Indiana University Press.

————. 1996. Jamaa el-fna. *Natural History* 105, no. 5: 38–45.

Seizer, Susan. 1997. Jokes, Gender and Discursive Distance on the Tamil Popular Stage. *American Ethnologist* 24, no. 1: 62–90.

Seligmann, Linda J. 1989. To Be in Between: The Cholas as Market Women in Peru. *Comparative Studies in Society and History* 31, no. 4: 694–721.

————. 1993. Between Worlds of Exchange: Ethnicity Among Peruvian Market Women. *Cultural Anthropology* 8, no. 2: 187–213.

————. 1998. Survival Politics and the Movements of Market Women in Peru in the Age of Neoliberalism. In Lynne Phillips, ed., *The Third Wave of Modernization in Latin America: Cultural Perspectives on Neoliberalism,* 65–82. Wilmington, Del.: Scholarly Resources Press.

————. Forthcoming. A Woman of Steel: The Life Story of a Peruvian Market Woman. In Judith Marti and Tamar Wilson, eds., *Women in the Informal Sector: Case Studies and Theoretical Approaches*. Albany: State University of New York Press.

Shaw, Jenny. 1995. Women, Time and Markets: The Role of Feminization and Contradiction in the New Forms of Exploitation. In Barbara Einhorn and Eileen Janes Yeo, eds., *Women and Market Societies: Crisis and Opportunity*, 146–59. Aldershot, Eng.: Edward Elgar.

Sheldon, Kathleen, ed. 1996. *Courtyards, Markets, City Streets: Urban Women in Africa*. Boulder, Col.: Westview Press.

Siegel, James T. 1986. *Solo in the New Order*. Princeton, N.J.: Princeton University Press.

Sikkink, Lynn. 1994. House, Community, and Marketplace: Women as Managers of Exchange Relations and Resources on the Southern Altiplano of Bolivia. Unpublished Ph.D. dissertation, Department of Anthropology, University of Minnesota.

————. 1995. The Household as the Locus of Difference: Gender, Occupational Multiplicity and Marketing Practices in the Bolivian Andes. *Anthropology of Work Review* XVI, nos. 1–2: 5–9.

————. 1997. Water and Exchange: The Ritual of *Yaku Cambio* as Communal and Competitive Encounter. *American Ethnologist* 24, no. 1: 170–89.

Simó, Tibor. 1983. *A Tardi társadalom* (The Society of Tard). Budapest: Kossuth.

Smith, Carol A. 1976. Exchange Systems and the Spatial Distribution of Elites: The Organization of Stratification in Agrarian Societies. In C. A. Smith, ed., *Regional Analysis, vol. 2: Social Systems*, 309–374. New York: Academic Press.

————. 1996. Race/Class/Gender Ideology in Guatemala: Modern and Anti-Modern Forms. In Brackette Williams, ed., *Women Out of Place: The Gender of Agency and the Race of Nationality*, 50–78. New York: Routledge.

Sozan, Mihály. 1983. Self-perception of Agricultural Workers. Paper presented at the XIIth European Rural Sociology Congress, Budapest, May 13, 1983.

————. 1984. Falu (Village). *Irodalmi Ujság* (Paris) I: 7–8.

Stamp, Patricia. 1989. *Technology, Gender, and Power in Africa*. Ottawa, Ontario: IDRC.

Stark, David. 1989. Coexisting Organizational Forms in Hungary's Emerging Mixed Economy. In Victor Nee and David Stark, eds., *Remaking the Economic Institutions of Socialism: China and Eastern Europe*, 137–68. Stanford, Calif.: Stanford University Press.

Steinhauf, Andreas, and Ludwig Huber. 1996. Redes sociales en una economía étnica: los artesanos de la Costa Norte del Perú. *Bulletin de l'Institut Français des Études Andines* 25, no. 2: 269–81.

Stephen, Lynn. 1991. *Zapotec Women*. Austin: University of Texas Press.

———. 1996. Export Markets and Their Effects on Indigenous Craft Production: The Case of the Weavers of Teotitlan del Valle, Mexico. In Margot Schevill, Janet Berlo, and Edward Dwyer, eds., *Textile Traditions of Mesoamerica and the Andes: An Anthology*, 381–402. New York: Garland Press.

———. 1997. *Women and Social Movements in Latin America: Power from Below*. Austin: University of Texas Press.

Stirrat, R. L. 1992. "Good Government" and "the Market." In Roy Dilley, ed., *Contesting Markets*, 293–313. Edinburgh: Edinburgh University Press.

Stolcke, Verena. 1981. The Naturalizations of Social Inequality and Women's Subordination. In Kate Young et al., eds., *Of Marriage and the Market*, 30–48. London: CSE Books.

Stoler, Ann. 1977. Class Structure and Female Autonomy in Rural Java. *Signs* 3, no. 1: 74–89.

Stoler, Ann. 1995. *Race and the Education of Desire: Foucault's History of Sexuality and the Colonial Order of Things*. Durham, N.C., and London: Duke University Press.

Strathern, Marilyn. 1982. Elmdon. In A. P. Cohen, ed., *Belonging, Identity and Social Organization in British Rural Cultures*, 72–100, 247–77. Manchester, Eng.: Manchester University.

Stromberg-Pellizzi, Gobi. 1993. *Coyotes* and Culture Brokers: The Production and Marketing of Taxco Silverwork. In June Nash, ed., *Crafts in the World Market: The Impact of Global Exchange on Middle American Artisans*, 85–102. Albany: State University of New York Press.

Sudarkasa, Niara. 1973. *Where Women Work: A Study of Yoruba Women in the Marketplace and in the Home*. Museum of Anthropology, Anthropological Paper, No. 53. Ann Arbor: University of Michigan Press.

Szabó, Zoltán. 1936. *Cifra nyomorúság* (Ornamental Misery). Budapest: Cserépfalvi Könyvkiadó.

———. 1937. *A Tardi helyzet* (The Situation in Tard). Budapest: Cserépfalvi Könyvkiadó.

Szántó, Miklós. 1977. *Életmód* (Ways of Life). Budapest: Corvina.

Szanton, M. C. B. 1972. *A Right to Survive: Subsistence Marketing in a Lowland Philippines Town*. University Park, Penn.: Pennsylvania State University Press.

Szelényi, Iván. 1994. *Socialist Entrepreneurs—Revisited*. Working Paper Series, No. 4. Ann Arbor: International Institute, University of Michigan.

Szelényi, Iván, with Robert Manchin, Pál Juhász, Bálint Magyar, and Bill Martin. 1988. *Socialist Entrepreneurs: Embourgeoisement in Rural Hungary*. Madison: University of Wisconsin Press.

Szendrey, Ákos. 1938. A népi élet társasösszejövetelei (Social gathering of folk life). *Ethnographia* XLIX: 124–37.

Tamil Nadu Corporation for Development of Women, Ltd. 1986. *Women in Tamil Nadu: A Profile*. Madras: Corporation for Development of Women, Ltd.

Tice, Karen. 1995. *Kuna Crafts, Gender, and the Global Economy*. Austin: University of Texas Press.

Tinker, Irene. 1987. Street Foods: Testing Assumptions about Informal Sector Activity by Women and Men. *Current Sociology* 35, no. 3: 1–110.

Tóth, Gusztáv. 1939. Cserépfalu és Bükkzsérc vallási szokásai (Religious Customs of Cserépfalu and Bükkzsérc). Typed Manuscript, No. Fsz. k. 79. Sárospatak: Sárospatak Archives.

Trawick, Margaret. 1990. *Notes on Love in a Tamil Family*. Berkeley and Los Angeles: University of California Press.

Tripp, Aili Mari. 1989. Women and the Changing Urban Household Economy in Tanzania. *Journal of Modern African Studies* 27, no. 4: 601–23.

Troin, Jean-Francois. 1975. *Les souks Marocains: Marches ruraux et organisation de l'espace dans la moitié nord du Maroc*. Aix-en-Provence, France: Edisud.

Tsing, Anna Lowenhaupt. 1993. *In the Realm of the Diamond Queen: Marginality in an Out-of-the-Way-Place*. Princeton, N.J.: Princeton University Press.

Ujváry, Zoltán. 1975. Szőlőhegyi jogszokások nagycétényben (Judicial Customs Relating to Vineyards in Nagycétény). *Varia Folkloristica*, 25. Debrecen: Hajdú Bihar Megyei Múzeumok Közleményei.

Uzzell, J. Douglas. 1994. Transaction Costs, Formal Plans, and Formal Informality: Alternatives to the Informal "Sector." In Cathy A. Rakowski, ed., *Contrapunto: The Informal Sector Debate in Latin America*, 251–69. Albany: State University of New York Press.

Valderrama, Ricardo, and Carmen Escalante, eds. 1996. *Andean Lives: Gregorio Condori Mamani and Asunta Quispe Huamán*. Translated by Paul Gelles and Gabriela Martinez. Introduction by Paul Gelles. Austin: University of Texas Press.

Vera-Sanso, Penny. 1995. Community, Seclusion and Female Labour Force Participation in Madras, India. *Third World Planning Review* 17, no. 2: 155–67.

Verdery, Katherine. 1994. From Parent-State to Family Patriarchs: Gender and Nation in Contemporary Eastern Europe. *East European Politics and Societies* 8, no. 2: 225–55.

VerEecke, Catherine. 1995. Muslim Women Traders of Northern Nigeria: Perspectives from the City of Yola. In Bessie House-Midamba and Felix K. Ekechi, eds., *African Market Women and Economic Power: The Role of Women in African Economic Development*, 60–79. Westport, Conn.: Greenwood Press.

Viramma, Josiane Racine, and Jean Luc Racine. 1997. *Viramma: Life of an Untouchable*. London: Verso Press.

Vörös, Miklós. 1996. Fogyasztás és kultura (Consumption and Culture). *Replika: Társadalomtudományi folyóirat* (Replika: Journal of Social Sciences) (Budapest) nos. 21–22 (May 1996): 77–79.

Waterbury, Ronald. 1989. Embroidery for Tourists: A Contemporary Putting-Out System in Oaxaca, Mexico. In Annette B. Weiner and Jane Schneider, eds., *Cloth and Human Experience*, 246–71. Washington, D.C.: Smithsonian Institution Press.

Weber, Max. 1976. *The Protestant Ethic and the Spirit of Capitalism*. New York: Scribner.

Weiner, Annette. 1976. *Women of Value, Men of Renown: New Perspectives on Trobriand Exchange*. Austin: University of Texas Press.

Weismantel, Mary. 1995. Masculine Women / White Indians: Andean Cholas. Paper presented at the American Anthropological Association Meetings, Washington, D.C., Nov. 1995.

———. 1997. Time, Work-Discipline, and Beans: Indigenous Self-Determination in the Northern Andes. In Ann Miles and Hans Buechler, eds., *Women and Economic Change: Andean Perspectives*, 31–54. Society for Latin American Anthropology, vol. 14. Washington, D.C.: American Anthropological Association.

Westermarck, Edward A. [1930] 1980. *Wit and Wisdom in Morocco: A Study of Native Proverbs*. London: George Routledge & Sons.

Westwood, Sallie, and Sarah A. Radcliffe. 1993. Gender, Racism and the Politics of Identities in Latin America. In Sarah A. Radcliffe and Sallie Westwood, eds., *Viva!: Women and Popular Protest in Latin America*, 1–29. London: Routledge.

White, Benjamin. 1991. Economic Diversification and Agrarian Change in Rural Java, 1900–1990. In P. Alexander, P. Boomgaard, and B. White, eds., *In the Shadow of Agriculture*, 41–69. Amsterdam: Royal Tropical Institute.

White, E. Francis. 1987. *Sierra Leone's Settler Women Traders: Women on the Afro-European Frontier*. Ann Arbor: University of Michigan Press.

Whitten, Norman, Dorothea Whitten, and Alfonso Chango. 1997. Return of the Yumbo: The Indigenous Caminata from Amazonia to Andean Quito. *American Ethnologist* 24, no. 2: 355–91.

Wilson, Fiona. 1993. Workshops as Domestic Domains: Reflections on Small-Scale Industry in Mexico. *World Development* 21, no. 1: 67–80.

Wilson, Tamar Diana, and Judith Marti, eds. Forthcoming. *Women in the Informal Sector: Case Studies and Theoretical Approaches*. Albany: State University of New York Press.

Wolf, Diane. L. 1992. *Factory Daughters: Gender, Household Dynamics and Rural Industrialization in Java*. Berkeley and Los Angeles: University of California Press.

Worcester, Dean C. 1913. Non-Christian Peoples of the Philippines Islands. *National Geographic Magazine* 24, no. 11: 1157–1256.

Index

In this index an "f" after a number indicates a separate reference on the next page, and an "ff" indicates separate references on the next two pages. A continuous discussion over two or more pages is indicated by a span of page numbers, e.g., "57–59." *Passim* is used for a cluster of references in close but not consecutive sequence.